LINCOLN IN LISTS

THOMAS R. FLAGEL

STACKPOLE BOOKS
Guilford, Connecticut

STACKPOLE BOOKS

An imprint of Globe Pequot, the trade division of
The Rowman & Littlefield Publishing Group, Inc.
4501 Forbes Blvd., Ste. 200
Lanham, MD 20706
www.rowman.com

Distributed by NATIONAL BOOK NETWORK

British Library Cataloguing in Publication Information available

Library of Congress Cataloging-in-Publication Data

Names: Flagel, Thomas R., 1966– author.
Title: Lincoln in lists / Thomas R. Flagel.
Description: Guilford, Connecticut : Stackpole Books, [2021] | Includes
   bibliographical references. | Summary: "In this book—both history and
   biography, informative and entertaining, meant to be read all at once or
   in bite-sized chunks—historian Thomas Flagel distills the life and
   legacy of Abraham Lincoln in twenty-five annotated lists representing a
   cross-section of Lincoln's life, career, and presidency"— Provided by
   publisher.
Identifiers: LCCN 2021015949 (print) | LCCN 2021015950 (ebook) | ISBN
   9780811739665 (paperback) | ISBN 9780811769648 (epub)
Subjects: LCSH: Lincoln, Abraham, 1809–1865—Miscellanea.
Classification: LCC E457.909 .F55 2021 (print) | LCC E457.909 (ebook) |
   DDC 973.7092—dc23
LC record available at https://lccn.loc.gov/2021015949
LC ebook record available at https://lccn.loc.gov/2021015950

*To Barb Ross
and
Hoyt Gardner*

Contents

Preface

The very first biography published on Abraham Lincoln appeared in December 1859, in the form of a brief political sketch in the columns of the *Chester County Times*. To construct this life story, the Pennsylvania paper relied on a few cryptic notes from Lincoln himself. True to form, Lincoln was evasive about his past, turning to specifics only when it came to his unique, odd, physical appearance. "If any personal description of me is thought desirable," the subject wrote, "it may be said, I am, in height, six feet, four inches, nearly; lean in flesh, weighing, on average, one hundred and eighty pounds; dark complexion, with coarse black hair, and grey eyes—no other marks or brands recollected." In sending these bits and pieces, Lincoln was apologetic, but he volunteered nothing more. In this extremely brief synopsis of himself, he closed with the remark, "There is not much of it, for the reason, I suppose, that there is not much of me." Less than a year later, this self-effacing man would win the 1860 election for president of the United States.

While many chief executives have faded into the afterthoughts of history, it is nearly impossible to imagine an American past without Abraham Lincoln. So forged is his being into the nation's evolution that he remains omnipresent. His likeness resides in virtually every home and business in the United States, primarily in the form of US currency. More books are written about him than any other figure in US history. Among presidential historians, he perpetually ranks among the top three chief executives, most often first.

Yet, much like the Constitution he vowed to defend, Lincoln was—and remains—open to interpretation. For better or worse, we still struggle to know him. In this quest, generations have taken liberties with his image, quoted him in and out of context, painted him as a peacemaker or a warmonger, a man of laughter or a perpetual depressive, a racist, a reformer, a deist, an evangelist, the American Bismarck, and a modern Moses. Such is the nature of human behavior. As Lincoln himself recognized in his First Inaugural Address, "Unanimity is impossible."

Offered here is an opportunity for readers to find their own conclusions through a series of categorized lists about the individual and his impact. For those who do not wish to wade through yet another thick biography and are not inclined to be satisfied with light overviews, the format of an annotated catalog offers a more compartmentalized look at any given subject within Lincoln's persona and the world in which he lived.

Not only can lists be succinct sources of information, but they also can bring better perspective through comparison and contrast. When placed in a larger context, the actions, events, and relationships frequently assumed to be the most important in Lincoln's life are often revealed to be something altogether different, while elements rarely considered can emerge as significant. A suitable example involves Lincoln's careers. Though he was president for a little more than four years, he was an attorney for a quarter century. While he remained amiable to nearly everyone he knew, his list of close friends was remarkably short, and even they frequently viewed him as an enigma.

As the man himself professed in his annual message to Congress in December 1862, "Fellow-citizens, we cannot escape history," and it seems American history cannot escape him. This work offers a different lens for the portrait. Each list begins with background information and criteria for respective rankings. Some lists are chronological to illustrate progression. Others are quantitative or qualitative. Where appropriate, names and terms appear in **bold type**, indicating that these subjects are referenced in another section. The book includes a collection and analysis of multiple and multifarious law cases, eyewitness accounts, biographies, state and federal reports, contemporary newspaper coverage, and monument analysis, as well as Lincoln's own actions, writings, and speeches. It is one more effort in the never-ending search for the real Lincoln.

Acknowledgments

THIS WORK IS BUT ONE CULMINATION IN THE CONTINUING LABORS OF thousands who study and preserve the details of our national past. By these people, I am inspired, and to them, I am eternally grateful. Many thanks to Charles A. Starling; the staff and volunteers at Lincoln's New Salem State Historic Site; Dr. Tom Schwartz and staff at the Lincoln Presidential Library and Museum; the staff of the Illinois State Archives; the John C. Hodges Library Special Collections staff at University of Tennessee at Knoxville; the Adams County, Pennsylvania, Historical Society; the National Park Service; and the Wisconsin Historical Society.

Along with my gratitude for the enormous moral support of my students, praise must go to the legal research of Masooda Folad and Petra Merkel, as well as social history research by Anna Clark. Abundant support and guidance came from my colleagues in the Columbia State History Department, including the late Hoyt Gardner, the late Dr. Bill Andrews, Dr. Barry Gidcomb, Greg Mewbourn, and Dr. Anna Duch, as well as invaluable writing advice from the English Department, particularly Bobby Thymn and Shane Hall. Thanks go to Dr. Robert Hunt for his direction on nineteenth-century material, along with the Pennsylvania State Archives in Harrisburg, John Heiser and Tom Greaney of the Gettysburg National Military Park Library, and Ken Allers Jr. for his Gettysburg expertise.

The last phases of this book were produced during personally trying times, including the deaths of several loved ones, a storm that destroyed much of my hometown, and the coronavirus pandemic. Thus, my deepest appreciation goes to Dave Reisch and Stackpole Books for their support and perseverance on this project, as well as to my family and friends, Barb Ross, Karl Green, Mike Bryant, Gus Schroeder, Drs. Rob and Laura Yost, John and Jacky Sylva, and many others. Your support has been, as always, immeasurable and invaluable. In this and all of my other publications, it would have never come to fruition without the wisdom and work of my chief editor and spouse, Theresa Ann Elworth.

Part I
The Private Lincoln

CHAPTER ONE

Lincoln's Homes

STRANGE THAT SO MUCH REVERENCE IS PAID TO PLACES LINCOLN LIVED, since Lincoln himself rarely showed much affection for the structures. While president, he spent nearly a quarter of his tenure in the main cottage of the Soldiers' Home on the northern edge of Washington, but he mentioned the locale in his writings just once, and only in passing. Of the Executive Mansion itself, he derided the crowded and creaky government building as "this damned old house."[1]

As the following list attests, he could be as restless as his birth nation. William Herndon, David Davis, and others equated this mobility with an unhappy home life. More likely, his wanderlust came from searching more than escaping. Certainly, he was not a homebody. He longed for mental engagement, whether through the company of others, burying himself in work, brooding over a book, storytelling, or playing with his kids. Though viewed as a lone figure, he generally disliked being alone.

In his lifetime, Lincoln dwelt in no fewer than six towns and cities, spread out over a thousand miles. It is almost fitting that even in death, Lincoln's body frequently moved, requiring tons of reinforced concrete to keep him in place. Below in chronological order are his successive primary residences, even though during his waking hours he was more apt to be out of the house than residing within.[2]

Sinking Spring Farm, Nolin Creek, Hardin (Now LaRue) County, Kentucky
February 1809–Spring 1811

When a child was born in the early nineteenth-century frontier, their chances of living to age five were fifty-fifty, their exact birthplace was rarely recorded, and the structure in which the delivery occurred almost never consisted of lasting materials. The same held true for little Abraham, his sister Sarah, and his little brother Thomas (who lived perhaps a few days). The Lincoln residence, as with many log cabins, was later parsed out for its trunks and lumber. In search of the exact spot, biographer Louis Warren gathered a multitude of testimonials, and found fifteen different birthplaces. Among the alleged locales were Swain County in North Carolina, Lynn Mountain in Tennessee, the old Lincoln home in Elizabethtown, and "Pop" Martin's place near the actual site. Lincoln was so unfamiliar with the place that he did not know for certain where his birth cabin stood.[3]

It can be said that nearly everything around the birthing was young. In 1809, Kentucky was only sixteen years old, and the United States was barely thirty-two. Hardin County itself had only recently been named, after a relative of Mary Todd. Indiana did not yet formally exist, nor did Illinois, Springfield, or Chicago.

Situated three miles from Hodgenville (Lincoln called it Hodgin'sville), the location had few attributes other than a consistent spring and a low market price. Otherwise, the surrounding land had marginal potential for crops or grazing. Not until the approach of the Lincoln centennial did the site garner much interest. The increasing hagiography of Lincoln, bonding with a resurgence of Horatio Alger's "rags to riches" novels and the American pastoralism of Frederick Jackson Turner, created a national movement to memorialize an otherwise wild, random plot (and a site that the Lincolns readily abandoned) into a secular shrine.[4]

Knob Creek, Hardin County, Kentucky
Spring 1811–December 1816

This was the home Lincoln first remembered, and where he went to school. Here his brother was born and soon died, and his father once again struggled to make a living. Just six miles north of the Sinking Spring Farm, the cabin itself stood along the Old Cumberland Trail, which was little more than a dirt path linking Nashville to Louisville. Much of the traffic, slow and lumbering, consisted of pioneers heading northward and across the Ohio River for better prospects.

In total, the property consisted of nearly 230 acres, although much of it was unusable. The homestead was in a flat valley with a few precious acres for farming. This aged sediment had been gleaned by rains and snowmelt from the rugged and steep surrounding knolls. Without the road alongside, the place would have felt utterly isolated. A two-mile walk due north brought Abe and his older sister to a schoolhouse, where the young boy attended at least two stints totaling but a few months. Sessions were usually in summer and winter, when there was little need of crop work. The family was so impoverished that Lincoln arrived for his first day in little more than a long sleep shirt, for which his classmates teased him. Otherwise, he hunted, fished, helped his dad with the cornfields, and played with area friends. Perhaps none was dearer to him than Austin Gollaher, a boy a few years his senior. During his presidency, Lincoln reportedly said, "I would rather see Gollaher than any man living." Though he felt close to several members of the community, he held no affection for the area's grinding poverty, extreme isolation, and harsh environment.[5]

PIGEON CREEK, PERRY COUNTY, INDIANA
December 1816–March 1830

In late autumn 1816, Thomas Lincoln followed a train of migrators ninety miles north to Indiana in yet another search for better conditions. Popular is the sentiment that he wanted to leave Kentucky because slavery repulsed him. While not the deciding factor, slavery played a secondary role. In Kentucky, the means of acquiring and owning humans was far clearer than the process of attaining land. Subsequent squabbles favored the wealthy, the wealthiest being slavers, leaving Thomas with little chance of holding on to his title. There was, however, relatively cheap land available in the Indiana Territory, made possible by whites driving indigenous populations from the area. From the 1787 Northwest

Ordinance onward, a rapid series of conflicts and treaties carved away Native communities. Just five years before Thomas's journey, Military Governor William Henry Harrison struck yet another blow at the Battle of Tippecanoe, where the Shawnee were trying to form a continent-wide resistance movement against the European tide.

Seventeen miles north of the Ohio River, thirty-eight-year-old Thomas marked out 160 acres with piles of brush and then headed back to retrieve his family. Upon their arrival—during one of the worst winters in regional memory—tradition states that Thomas constructed a "half-faced camp," a shelter open on one side and warmed by a roaring campfire. Abraham was seven, about to turn eight. By late spring, an eighteen-square-foot log cabin went up. The setting was exceedingly rustic and slow to evolve. Four years later, there were still only eight families living within a mile of the Lincolns' cabin, and there were no doctors, schools, or churches anywhere near them, though there was a growing number of chickens, hogs, corn rows, oat shoots, and wheat stalks.[6]

After Abe's mother, Nancy, died in 1818 and his father married Sarah Bush Johnston the following year, the cabin's population density increased dramatically. Abe slept in the loft alongside cousin Dennis Hanks and stepbrother John Johnston. Sleeping downstairs were his father, stepmother, sister Sarah, and stepsisters Elizabeth and Matilda. Thomas constructed most of the furnishings—the beds, a bureau, a table, and a few chairs. Sarah came with additional accoutrements and cookery, which added greatly to the home's functionality.[7]

The 1820 census listed the household as:

Thomas, 42	Elizabeth, 13
Sarah, 32	Abraham, 11
Dennis, 21	John, 10
Sarah, 13	Matilda, 9

Ten years later, Thomas, Sarah, Abe, and ten extended family members left for Illinois. In search of yet better soil, the Lincolns left behind one hundred productive acres, selling along with them some one hundred hogs and several hundred bushels of corn. They also walked away from a number of gravesites, including Abraham's mother, sister, and his sister's child. The journey would be a difficult one, spanning nearly 230 miles and traversing a number of streams and rivers swollen by spring rains, and ending with another set of homes yet to be built.[8]

TEN MILES SOUTHWEST OF DECATUR, ILLINOIS
March 1830–April 1831
On the banks of the Sangamon River, John Hanks, Thomas, and Abe began construction of a log cabin on March 30, 1830, having the shell completed in four days. By the end of spring they had completed the home, as well as a barn and smokehouse. Through the power of their teams of oxen, the Lincolns busted fifteen acres, fenced in by Abe's skilled axe work.

Through the remainder of the year, neighbors assisted each other in forming their own plots and homesteads. Here the young adult Abe did his most prolific work as a rail splitter, though neither he nor his parents stayed for long. The following summer, Lincoln, cousin John Hanks, and Denton Offutt were off to New Orleans on a flatboat, hauling a cache of crops and hogs, and father Thomas was on the move again to Coles County farther to the south and east. At age twenty-one, Lincoln was free to pursue his own future, which he did when Offutt proposed opening a store in the growing Sangamon village of New Salem, where Lincoln could work and live.[9]

NEW SALEM, ILLINOIS
July 1831–April 1837
Despite living as an adult for seven years in New Salem, Lincoln never resided in any one place for an extended period. He moved about frequently, often sleeping in one place and partaking of a meal in another. Such fluidity was not uncommon for unattached young men at that time and place. For that matter, permanence was a luxury enjoyed by very few in a new and shifting landscape. At its apex, New Salem contained merely a score of homes.

Returning to Illinois after **piloting a flatboat** for Denton Offutt to New Orleans, Lincoln opted to leave his father and stepmother for New Salem, first staying with the town's cofounder Reverend John Cameron and his large family. When Offutt opened a store in town and hired Lincoln to **clerk** it with Tennessee native William Greene, effectively part of their pay included the ability to bunk in the small log cabin. Unfortunately for both young men, they lost their accommodations and their jobs when the store failed in the summer of 1832, most certainly through no fault of either employee—both were gone at the time, serving in the Black Hawk War. Upon Lincoln's return from his uneventful time as a **soldier,** he went into business managing a store with William Berry, in a frame building unlike the ubiquitous log cabins of the town. The pair likely slept in the small back storage room where whiskey was stored. In early 1833, Lincoln and Berry bought another establishment, moving into the slightly larger structure to try their luck, eating at various homes whenever possible. Most certainly, Lincoln's life changed for the better when the county elected him in 1834, and again in 1836, to work and live in Vandalia in the **Illinois Legislature**.[10]

One of the reasons Lincoln eventually left New Salem was due to the dwindling number of places to stay. When the river proved too shallow and roadways too winding for heavy traffic, families moved to more promising vistas, including the newly established Petersburg just two miles northward, a town Lincoln himself helped plat as a **surveyor.** Lincoln himself left in 1837 for the city he helped become the state's new capital. As for the little bluff town that took him in when he was first on his own, it died not three years after Lincoln's departure, to become one of hundreds of ghost towns across the Midwest.

JOSHUA SPEED'S STORE
April 1837–1840
It was a Saturday in April when a homeless Abraham entered the merchant shop of **Joshua Speed** on the town square and inquired about the price of a bed and sheets. Seventeen dollars, Speed responded, an amount, Lincoln admitted, that was far beyond his means. "I never saw a sadder face," Speed later remarked; taking pity on the young man, he offered to

share his lodgings on the second floor. Immediately, Lincoln carried his saddlebags upstairs, plopped them on the floor, and returned with a far brighter countenance and declared, "Well, Speed, I am moved!"[11]

Thus began nearly four years of sharing a room—in fact, a bed, a common practice in a world of limited space and stark gender divisions. But Speed and Lincoln grew close as well. Prone to episodes of extreme sadness, Lincoln was at his most distraught when Speed moved back to Kentucky on January 1, 1841, to manage his family's plantation. Lincoln was to wed Mary Todd on the same day, but she ended their courtship for reasons unknown, which only added to his torment. He busied himself that spring by traveling the Eighth Judicial Circuit of Illinois, managing cases, switching law partners from **John Todd Stuart** to **Stephen T. Logan**, and consequently leaving his office in Hoffman's Row on the north side of the town square for a new, Greek Revival building across the way. That August, he traveled to Kentucky and spent a month with Speed and his new spouse Fanny Henning outside of Louisville. By September, mentally and physically recovered, he traveled back to Illinois to ride the court circuit yet again. In the interims, he likely resumed his New Salem survival strategy of lodging at taverns, in shops, and with friends. In other words, Lincoln was most at home when he was not at home.[12]

GLOBE HOTEL, SPRINGFIELD, ILLINOIS
Wedding Night, November 4, 1842–Late 1843

Mary was an investor. She saw enormous potential in Mr. Lincoln, though by outward appearances, it may have looked as if her marriage was a step down and her life had taken a downward trajectory. Giving up her life with older sister Elizabeth Todd Edwards and the relatively palatial Edwards home in a wealthier section of Springfield, she entered a boarding house with her new husband on Adams and Third Street, a few hundred yards from the main square. There was no honeymoon. Rent was around $4 per month, including meals, in a room of less than three paces by five paces. Many people knew the building as the Globe Tavern.[13]

However, there were advantages. Lincoln's new law office with Logan was just around the corner. She had family nearby. Living a short walking distance from downtown, the couple enjoyed easy access to plays, shops,

The Globe Hotel, also known as the Globe Tavern, where Mary and Abe's first child, Robert, future secretary of war under James Garfield and Chester A. Arthur, was born. Library of Congress.

and levees. The main floor featured parlors and a dining room that could seat nearly one hundred people. Even the Lincolns' horse ate well. Newspaper advertisements touted, "Attached to the hotel is a stable, where horses will have the best of fare."[14]

Their opportunities to partake of the pleasures of metropolitan life waned when Mary became pregnant with their first child. On August 1, 1843, she delivered Robert Todd Lincoln in their bedroom at the Globe Hotel. Though she enjoyed the support of her sisters close by, life in the bustling boarding house made new motherhood all the more challenging.[15]

214 FOURTH STREET, SPRINGFIELD, ILLINOIS
Late 1843–May 1844

Not long after Robert Lincoln's birth, the family rented a three-room, clapboard house on Fourth Street. Though his law practice was on the rise, Lincoln still earned a lower-middle-class income. On January 1, 1844, his bank savings totaled $134.30. His holdings, credit, and credentials needed to improve before the family could enter homeownership.[16]

But sometimes it is not what you know but who you know. While the Lincolns' financial position still languished, the minister who had performed their wedding needed to sell his home at Eighth and Jackson. To facilitate a purchase, Mary's father, Robert, granted the new parents a tidy sum—a fitting gesture, considering that their firstborn was named after him. Rev. Charles Dresser eventually received $1,200 in cash and a $300 lot (totaling approximately $52,000 in 2021 money) in exchange for the deed.[17]

EIGHTH AND JACKSON, SPRINGFIELD, ILLINOIS
May 1844–October 1847

This would be the only home that Mary and Abe would ever own. When they moved in, the place was not much larger than the rental they had just left. A one-story, white frame house with green shutters, it stood as solid, bucolic proof that Mr. Lincoln could achieve great things, just as Mary believed when others held some doubts. Mary may have been her happiest at this time, albeit in brief intervals. Her niece described the abode as "sweet and fresh, and Mary loved it. She was exquisitely dainty and her house was a reflection of herself, everything in good taste and perfect order."[18]

The idyllic scene grew with the arrival of little Edward Baker Lincoln in March 1846. Reportedly sweet-natured and loving, Eddie and his older brother Robert slept upstairs, often with one parent or the other—a common practice. With Lincoln's victory in the US midterm elections of 1846, the family eventually moved to Washington, D.C., renting their new home to a Mr. Cornelius Ludlum for the interim.[19]

SPRIGG'S BOARDING HOUSE, WASHINGTON, D.C.
December 1847–November 1848

Across the street from the Capitol, where the current Library of Congress resides, there stood a block of row houses known as Duff Green's Row, so named because of their wealthy owner. Lincoln, Mary, Robert, and baby Eddie took up residence in a building run by Mrs. Sprigg, along with several other congressional members who found the rent and location to be a wise business decision. Sprigg's was a Whig enclave, although, like the party as a whole, the tenants split along sectional lines on the issue of slavery—his resident colleagues hailed from Pennsylvania, Indiana, Ohio, and Mississippi. To keep the peace at the first-floor dining table, Lincoln diffused tense discussions by interrupting with a story or two. Lincoln was well liked. Mary struggled. Away from family and friends, she cared not for the weather or the disheveled, half-built Washington. By comparison, Springfield seemed refined. She was the only congressional spouse present. The sickly Eddie also left her longing for healthier environs and her familial support base. Before long, she and the children left for Kentucky.[20]

Eighth and Jackson, Springfield, Illinois
October 1848–February 1861

Following a rather unsuccessful term as a **US representative**, Abe and his growing family could expect to spend their lives firmly in the middle-class comforts of burgeoning Springfield. A quiet life awaited. But then, in July 1849, Mary's father perished in a cholera epidemic. Adding to her pain, her father's will triggered severe family infighting, with Mr. Lincoln pulled into the fray serving as her legal representative as well as representing three of her sisters then living in Springfield. In January 1850,

The remodeled Lincoln home on Eighth and Jackson. Lincoln's presidential campaign managers distributed images similar to this one to assure East Coast voters that their candidate was more than the "rail splitter" frontiersman that eager westerners portrayed him to be. Liljenquist Family Collection, Library of Congress.

her maternal grandmother passed away. Less than a month later, after suffering for weeks from a mysterious lung ailment, her "Little Eddie" died just shy of his fourth birthday. A devastated Abe and Mary held his funeral in the parlor of their home.[21]

From then on, these dark memories and the growing stresses of social climbing steadily eroded the pleasures of home life. In 1856, the Lincolns doubled the size of their home and their investment with a $1,300 addition, via Hannan and Ragsdale Architects and Builders of Springfield. Suddenly theirs was the largest home on the block, two full stories with a stone wall and iron fencing adorning front lawn, five bedrooms within, plus another for storage. While several homes in Springfield were far larger and grander, the Lincoln abode became a common destination for Mary's growing social calendar. Hundreds of people would come to her levees, made possible by their upgrades and the labor of house servants. Finally, the Lincolns could count themselves among the upper-middle class, with a public image suitable for renewed political ambitions.[22]

THE EXECUTIVE MANSION
March 1861–May 1865

When Mary first arrived in 1861, she exclaimed, "I am beginning to feel so perfectly at home, and enjoy everything so much." Years later, she attested, "All the sorrows of my life, occurred there."[23]

White House life was a constant struggle for the Lincolns, to the point that the weary president labeled the place "that damned old house." In its defense, the building had endured more than six decades of use and abuse, including a gutting fire in 1814 and several smaller ones thereafter, a public trashing on Andrew Jackson's Inauguration Day, and year after year of churning civil service work, not to mention the pleading office seekers who repeatedly infested the place. Last but certainly not least, the Lincolns were the fifteenth family to take up residence. The president's office on the second floor was anything but a refuge, as bad news from the war and pestering politicos from everywhere else left Lincoln on the brink of exhaustion. Manifold were the reasons to venture away from home, which Mom, Dad, and the kids did frequently, including long summers at the **Soldiers' Home** north of town. The death of beloved son and brother Willie in February 1862 inside the house only deepened their loathing.[24]

Nor was the immediate setting terribly inviting. Hardly a bucolic area, the District of Columbia had gone undeveloped throughout the colonial period for a reason. Largely marshland, its warm months produced sloppy humidity and whining clouds of mosquitoes. Winters brought freezing wet winds from the Atlantic and irrepressible infestations of house mice. Even after a lifetime of incorporation, the District's infrastructure remained poor, a fact punctuated by streets that alternated between mud and dust. Even the government itself looked haphazard and incomplete. The Capitol dome was little more than a truncated, skeletal shell (to remain unfinished until 1863). Situated between the White House and Capitol Hill, the Treasury Department was not yet finished. The obelisk Washington Monument stood less than half done (and would remain so until 1884). Add the fact that in a few weeks after his inauguration, Lincoln would be living on the front lines of a major war. The ensuing influx of refugees, soldiers, sailors, sex workers, manufacturers, and profiteers by the thousands would soon stress the place to the breaking point and push the population to more than one hundred thousand. The year 1863 alone saw twenty-four thousand arrests, with July averaging a murder every twenty-four hours. Plus, the town eventually contained approximately five thousand ladies of the evening plying their trade by war's end, spreading their infectious charms night and day. Intensifying the sense of misery and dread, sixty-eight forts surrounded the city, along with dozens of hospitals caring for sick, mangled, and dying young men.[25]

Mary's many detractors certainly condemned her for incessant attempts to improve the appearance of the place, but it could be argued that she tried her best to refurbish the government building for the same reason her husband insisted that construction of the Capitol dome should continue: both husband and wife wanted to offer concrete signs of national progress, in spite of the war's horrible setbacks. It was also how they operated. Abraham and Mary remodeled their home on Eighth and Jackson in Springfield at least seven times, reflective of their constant ambition to improve their existing condition, regardless of how far they had already come. Yet, unbeknownst to them both, in the spring of 1865, Abraham would leave the house a month before she would.[26]

CHAPTER TWO

Lincoln's Greatest Mentors

ENTICING IS THE THOUGHT OF THE PURELY SELF-MADE LINCOLN, FORG-
ing his own principles and success out of the American wilderness into
which he was born. In many ways, the chief architect of this image was
Lincoln himself, who tacitly crafted this semblance as an appeal to the
voting masses. Soon after his death, a litany of somber tributes perpet-
uated the legacy of his modest origins. As Charles Sumner said in his
famous eulogy, "His style was his own; formed on no model, and spring-
ing directly from himself."[1]

This romanticized view ignores the basic nature of Lincoln's development. Though painfully aware of his social clumsiness and awkward
appearance, Lincoln was more concerned about a natural gravitation
toward depression and its ensuing specter of isolation. Late in age, he
expressed an inherently high degree of self-reliance, but much of that
autonomy came after years of guidance and assistance from others. Yet
throughout his life he rarely worked or traveled on his own and actively
sought the company of others, especially those with experience. For
example, Lincoln served as a junior law partner until age thirty-five, past
middle age for the time. His stepmother Sarah noted that Lincoln loved
to play with children and argue with his contemporaries, but she said,
"He duly reverenced old age. . . . He listened to the aged."[2]

Lincoln's mentors were a varied lot, from the semiliterate to university graduates, from the impoverished to the upper-middle class. Still,
their similarities are striking. Geographically, Lincoln's teachers were
firmly tied to the border states, neither fully Northern nor Southern in

background or sentiment. Politically, the majority were moderate, if not partial to the working and middle classes. Many hailed from slaveholding states but were not supportive of the institution. Lastly, despite the misogynistic world in which he lived, and his own gaucherie around women, Lincoln tended to venerate females with the same sincerity as he did males. Consequently, very much like the borderlands from which he came, Lincoln continuously lived in a multitude of worlds simultaneously, making him a complex subject for biographers thereafter. Below are the individuals most prominent in the development of the adult Lincoln, in order of their appearance in his life. The list is certainly not complete, but it contains the primary contributors to his character and trajectory.

NANCY HANKS LINCOLN (VIRGINIA, 1784–1818)

In nearly every sense, Abraham unquestionably belonged to his mother. Neighbors and family described her as sensitive, tenderhearted, and uncommonly intelligent, attributes she evidently instilled in her son. She was born in the northwest hills of Old Dominion (today's Mineral County, West Virginia). Uncertainty prevails concerning who her birth parents were. She would be called Nancy Sparrow in her teens, being the daughter, stepdaughter, or close relative of one Henry Sparrow. Years later, Nancy's ambiguous lineage spawned wild speculations, including unsubstantiated rumors that she, and consequently her famous son, had African ancestry. More is known of her mother, Lucy, who by some accounts was a skilled seamstress, neat, orderly, and kind. As an infant, Lucy Hanks was brought by her mother to the Kentucky Territory. Her uncle Thomas and aunt Elizabeth Sparrow, effectively her foster parents, moved the family to Nolin Creek.[3]

Physically, Abe resembled his mother more than his father. She was relatively tall for a woman of the time, somewhere near five feet, seven inches. Although accounts differ as to whether she was thin or relatively sturdy, she reportedly did possess a head of thick raven locks. Her eyes were probably hazel and were said to have been uncommonly clear in their gaze. No living image of her exists, though artist Lloyd Ostendorf's 1963 conjectural painting of her (located at the Lincoln Birthplace near Hodgenville) remains a popular hypothesis of her likeness.[4]

Nancy married Thomas Lincoln in 1806, possibly while she was already pregnant with their first child, Sarah, who arrived eight months after the wedding. Two years later, nearly to the day, Nancy again gave birth, this time to a healthy and soon-to-be quite tall Abraham. Nancy herself was barely literate, but she reportedly encouraged her son to break the cycle. Altogether, she more than Thomas showed greater reverence for the written word and a desire to be more than she was. Mother Lincoln also suffered from depression, a condition shared with her Abraham. Yet if her son could learn how to read, he might one day write a happier story for himself, a life beyond the hardships she endured every day.[5]

THOMAS LINCOLN (VIRGINIA, 1778–1851)

Some individuals have minimized, even belittled, Thomas Lincoln's role in his son's development, and it is fair to say that Abraham was among them. In a letter to a distant relative, then Congressman Lincoln called his father "a wholly uneducated man; which I suppose is the reason why I know so little of our family history." In notes given to John Locke Scripps of the *Chicago Tribune* for a campaign biography in 1860, Abe claimed his dad "never did more in the way of writing than to bunglingly sign his own name." Early biographers parroted the son, especially Josiah G. Holland in his 1865 *Life of Abraham Lincoln* and William Herndon, who portrayed Thomas as "roving and shiftless."[6]

The evidence points to a different character, a person who was certainly in motion but far from lazy. At one time, Thomas owned three farms, for which he paid cash. Reflecting a restless nation, he lived in perhaps ten different places in is lifetime. Responsible with money, a storyteller, with a strong physical work ethic, he tried several trades, including farming, carpentry, jail guard, and land ownership. Thomas also labored as a surveyor, as would his son. A Whig, he often signed petitions for the improvement of roads in the community. Seeing his father repeatedly fail due to circumstances far beyond his own control likely inspired Lincoln to favor a political system that supported the laborer over the landed gentry.[7]

Concerning education, Sarah Bush Johnston Lincoln recalled, "As a usual thing Mr. [Thomas] Lincoln never made Abe quit reading to do anything if he could avoid it. He would do it himself first. Mr. Lincoln could read a little and could scarcely write his name: hence he wanted, as he himself felt the uses and necessities of education, his boy Abraham to learn and encouraged him to do it all the way he could."[8] David Turnham, a neighbor of the Lincolns in Indiana, observed, "Abe favored him in many particulars. Both were humorous—good natured—slow in action somewhat."[9]

As a member of the Separate Baptist Church at Pigeon Creek in Indiana, he had Abe assist in services, though the son never joined. But Thomas himself, and the church itself, was not at all dogmatic. The congregation did endorse two concepts that the young Abraham apparently shared: a strong sense of fate and an open disdain for slavery. Thomas also taught his son basic carpentry, how to wield an axe, and the fickle fortunes of agriculture.[10]

Last and certainly not least, Thomas brought Abraham and his beloved stepmother together, an otherwise improbable kinship that helped the young boy endure some of the most physically and emotionally difficult periods of his young life. For this and many other acts, Abraham would name one of his own sons Thomas. Without question, the relationship was fraught with discord, and the greater share of love emanated from the father. Notably, this uneasy, frustrated connection with a less educated and rough-hewn father would be remarkably similar to how Robert Lincoln would see his own dad.

SARAH BUSH JOHNSTON LINCOLN (KENTUCKY, 1788–1869)

After Lincoln's mother died, his father left Abraham and his sister for several months, which may have contributed to Abe's sense of disconnection toward Thomas. However, upon his return, the Lincoln family was suddenly much greater in size and wealth. Sarah Bush Johnston, herself a widow, married forty-one-year-old Thomas when she was a youthful thirty-one. She brought with her bedsteads, feather bed mattresses, quilts, rudimentary pots and utensils, and a pair of spinning wheels. Thomas, poor as he was but in land, had to borrow a wagon and team to haul the lot from Elizabethtown. She also brought her children—namely, twelve-year-old Elizabeth, nine-year-old John, and eight-year-old Matilda.

Suddenly Abraham at ten and twelve-year-old sister Sarah could feel a greater familial connection and experience the otherwise foreign world of childhood among their new playmates.[11]

Intolerant of frontier life's barbarities, Sarah insisted on cleanliness of mind and body. A believer in discipline, she also offered praise, especially to Abraham, for which he felt warmly grateful, and to which he was unaccustomed. In short, she replaced a life of mere survival with one of planning and working toward a better future. Concerning her adopted son, she insisted, "Abraham gave me never one hard word . . . was temperate in all things—too much so I thought sometimes." Regardless, she confessed, "Abe was the best boy I ever saw or ever expect to see. . . . His mind and mine—what little I had, seemed to run together—move in the same channel."[12]

JAMES RUTLEDGE (SOUTH CAROLINA, 1781–1835)

Compared to the foreboding forests of barely settled Spencer County, Indiana, the open fields and growing town of New Salem must have felt like the promised land to the twenty-two-year-old Lincoln. When he arrived in July 1831, the town itself was only two years old (and unbeknownst to its inhabitants, would all but disappear by 1840). It was a tiny but promising hamlet on a bluff, made possible by the construction of a water mill, a store, and a tavern. At the time, the town looked like a solid place to reside, for it held status as one of the focal trading spots on the Sangamon River. Furthermore, it attracted one of the scarcest commodities in the West—erudite minds.

Back in southwestern Indiana, Lincoln was among the most educated among his neighbors, where simply being literate placed him in high standing. In New Salem, he was but a sponge in a new sea. Among his fellow residents were Dr. John Allen, graduate of Dartmouth; Dr. Jason Duncan, who led the effort to make young Abe postmaster of the village; and Thomas J. Nance, schoolteacher for the community. While Abraham possessed a few months of elementary schooling, five of his new neighbors studied at Illinois College at Jacksonville.[13]

For the entirety of his six years here, he never owned his own place, staying instead at the shops in which he worked or with families in the area. One of his sanctuaries was the home and tavern of the man who made the town possible. James Rutledge, along with one John Cameron, founded New Salem in 1829. Lincoln biographer Benjamin Thomas describes Rutledge as "medium height, quiet, dignified, sincerely religious, and fairly well educated." Along with giving Abraham a place to settle, Rutledge provided a cache of books from his personal library, possibly as many as thirty volumes, which Lincoln borrowed and read frequently. In addition, Rutledge gave the community and its promising minds an outlet of immeasurable worth—he founded a debating society. By entering this chorus of educated voices, Lincoln started his journey from mere storyteller to proper public speaker. Denied such pleasures back in rural Indiana, he was suddenly able to share in topics of academic gravity, such as the nature and responsibilities of representative government, the merits of free versus slave labor, and the complexities of religion.[14]

Perhaps most critical in his fostering of Lincoln's evident abilities, Rutledge was one of the individuals who encouraged him in 1832 to run for the Illinois Legislature, when Abe was just twenty-three. The young candidate lost, but he found a new passion and a great deal of confidence. Unfortunately, legend reduces Mr. Rutledge's contributions to a single event—he produced a daughter, centerpiece to the myth that Lincoln had only one true love of his life who wasn't Mary Todd.[15]

(WILLIAM) MENTOR GRAHAM (KENTUCKY, 1800–1886)

It was in New Salem that Lincoln truly began to grow, but the town itself did not. The Sangamon River, hoped the locals, would become a major artery of new blood and business, but its quiet and shallow draft proved to be little more than a capillary in the body of Illinois. Nonetheless, the people of New Salem helped the sprouting Abe navigate his transition into adulthood. Among its most influential figures was the appropriately named Mentor Graham. Nine years Lincoln's elder, Graham lived just west of town, and the young Lincoln stayed with him for several months in 1833. A schoolmaster who helped him learn mathematics, Graham also championed the art of rhetoric, which enabled Lincoln to learn a second language, as it were. In this pursuit, Graham directed Lincoln to the nearest copy of grammar in New Salem, **Samuel Kirkham's** *Grammar in Familiar Lectures*, owned by an individual who lived six miles from town.[16]

Evidently, much of his guidance came by way of avid encouragement rather than capable teaching. Graham's qualifications as an educator were suspect, and his spelling involved a great deal of phonetical guesswork. Still, many years later, Lincoln referred to him as "my old teacher." R. B. Rutledge, brother of Lincoln's friend Ann, contended, "I know of my own knowledge that Graham did more than all others to educate Lincoln."[17]

Interestingly, Graham was a hard-line Democrat. In 1844, he voted for James K. Polk. In 1846, when Lincoln ran for US Congress, Graham voted for his opponent, Peter Cartwright. He was, however, a Unionist, and he voted for Lincoln at least in 1864.[18]

BOWLING GREEN (NORTH CAROLINA, 1787–1842)

Green was educated, though unrefined, and a lawyer with a politician's charisma and a protruding gut—he tipped the scales at three hundred pounds. Perhaps the latter quality came from his preference for strong drink. His home just north of New Salem was Lincoln's shelter for a time, right after Ann Rutledge passed away in August 1835. Green's personal library was an oasis of information for the curious scholar.[19]

Lincoln, in one of his first political acts, voted for the Democrat Green in 1831 to justice of the peace. The following year, partly to support the promising lad, and partly in hopes of knocking the more influential Whig John Todd Stuart out of office, Green supported Lincoln in his first run for the 1832 Illinois House, as he would do again in 1834 in Lincoln's first win.[20]

Legend has it that when Lincoln left New Salem for a new life in Springfield, he was mounted on a horse loaned to him by Bowling Green. Years later, Lincoln was given the honor of speaking at Green's funeral.[21]

JOHN "JACK" KELSO (KENTUCKY, 1795–1868)

Described as the local dreamer, the "village philosopher," though also a rustic hunter and fisherman, New Salem's Jack Kelso immersed the young Lincoln in William Shakespeare, Robert Burns, and Lord Byron.

Neighbors recalled the two men sitting for hours at a time, resting in the cool shade of a ravine. The homeless Lincoln also resided with Jack and his wife Hanna for several months.[22]

Kelso was also Lincoln's source for critics of religion and political tyranny. Among Kelso's favorites were Thomas Paine and Voltaire, while Lincoln gravitated toward the equally skeptical Burns. Adding to Lincoln's arm's-length treatment of organized religion and active disdain for injustice, Kelso also helped teach him in surveying, and the two plotted a road project from nearby Musick's Ferry through New Salem.[23]

SIMEON FRANCIS (CONNECTICUT, 1796–1872)

While serving as postmaster in New Salem, Lincoln enjoyed access to stacks of subscribers' newspapers, including the *Cincinnati Gazette*, *Louisville Journal*, and *St. Louis Republican*, and most were heavily Whig in their leanings. One closer to home, and just as partisan, was the *Sangamo Journal* under the editorship of East Coast native and Freemason Simeon Francis.[24]

Francis himself had apprenticed at a young age in a Connecticut printing office.[25] He came to Springfield in 1831 and started the *Journal* soon after, working from a two-story frame building on the northeast corner of Washington and Sixth. His modest office may have been one of the strongest magnets that eventually pulled Lincoln into Springfield. Simeon himself exuded energy. Bright, hopeful, and extroverted, he was among the most optimistic and outspoken about the promise of Springfield, a buoyant disposition that evidently persuaded Lincoln to think the same of Springfield and Illinois as a whole.[26]

Along with John Todd Stuart and others, Francis formed the community's Lyceum in 1833, a group in which Lincoln would make his first public speeches and form several of his fundamental political views. In 1836, the New Salem–based Lincoln used the *Journal* to promote his own ardently Whig views and to announce his candidacy for reelection to the state house. "Whether elected or not, I go for distributing the proceeds of the sales of public lands to the several States to enable our State, in common with others, to dig canals and construct railroads without borrowing money and paying the interest on it." The *Journal*'s clearly partisan rhetoric at times became more than some men could bear, including the Little Giant himself. In 1840, Stephen Douglas encountered Francis in the street and proceeded to beat the editor with his cane.[27]

On a sentimental note, Francis's wife played a major role in paving Abe's path. Distressed that her dear friend Mary Todd had estranged from her fiancé Abraham, Mrs. Francis, apparently without the two parties knowing, invited the broken couple to a gathering at the Francis home in 1842, with the ulterior motive of binding up the wounds of separation. The plan apparently worked, and the courting reconvened.[28]

Simeon and Abe had something of a falling-out in 1856, as the splinter faction "Know-Nothings" threatened to start a rival paper in town. Fearing he would soon be demolished financially, Francis sold his business, a move Lincoln later told him was a mistake. This dis-agreement, however, did not prevent Francis from supporting Lincoln thereafter. In 1860, from his new home in Oregon, Francis supported Lincoln's bid for the presidency, and he served as a paymaster in the US Army during the war.[29]

JOHN TODD STUART (KENTUCKY, 1807–1885)

They met in the Black Hawk War, and their paths crossed again when they shared the Whig ballot for the 1834 state election to the lower house. Stuart would later become Lincoln's first law partner, and Lincoln would marry into Stuart's extended family. The inclination might be to believe Stuart was fortunate to stumble upon a rising icon. In reality, it was Lincoln who benefited most from the charming, venerated, and established Stuart.

In 1834, they ran for the four district spots available for the Illinois House. Lincoln finished first, while Stuart finished fourth. But the standings were more because Lincoln was a relative unknown, inoffensive to both Whigs and Democrats, while Stuart was a Whig chieftain, and consequently the target of opposition. In the state legislature, Stuart and Lincoln roomed together, making their residence a virtual situation room for the Whig Party. Stuart had been selected as floor leader for the faction, but he had his sights set on the national legislature, allowing Lincoln to act as his proxy during his many absences.[30]

Highly supportive of Lincoln when both were rising in the world of law and politics, the older Stuart split with Lincoln at a critical moment of US history. When the Thirteenth Amendment came to the floor of the US House, Congressman Stuart voted against the measure to end human slavery in the nation.

John lived in Springfield while Abe was in New Salem twenty miles distant. By 1836, Lincoln was coming to his office on a regular basis, plodding up to the second floor of the brick-façade Hoffman's Row, a short walk off the town's main square. Stuart's partner at the time, Henry Dummer, attested, "He was the most uncouth looking man I ever saw. He seemed to have but little to say; seemed to feel timid, with a tinge of sadness . . . but when he did talk all this disappeared for the time. . . . He surprised us more and more at every visit."[31]

Despite just two years' difference in age, their relationship was that of paternal figure and student, as Stuart was much of everything Lincoln was not—handsome and college educated, he was also the son of a classical professor at Transylvania College.

With an established practice, ready client base, and venerated status, John accepted Abe as his junior partner from 1837 to 1841. Overall, Stuart was sloppy in record keeping and correspondence and kept an imprecise office, as his attentions were more loyal to the lure of politics. Lincoln picked up both habits. Part of Stuart's incentive to take on the unique but inexperienced Lincoln was a personal desire to get back to his true love of politics. Stuart looked to have Lincoln take on the basic cases, while he would look to win a congressional seat from a rival Democrat, one Stephen A. Douglas. Indeed, in 1838 Stuart beat Stephen Douglas for the US House by a mere thirty-six ballots of more than thirty-six thousand. In turn, his frequent absences enabled Lincoln to become a prominent figure in Springfield law and the state house.[32]

STEPHEN T. LOGAN (KENTUCKY, 1800–1880)

John Todd Stuart may have been the major figure in nudging Lincoln into law, but Stephen Trigg Logan drilled into Lincoln's head the necessity of legal and linguistic precision. In an 1862 letter to Gideon Welles, Lincoln described Logan as "almost a father to me." Logan prized Abraham's sheer tenacity. "I have seen him get a case and seem to be bewildered at first, but he would go at it and after a while he would master it. He was very tenacious in his grasp of a thing that he once got hold of."[33]

Logan was first impressed by the fellow Kentuckian in 1832 when he saw Lincoln in Springfield's old courthouse campaigning in that year's election. "He was a very tall and gawky and rough looking fellow," said Logan. "His pantaloons didn't meet his shoes by six inches. But after he began speaking I became very much interested in him."[34]

Though Logan was just as sloppy in dress, he was far more business-like and exact. He also had a temper and a limited sense of humor, and he was frequently impatient and demanding, but he imposed a discipline on Lincoln's practice. Nonetheless, Logan did not have his younger partner's ability with people. Historian Brian Dirck determined he was "surpassingly ugly, a smallish, wizened little man who some likened to a gnome." Nonetheless, he was one of the most prominent and respected attorneys in the state. Legal historian John Duff contends that "no man contributed more towards bringing Lincoln's natural gifts as a lawyer to their fullest fruition."[35]

They dissolved their legal partnership in late 1844 on good terms. Logan wished to make his own son his junior partner, and Lincoln was ready to establish his own practice. They would remain in close proximity, but not necessarily as friends, going head-to-head in the Illinois Supreme Court no fewer than thirty-two times, with the results nearly even. In 1860, Logan attended the Republican National Convention and was a leading Lincoln promoter at the Wigwam. In turn, Lincoln as president trusted him so much that he appointed Logan to an Illinois commission that investigated claims against the federal government.[36]

CHAPTER THREE

Mary and Abe Commonalities

HE WAS BORN IN POVERTY, AND SHE IN OPULENCE. LANKY AS A TREE, HE
moved in plodding steps, while Mary was short and portly, traversing
on impulse. He forgave readily, while she took slights to heart. He cared
little for material things, whereas she was a compulsive shopper. Yet these
are differences often amplified by Mary's many detractors. In style, they
starkly contrasted, but in substance they could be close. He had courted
others before Mary, and may have been in love once or twice, but in her
he found a lasting match. Opposites may attract, but it was the similarities that truly bound Abe and Mary.

BOTH WERE BORN IN KENTUCKY
Each arrived on a cold Sunday in winter, though their births occurred
ninety miles and nearly a decade apart. The names Abraham and Mary
were favored in their respective families and were given to children
frequently over many generations. Specifically, he was named after his
paternal grandfather, she after her mother's only sister. In youth, he went
mostly by "Abe," a name he apparently disliked. In maturity he became
invariably "Lincoln" or "Mr. Lincoln," even to his wife. Little Mary was
known as "Mary Ann" until the age of five, when her sister Ann was
born. After marriage it was commonly "Mrs. Lincoln," while her husband
habitually called her Mary, Molly, or Mother.

Few details are known of their early childhoods. Due to high mor-
tality rates, mostly from a myriad of infections and diseases, infants were
often viewed as precarious entities. Indeed, Abe was three when he lost

The first known photos of Lincoln and Mary, circa 1847. To date, Lincoln is the only US president born in Kentucky; so, too, Mary is the lone First Lady born in the Bluegrass State.

a baby brother to illness. Mary was four when a younger brother died. Virtually no family in their immediate circles was spared. Senator Henry Clay and his wife Lucretia, close friends of the Todds, experienced the anguish of losing five of their six daughters.[1]

BOTH LOST THEIR BIRTH MOTHERS EARLY

Without question, Mary could be clingy. In contrast, Lincoln was amiable but could be emotionally detached. Arguably, both personalities were formed, in part, by a mutual trauma from their childhood. Lincoln's loss of his mother, **Nancy Hanks Lincoln,** as well as an aunt and uncle, to toxic cow milk left the nine-year-old Abe firmly aware of life's harsh transience.

Mary Todd grew up in a similar state of biological fear. In 1825, when she was only six, a litany of epidemics struck her hometown of Lexington, particularly the urban curses of cholera and typhoid. But it was an infection that struck her beloved mother, resulting from the dangerous event of childbirth. At the time, one in seven deliveries on average were fatal to the mother, as the seventh was for Eliza Todd. Soon after her little George was born, Eliza developed "childbed fevers," a common effect of unsanitary environments in which the births took place, which was most often at home. When she took ill, three male doctors treated her (a rare occurrence in the gender-segregated world of nineteenth-century Lexington). Despite their efforts, she slowly slipped away. Most likely it was puerperal sepsis or a related strain, although the doses of mercury and opium and the fading art of bloodletting administered by her doctors likely did not help. She was thirty-one. Mary's reaction to her mother's death was not recorded. What pain she felt remains a mystery, but what transpired next likely exacerbated a sense of loss. Within six months, her father proposed to another woman, and, unlike Abe with his new step-mother, Mary grew to hate her father's second wife.[2]

BOTH WERE WELL READ

As youngsters, both Mary and Abraham were more cerebral and con-templative than nearly everyone their same age. Though both claimed to learn slowly, they clearly excelled in school and displayed an exceptional ability to retain information. Of the two, Mary received far more school-ing. With ten years of personal tutoring and private academy, she was more educated than most of society, including much of the elite. Like her future husband, Mary essentially attained most of her knowledge through reading.[3]

Poems were their first love. Even as a young teen, Mary became partial to the greats. Cousin Margaret Stuart Woodrow observed that, above all, Mary had a "love for poetry, which she was forever reciting." In Lincoln she found a kindred spirit, as they shared a deep affection for the writings of Robert Burns, and each could recite some of his more famous works.[4] In prose, ironically, it was Mary who preferred Charles Dickens and his sentimental depictions of the underclass. Lin-coln appeared to steer in the opposite direction, especially in his youth, when he devoured biographies of heroic figures such as Benjamin Franklin and George Washington.

In later years, he carefully read mathematics, guide books on grammar and elocution, and piles of newspapers. Her reading list consisted heavily of romances, classics, novels, and the occasional history, all of which she

English poet and playwright Edward Bulwer-Lytton. Among the novels that Mary read as an adult was Lytton's novel *Paul Clifford*, which contains the famously hackneyed line "It was a dark and stormy night . . ."

could read in French. And both venerated Shakespeare. Mary encountered him sooner than Lincoln, studying the classics as a teen in her pristine Lexington boarding school, while he first read of the English master while in his twenties along the banks of the muddy Sangamon.[5] In time, they would both use the Bard of Avon to describe each other. When the couple was first engaged, their independent minds clashed over the commitment, and they parted in anger and accusation. Thereafter, Lincoln sank away from her and into a dark gloom. Mary feared for his mental health, and she admitted to a friend, "Imagine that others were as seldom gladdened by his presence as my humble self, yet I would the case were different, that 'Richard' would be himself again, much happiness would it afford me." By "Richard," Mary meant Shakespeare's Richard II, a king who had fallen into an immeasurable despair, to the point that his queen feared she had lost him. In warmer tones, and after years of wedlock, Lincoln described his wife to a friend by quoting from the iconic *Macbeth*. Praising Mary's consistent faith in his abilities, Lincoln called her "my dearest partner of greatness," a line uttered by Lady Macbeth.[6]

BOTH MOVED TO SPRINGFIELD IN SEARCH OF OPPORTUNITY
They were from Kentucky, but they did not meet until they moved to Illinois, "they" being Lincoln and his confidant Joshua Speed, his

friend O. H. Browning, the schoolteacher Mentor Graham, and Lincoln's three law partners John Todd Stuart, Stephen Logan, and Billy Herndon. Much of Bluegrass country was in a state of decline in the mid-nineteenth century. From 1830 to 1860, its population grew an average of less than 2 percent per year. As for Mary, all three of her sisters first transferred from Kentucky to Springfield, including the oldest, Elizabeth, who introduced Mary to Lincoln. Reasons for their respective migrations were manifold, but, in general, the greatest pull was the promise of greater wealth.

While the Todds represented the "go west" movement, Lincoln was heading south and east. It was a modest move of fifteen miles for him, but it may have seemed like a world away. His adopted hometown of New Salem was suffering from a river too shallow for steamer traffic and roads too few and distant. With a cooper, a blacksmith, a few shops, and a milldam, the town had the heart but not the arteries for survival. Unlike nearby Springfield, growing by strides as the seat of Sangamon County, New Salem only had one doctor, no lawyers, no churches, and no hotel. At its peak, the settlement's population was a mere twenty-five families. In 1837, Lincoln subtracted himself from the equation, packed his few belongings, and headed to a town that numbered one thousand residents and growing.

Coming to Springfield a month after him was his future bride, though they did not meet until the following year. For Mary, visiting her sisters Elizabeth and Frances may have been a bit of a shock. Springfield was still taking its first crude steps out of the roughshod prairieland. By comparison, Lexington, though isolated, was established and revered. It was also her home, and she made her way back to Lexington later that year.

But "home" contained little independence and an overbearing stepmother. Ever since her teens, she felt "my early home was truly at a boarding school," meaning Shelby Female Academy, where she returned to apprentice as a teacher.[7]

That same year, a crippling economic depression confirmed what many Lexington natives had already feared: their town was dying. Like a New Salem writ large, the old city had few roads leading to it, and the closest major river was the Ohio, eighty rugged miles away. While Louisville, Cincinnati, and Springfield were doubling in population every five years, the once burgeoning "Athens of the West" had clearly stagnated. As if to drive the point home with a lancet, the medical school at Transylvania University (the long, great pride of Lexington), transferred to Louisville.[8]

Much to the dismay of her father, Mary returned to her sisters and Springfield in 1839, excited by the prospect of meeting new people and possibly becoming a teacher, to live on her own terms. Her timing was fortunate. The town was about to become the new capital of Illinois, thanks in part to a man she would later meet.

BOTH WERE CLOSER TO HER SIDE OF THE FAMILY

Lincoln was foremost a pragmatist. In his wife he found love. In her family, and not his own, he found useful contacts. Likewise, Mary remained attached to her sisters and some of her stepsiblings, but she apparently made no attempt to reach out to her husband's side while he was alive. This is not to suggest that the Todds were more enjoyable company than the Lincolns. The Todds were a proud family, prone to exaggerated thoughts of self-worth. As tradition states, Lincoln noticed that God only needed one *d* in his name, but the Todds demanded two.[9]

In truth, by the time of their wedding—conducted in Mary's sister and brother-in-law's parlor—Lincoln did not have much of a family left. With mother, sister, and baby brother long since dead, all that remained were distant cousins, his stepmother, and his father. So strained was the last relationship that when Thomas Lincoln became gravely ill in late 1850, Lincoln did not travel the eighty miles to be by his father's death-bed. Nor when the man died in January 1851 did Abraham attend the burial or funeral, nor did he provide a headstone for the grave. It is true that the last of Abe's four sons was named after Lincoln's father, but it is not known whether Abraham ever disclosed that fact to his surviving stepmother. In fact, Lincoln never introduced his wife or any of his children to his father or his stepmother. In contrast, his very first son was christened Robert Todd in honor of Mary's father.[10]

For a young and upwardly mobile couple, the Lincolns knew the power of networking, and the Todds had wealth and education that the Lincoln side simply did not. In addition, brother-in-law Ninian Edwards was the son of a former Illinois governor. William Wallace, a younger brother-in-law and namesake of his third child, was a prominent doctor in Springfield. On many occasions, Lincoln performed legal work for the family, though in one instance Mary's brother Levi proved less than cooperative (see **Lawyer Lincoln**).

These lucrative bonds continued, and they were partly responsible for Lincoln's rise in politics. When he ultimately achieved the presidency, he hosted several of his in-laws at the White House, including Confederate ones, but from his own side only distant cousin Dennis Hanks came to visit. For his brothers-in-law, Lincoln appointed Ninian Edwards a commissary officer, even though Edwards voted against him in the 1860 elections; William Wallace was named a paymaster; and Charles Kellogg also received a job as army commissary officer, despite being pro-slavery.[11]

BOTH WERE DIE-HARD WHIGS

They came from Whig households, primarily because of their fathers, who favored the relatively new principles of progressive social reform and active government. Their party derived its name from the old English brand of those in opposition to an unresponsive monarchy, which for the Whigs of America came in the guise of autocratic Andrew Jackson.

The faction was more of a natural fit for Mary, for it appealed to, and was led mostly by, philanthropic members of an educated upper class. In many ways she was born into it. Her father Robert Smith Todd thoroughly believed that, as a prominent and successful figure in society, he possessed noblesse oblige. Rising to assemblyman and then senator of Kentucky's state legislature, he frequently mixed with the highest names in state politics, and his Lexington home became a hub of political discussion.[12] Eager to take part in such lively exchanges, and humored by her loving dad, Mary sat among the adults and expressed her support as early as age nine. Certainly, it was a rare thing in the existing environment for a female to be outspoken on politics, let alone a child. But as she

While in Springfield, a single Mary Todd knew and was courted by Stephen Douglas. She resisted any motion toward matrimony, however, partly because she could not stomach the fact that he was a Democrat.

matured, she maintained her interest in the subject. Becoming one of the most educated in her family, she also aimed to stay among the most politically connected, despite the societal limitations placed upon her gender.

Though hardly wealthy or connected, Lincoln's father favored the idea that local governments should help in advancing the general condition. Abe adopted these views, including the promotion of internal improvements. In his very first run for office in 1832, Lincoln hammered the theme of river and road development as his main plank. The following year, the New Salem resident eagerly signed a community petition for the construction of local roads.[13]

This harmony of political disposition brought Mary and Abe closer than perhaps any other factor. While they moved tenuously into courtship, they rushed headlong into campaigns. In 1840, while Lincoln became a Whig elector and stump speaker, Mary surprised even herself in the degree of her involvement in the pending presidential election. Scouring the Whiggish *Sangamo Journal* for campaign news, attending speeches, marveling at the partisan parades and political debates around her, she observed, "This fall I became quite a politician, rather an unladylike profession, yet at such a crisis, whose heart could remain untouched while

A rare voice of reason in midcentury US politics, Henry Clay labored for years to temper sectional divisions. His death in 1852 left moderates without their greatest advocate. Library of Congress.

the energies of all were called in question?"[14] Though each supported the Whig nominee William Henry Harrison, they privately preferred a mutual hero: the celebrated father of their cherished party, Henry Clay.

BOTH REVERED HENRY CLAY

Mary knew Clay since her childhood as a dear family friend. Lincoln called him "my beau of an ideal statesman, the man for whom I fought all my humble life."[15] Handsome, refined, dashing, Speaker of the House, secretary of state, senator, Henry Clay became a giant in Congress when that branch dominated the course of federal politics. Among his many monikers, including "Harry of the West," "Star of the West," and "Prince Hal," the most fitting was the "Great Compromiser." With his shepherding, the legislature created the Compromise of 1820, establishing the states of Missouri and Maine, maintaining a balance of free and slave states in the Senate. When South Carolina threatened to leave the Union in 1833 because of high federal tariffs, Clay negotiated a gradual reduction of import duties, staving off a national crisis. In 1850, he again rescued the country from its own passions, constructing a delicate (yet ultimately doomed) set of pro- and antislavery laws in an attempt to temper growing sectional animosity.

For the Todd family, Lexington's most famous resident stood like a towering obelisk, stalwart in standing and conviction. His runs for the presidency in 1824, 1832, and 1844 may have ended in defeat, but each attempt cemented his place as the greatest of Kentucky's statesmen. Mary's youthful admiration may have bordered on infatuation. One story tells of a thirteen-year-old Mary riding to Clay's Ashland estate to show off her new white pony. Despite interrupting a dinner party, she was invited in. She then asked her famous host whether it was true that he could become president. Clay was said to have answered, "If I am ever President I shall expect Mary Todd to be one of my first guests." Mary responded, "If you were not already married, I would wait for you."[16]

For the aspiring Lincoln, wandering into politics at age twenty-three, Clay was his chosen compass. Following Clay's direction, Lincoln promoted internal improvements. He would also adopt Clay's faith in strong protective tariffs and the creation of a national bank. When slavery grew into the dominant question of the age, Lincoln echoed Clay's endorsement of gradual emancipation and eventual recolonization to Africa, though Clay, like the Todds, owned many slaves. In Lincoln's "Great Debates" with Stephen Douglas, he praised the immortal Clay's name more than forty times.[17] And as president, Lincoln held fast to the pillar of the Great Compromiser's monument and mantra: "It has been my invariable rule to do all for the Union. If any man wants the key of my heart, let him take the key of the Union."[18]

Both Were Uncomfortable with Their Own Appearance

In 1840, when Abe Lincoln was just one of many potential suitors, a niece described her aunt Mary, age twenty-two, as the centerpiece of a social gathering. "[S]he danced and swayed as lightly and gaily as a branch of fragrant apple blossoms in a gentle spring breeze," said the niece. "From her pink dimpled cheeks to her sophisticated pink satin slippers, she was a fascinating alluring creature." Yet even then, Mary considered herself unattractive, squat, a "ruddy pine knot."[19]

Through the years, she did not age well, and she knew it. Her face grew round with pronounced jowls. Her lily-white complexion, once like a china doll's, wrinkled deeply at the eyes, and the creases seemed deeper in the shade of her dark brown locks. Constantly fighting her weight, she mercilessly squeezed her pear-shaped body into constricting hourglass corsets. While her husband had his picture taken at least 130 times in his life, she avoided photography, believing that the camera made her look even heavier. When Matthew Brady took several portraits of her in an 1861 sitting, she was so disappointed with the results that she ordered all the negatives destroyed, save one full profile taken at a distance.[20]

While Mary could hide her poor self-image under bountiful dresses, overt jewelry, and flowered headwear, there was no hiding Lincoln. Ridiculously tall, with gangly limbs almost devoid of coordination, a face of dark furrows, and an ample nose, he routinely made a poor first impression. His wife would say of him, "As you can see, he is not pretty." A New Yorker, seeing Lincoln before his Cooper Union speech, considered him "bluff and awkward, his every utterance an apology for his ignorance of metropolitan manners and customs."[21]

No one was more conscious of this initial unattractiveness than Lincoln himself, and he often dealt with his unique look by joking about it. In their Great Debates, Stephen Douglas accused Lincoln of being two-faced, to which Lincoln famously responded, "If I had two faces, would I be wearing this one?" Yet through his storytelling and his warm demeanor, the alleged "ugliness" disappeared. Many commented on how his face became altogether charming, in an odd way, whenever he spoke or smiled.[22]

BOTH WERE LENIENT PARENTS

Abe and Mary were children in an era when "childhood" effectively did not exist. In dress, demeanor, and duties, the offspring of poor and wealthy alike in early America were expected to function like miniature adults. This was by necessity. In Lincoln's harsh frontier upbringing, the young were a fundamental part of the family labor force, helping with chores as soon as they could lift and carry. For Mary, as the daughter of a well-to-do merchant, her expected role from cradle to grave was to be the obedient female, serving and suffering in silence.

Yoked and bridled as they were in youth, the parental Lincolns evidently believed that a much softer hand was more effective and preferable. They tried to instill some discipline in firstborn Robert, and for the most part they were successful. But Edward, next to arrive, consumed much of their attention, as he was constantly sick. His perpetual frailty trumped any need for correction. Despite the care of his parents, especially his mother, little Eddie lived less than four years.

In time, "Bobby" grew distant, especially when he began to attend boarding schools. In contrast, third and fourth sons Willie and Tad had the run of the house, and neither parent did much to stop them. Billy Herndon called them "brats" and loathed every visit they made to the law office. On one occasion, according to Herndon, the boys proceeded to destroy the place, "gutted the shelves of books—battered the points . . . of gold pens against the stove—turned over the ink stands on the papers and danced over them."[23] Herndon admitted he wanted to "wring their necks," while Lincoln seemed oblivious to the damage. To Mary, Willie and Tad were her "angel boys," "darlings," and "dear boys." To Lincoln, they were a steady source of play and entertainment. To many others, the two boys were little more than untamed imps. As Lincoln once admitted to Springfield neighbor Dr. Anson Henry, "We never controlled our children much."[24]

It is not known whether Tad Lincoln was mentally challenged or simply coddled beyond measure. Regardless, he did not learn how to read until age twelve, after his father's death.

The situation didn't change when the Lincolns became the First Family. At the Executive Mansion, a place Bobby rarely visited, the two younger boys made a playroom of their father's office and a play fort atop the White House roof; they were also allowed to own a veritable zoo of cats, ponies, and turkeys. Tad infamously interrupted a public reception in the East Room by riding a makeshift chariot (a chair on its back) dragged by his pet goat Nanko through the stunned crowd.[25]

After Willie tragically passed away in February 1862, the spoiling of Tad continued unabated. Near the war's end, with so much left to be done, Lincoln still acquiesced to Tad's demands and tantrums. Right after the capture of the Army of Northern Virginia, Lincoln wrote to his secretary of war, "Tad wants some flags. Can he be accommodated[?]" To his secretary of the navy, he was even more insistent: "Let Master Tad have a Navy sword."[26]

CHAPTER FOUR

Lincoln's Closest Friends

THIS LIST IS SHORT FOR A REASON: LINCOLN REFERRED TO NEARLY everyone as his friend but was truly intimate with a miniscule number of people. To heads of state, including Donja Isabel II of Spain, the king of Siam, and Queen Victoria, he ended his communications with the assurance that he was their "Great and Good Friend." Even people who were suing him received his good graces. Excepting his tense relationship with his father, Lincoln very rarely held grudges; however, a difficult childhood may have had left him physically and emotionally detached from close relationships. For example, he did not care for "Abe" or Abraham. According to his oldest son Robert, "after his youth at least, my father was never addressed familiarly and personally by anything but his last name, even by his most intimate friends." At times he would open himself up, and yet invariably drift away. Biographer David Donald assesses that Lincoln had very few close friends from his younger days, and of that handful, he grew apart from them all. Otherwise, as Joshua Speed attested, "he did not seek company; it sought him."[1]

In this, Lincoln resembles the most powerful and imposing US presidents. Andrew Jackson, the Roosevelts, Lyndon Johnson, Richard Nixon, Ronald Reagan, Barack Obama—virtually all liked to be, or needed to be, the center of attention. Nearly all were far closer to their mother than to their father. All were by their nature exceedingly stubborn when they felt that they were in the right. They called many people their friends, and yet they were close to very few people for most of their lives. Certainly amiable, Lincoln could also be just as calculating. As he said in 1842 during a speech on temperance, "If you would win a man to your cause, *first* convince him that you are his sincere friend." Lincoln returned to that position in private and public, time and again, as he did in closing his First Inaugural: "We are not enemies, but friends."[2]

Why did he, a person so humane, keep humanity at arm's length? The hypotheses are plentiful—the repetitious loss of loved ones in his youth, clinical depression, a fatalist demeanor, a personality externally warm but internally troubled, keen awareness that death could take anyone at any time. What is certain is that he enjoyed kindness for its own sake, but anything more remained just beyond his reach. A prime example of his ability to distance himself includes David Davis. A corpulent, story-loving, audacious character in person, and a consummately professional judge, Davis served on the bench of the Illinois Eighth Circuit and grew to know Lincoln extremely well, presiding over more than a thousand cases that involved the Springfield lawyer. So impressed was the magistrate that he allowed Lincoln to sit in his place in a multitude of court proceedings, lobbied industriously for Lincoln in the 1858 Senate race, and became his campaign manager in Lincoln's successful bid for the White House. He also traveled with the president-elect to Washington and, in 1862, was appointed by Lincoln to the US Supreme Court. After the assassination, the Lincoln family selected Davis to preside over Abe's estate. However, as author Thomas Craughwell finds, "Lincoln liked and respected Davis, yet he never opened his heart to him." Davis himself confirmed, "Lincoln never confided to me anything." Along with Davis, honorable mentions include Lincoln's bodyguard Ward Hill Lamon, political adviser Orville Hickman Browning, political supporter Jesse Fell, surgeon Dr. Ozias M. Hatch, fellow lawyer and politician Joseph Gillespie, his secretary of state William H. Seward, and his personal secretaries John Hay and John Nicolay.[3]

MARY TODD LINCOLN (KENTUCKY, 1818–1882)

Her many critics would balk at the idea that Mary more than any other was Lincoln's closest friend, but he kept her closer than anyone to the very end. During a social gathering at the White House, Lincoln confessed, "My wife is as handsome as when she was a girl and I a poor nobody then, fell in love with her and once more, have never fallen out."[4]

To be sure, Mary Todd had the ability to test anyone's patience, including Lincoln's. Yet it should be recognized that of the two, Mary made the better first impression, especially with the other gender. She came from an established and respected family, knew French, was a vibrant dresser, and could be an engaging and witty conversationalist. Of the four sisters who moved to Springfield, Mary was considered by many the kindest and most approachable.

In contrast, Lincoln had a more difficult time socializing. "I am quite as lonesome here as I ever was anywhere in my life," he said when taking up residence in Springfield. "I have been spoken to by but one woman since I have been here, and should not have been by her if she could have avoided it." Once more, the thought of any woman eventually wanting to marry him was beyond his comprehension. At one point, the bachelor Lincoln confessed, "I can never be satisfied with anyone who would be blockhead enough to have me."[5] While Mary grated on many—Lincoln's secretary John Hay referred to her as "the Hell-cat"—Lincoln was also no treat to live with.[6] He was prone to brooding, was gone for months at a time riding the legal circuit, and often neglected his dress and appearance. Mary was one of the very first people to fully appreciate his potential, and he in turn adored her.

When they were apart during his term as a US representative, his love letters were less than alluring. "Are you entirely free from head-ache?" he inquired. "That is good—good—considering it is the first spring you have been free from it since we were acquainted. I am afraid you will get so well, and fat, and young, as to be wanting to marry again. . . . Get weighed, and write me how much you weigh." Yet he could also be openly tenderhearted when he tried. During his term in Congress, Lincoln admitted to his wife, "When you were here, I thought you hindered me some in attending to business; but now, having nothing but business—no variety—it has grown exceedingly tasteless to me. I hate to sit down and direct documents, and I hate to stay in this room by myself."[7]

Theirs was a difficult marriage, but Lincoln openly cared for her more than for any other person in his life. Library of Congress.

In turn, she missed him when he was away, which was often. "I consider myself fortunate," she once attested, "if at eleven o'clock, I once more find myself, in my pleasant room and very especially, if my tired and weary husband is there, resting in the lounge to receive me—to chat over the occurrences of the day."[8] Those wanting to be closer to him often felt her overly possessive, but outside observers noticed that the attachment was mutual and sincere. A telegrapher in the War Department recalled, "Lincoln at all times showed a most tender regard for Mrs. Lincoln." Often, when the First Lady was away from Washington, Lincoln stayed in contact by way of the telegraph. Said the operator, "between husband and wife there was deep affection and close confidence."[9]

JOSHUA FRY SPEED (KENTUCKY, 1814–1882)

When Lincoln traveled to New Salem by himself at age twenty-two in 1831, he described himself as "strange, friendless, uneducated, penniless."[10] At twenty-eight when he moved on to Springfield, he was better read but otherwise in the same predicament. Lincoln had visited the new capital before, stumping for himself during the state election of 1836. It was during that campaign when a young Joshua Speed first saw him. "I remember that his speech was a very able one," recalled Speed, but the speaker himself was a "long, gawky, ugly, shapeless man."[11]

Speed would meet that same shapeless man again in 1837, when Lincoln entered his Springfield dry goods store. Speed offered boarding to him. The two became roommates for nearly four years and Lincoln's closest male friend for life.

When Lincoln was at his very lowest, so was Speed. The two struggled with pending marriages. Lincoln broke up with Mary just as his dear friend had to move back to Kentucky; Speed's father had died, leaving responsibility of the family plantation on his shoulders. Lincoln was so distraught that people close to him worried that he was turning suicidal. Through a series of long letters, they pulled each other through. Notably, in communicating with nearly everyone else, the older friend signed his name "A. Lincoln." With the young Speed, it was always "Lincoln." In August 1841, he traveled to the Speed family home and spent nearly a month with them, growing even closer to Joshua and his mother, Lucy, with whom Lincoln corresponded frequently and warmly. That September, a rejuvenated Lincoln returned to Springfield but remained closely connected to his second family thereafter (Lincoln's first family at this point were the Todds in Springfield). The two commiserated over their fears of marriage, talked politics, and ultimately convinced each other that they deserved to give and receive love from their significant others. When Mary was with child and Lincoln was out riding the Eighth Circuit, it was Joshua who sent him the good news. When the Lincolns traveled to Washington for Abe's sole congressional term, Speed went with them.[12]

Their closeness suffered horribly in 1854 when Speed voiced his support for the Kansas-Nebraska Act, the law that permitted the spread of slavery into western territories. They corresponded several times over the matter, until August 1855, when, at the end of a long and heartfelt letter, Lincoln condemned the Nebraska bill as an ordinance of, by, and for violence, condemning Speed's views more than he ever did before or since. A distraught Lincoln ended the letter saying, "My kindest regards to Mrs.

Speed. On the leading subject of this letter, I have more of her sympathy than I have of yours. And yet let [me] say I am your friend forever."[13]

Of course, Lincoln discussed a wide spectrum of subjects with colleagues, constituents, and press, but his language was far more candid and heartfelt with his old roommate. In 1855, regarding slavery, he confessed, "Dear Speed, . . . I hate to see the poor creatures hunted down, and caught, and carried back to their stripes, and unrewarded toils; but I bite my lip and keep quiet. In 1841 you and I had together a tedious low-water trip, on a Steam Boat from Louisville to St. Louis. You may remember, as well as I do, that from Louisville to the mouth of the Ohio there were, on board, ten or a dozen slaves, shackled together with irons. That sight was continual torment to me; and I see something like it every time I touch the Ohio, or any other slave-border."[14]

During his presidency. Lincoln relied heavily on Joshua and his brother James for insights and support in Kentucky, and he eventually appointed James as the US attorney general in 1864. They last saw each other around April 1, 1865, when they shared some time together in Lincoln's office. Joshua had visited his friend several times before at the Executive Mansion, but on this occasion, Speed remembered, "He looked jaded and weary." A year after the assassination, reflecting upon their twenty-eight-year relationship, Speed said of him, "Mr. Lincoln was so unlike all the men I had ever known before . . . or known since, that there is no one to whom I can compare him."[15]

JOHN "JACK" ARMSTRONG (TENNESSEE, 1803–1854)
Villages and neighborhoods are by nature territories, and in many cases the human tendency toward tribalism will manifest itself. Such was the case in and around New Salem, where a group of toughs dubbed the Clary's Grove Boys declared their authority through loud and aggressive behavior. Their alpha was a blacksmith named Jack Armstrong, who often demonstrated his prowess through feats of strength, such as wrestling matches, including one with a tall twenty-one-year-old newcomer. The origins and winner of that grappling row remain in the realm of conjecture, but the outcome was the initiation of a reader into the rabble. Lincoln's combination of physical strength, sharp wit, intellect, and good

nature ingratiated him in a unique way. Lincoln never had to join the gang to be admired by it, especially by Armstrong.[16]

From then on, the pair often spent time together, mostly for the storytelling. Lincoln evidently excused himself from participating in the more violent activities, such as fisticuffs and cockfights, choosing instead to opt out or act as impartial judge, the latter course earning him the nickname "Honest Abe." In the seven years that Lincoln lived in New Salem, having no home of his own outside of his store cabins, he frequently stayed and dined with Jack and his wife, Hannah.[17]

After Jack died, his son became a primary suspect in a murder case. When Hannah approached Lincoln and asked for help, he accepted in gratitude for their long history of kindness toward him. The ensuing *People v. William Armstrong* trial (a.k.a. the Almanac Case) became one of Lincoln's most famous. Renowned or not, the Armstrongs were far more grateful that Lincoln attained an acquittal.[18]

WILLIAM HENRY HERNDON (KENTUCKY, 1818–1891)

Their relationship was more like father and son, but it was a kinship based on honest affection and sincere loyalty. In his law practice, Lincoln partnered with John Todd Stuart for more than four years, and with Stephen Logan nearly as long. The business firm with Billy Herndon would last for over twenty years and would have lasted longer. The call was invariably "Mr. Lincoln," and the response was always "Billy," but the enormous amount of time Herndon spent with Lincoln gave us one of the first and most candid insights into Lincoln's world.

Herndon first remembered seeing Lincoln on the same day he saw his first steamboat. In 1832, when still a teenager, he saw Lincoln and others busily shepherding the *Talisman* up the Sangamon River. Herndon had relatives in New Salem. Said Herndon, "There was something in his tall and angular frame, his ill-fitting garments, honest face, and lively humor that imprinted his individuality on my affection and regard."[19]

Billy had lived in Springfield since he was five years old. He grew up to become passionate, assertive, idealistic, and abolitionist. His father was a member of the Long Nine, and Billy scoffed at his (and at Lincoln's) cautious approach toward the peculiar institution. Why did Lincoln choose him as a partner? Herndon admitted, "I don't know and no one else does." Mrs. Lincoln certainly loathed him, and he loathed her. Mary described him as a "miserable man" and "almost a hopeless inebriate." Neither charge was true, but Lincoln didn't press Mary to change her mind, and so Billy almost never darkened their door on **Eighth and Jackson**. Mutual jealousy prevailed, as they viewed each other as their chief rival for Lincoln's attention.[20]

When prudence demanded, Lincoln could leave a homestead, play the political middle ground, cut himself from business ties, and ditch cabinet members, but his partnership with Herndon remained in place. After years together in their Springfield law office, Lincoln assured his junior that even his ascension to the highest office in the land would not sever their bond: "Give our clients to understand that the election of a President makes no change in the firm of Lincoln and Herndon. If I live I'm coming back some time, and then we'll go right on practicing law as if nothing had ever happened."[21]

As we know, something happened. When assassination turned Lincoln from public official to heralded martyr, ensuing biographies presented him as virtually flawless, idealized, even godlike. Such unctuous outpourings repulsed Herndon, who felt a more honest assessment would better serve Lincoln's legacy. Herndon set about interviewing as many people as he could, many of them contemporaries in Springfield who knew Abe personally. Herndon, unable to weave the piles of threads into a cohesive text, eventually attempted to work with a coauthor. After bitter differences concerning format and tone, Herndon and Jesse Weik's *Herndon's Lincoln: The True Story of a Great Life* finally reached publication in 1889. Certainly, Herndon was guilty of falsehoods, including the **myth that Ann Rutledge was Lincoln's only true love**. His treatment of Mary Todd was particularly harsh and exaggerated. Simultaneously, he rightly questioned the exceedingly religious images advanced by far less knowledgeable authors and was willing to present a more earthy and honest depiction of Lincoln's demeanor and inner circles. As Douglas Wilson states, "While he was far from an ideal biographer . . . the biographical resources he gathered and developed are simply indispensable to our knowledge of Lincoln."[22]

Edward Dickenson Baker (London, England, 1811–1861)

A captivating orator and ambitious politician, with an erudite mind and affable nature, Edward Baker also shared Lincoln's ability to be competitive yet upstanding and friendly. In addition, both were bibliophiles and loved poetry, and they formed a bond that would last for twenty-five years. To be sure, the two were dissimilar in many ways aside from Baker's foreign birth. Unlike the more measured Lincoln, Baker could be overly courageous in speech and action. Baker became a professional soldier, fighting in the Mexican War, while Lincoln lacked a militant streak. Yet the two were loyal to the Whig Party and each other's word; they diligently avoided running for the same office when seats for them both could not be assured (they were, however, quite competitive when it came to playing games of handball). In 1846, Lincoln honored his spirited friend by naming his second child after him.[23]

When Baker moved out west, he became one of the few members of the new Republican Party to win a race for office in that region, becoming one of Oregon's US senators in 1860. His personal and political ties made Baker all the more indispensable to Lincoln, a point the president-elect made abundantly clear when he crashed a family gathering in Springfield

More refined than Lincoln, better educated, and far more competitive, Edward Baker was not afraid of making enemies, but he grew close and loyal to his American-born friend, to the very end of his life.

to greet his old friend who was on his way to Washington. So close was their connection that on Inauguration Day, Baker rode in the carriage with Lincoln on the way to the Capitol, and when it was time for the newly sworn president to deliver his address, it was Senator Baker who introduced him.[24]

When the war broke out, Baker made good on a promise to defend the Union with his life by joining the army and gathering recruits. Lincoln thought so much of Baker's military abilities that in the summer of 1861, he sent a letter to War Secretary Simon Cameron recommending that Baker be promoted to brigadier general, along with a few other individuals including U. S. Grant, Franz Sigel, and Joseph Hooker. Baker refused the star and remained a colonel. Less than three months later, Baker would die in battle, marking one of Lincoln's **worst days as president**.[25]

LEONARD SWETT (MAINE, 1825–1889)

A veteran of the Mexican War, Leonard Swett moved to Bloomington, Illinois, where in 1849 Judge David Davis introduced him to fellow attorney Abe Lincoln while riding the Eighth Circuit. Like Lincoln, Swett joined the Republicans after the 1854 Kansas-Nebraska Act threatened to expand slavery far into the continental West. By the late 1850s, he was fiercely loyal to Lincoln and labored tirelessly to get his friend into the US Senate. Swett played a more prominent role in the Wigwam of Chicago at the Republican National Convention. Speaking on Lincoln's behalf, and probably without his consent, Swett influenced Seward and Cameron supporters to consider Lincoln as their second choice in exchange for unnamed favors.[26]

When the president-elect traveled to Washington, so went Swett, where he kept Lincoln well informed and supported the formation of strong cabinet, including the addition of William H. Seward to a major post. Later, he also lobbied strongly to have David Davis be placed on the Supreme Court. He asked little in return, despite being in debt for much of his professional life. In later 1862, Swett ran against **John Todd Stuart** for the US House, dedicating himself to support the controversial Emancipation Proclamation. He lost narrowly, a defeat seen as a setback for Lincoln's war policies in Illinois. After a brief and unsuccessful foray into mining in California, Swett returned to Washington in 1864 to campaign vigorously for Lincoln's reelection. When asked who knew Lincoln best in his adult life, then Justice Davis told a reporter, "Herndon and Swett were his intimate personal and political friends and can . . . give you more detailed information concerning the past fifteen years of his life than perhaps any other parties."[27]

CHAPTER FIVE

Books That Most Impacted Lincoln

HIS SCHOOLING WAS BRIEF AND SPORADIC. THREE SHORT RUNS UNDER locally paid instructors gave him less than a year total of formal education. Not until age ten did Abe become functionally literate. Once he had conquered the basics, however, his fondness for reading grew almost as fast as he did, and it magnified the differences between him and most everyone he knew. By his sixteenth birthday Abe was already an oddity, taller than nearly all around him, quietly inquisitive, and panged for print. His most uncommon trait was a desire to peruse writings almost anywhere at any time, a preoccupation alien to a region where few people owned books, and even fewer had the time to read them. The dearth of available material only seemed to fuel his hunger; as his stepmother recalled, "Abe read all the books he could lay his hands on."[1]

He preferred studying in a lounging position, his long legs propped up against the trunk of a tree or prone stretched out along the floor of a room, as if to accentuate the fact that he lived in a world that didn't quite fit him. Some viewed Lincoln's preference for reading as laziness. One who had hired him for fieldwork admitted that Abe "was always reading and thinking—[and I] used to get mad at him." By the time he was twenty, Lincoln knew full well that he could not live as his parents did, hand to mouth and semiliterate. Instead, young Abe concluded, "The things I want to know are in books."[2] By his mid-twenties, a job as postmaster in New Salem gave him access to incoming newspapers, which he scanned voraciously for anything economic, international, or political in nature.[3]

To absorb material fully, he adopted the habit of reading out loud, often to the annoyance of those around him. He defended the practice by saying, "When I read aloud, two senses catch the idea." Lincoln also employed a third—writing on scraps of paper any points or phrases he wished to memorize.[4]

Despite his love of literature, he was never a collector, choosing instead to maintain the frugal frontier practice of borrowing rather than buying. While serving as a US representative, Lincoln frequently borrowed volumes from the Library of Congress and the Library of the Supreme Court, both of which resided in the Capitol building at the time. As president, though he added scores of titles to the White House reading room, he never possessed much of a personal library himself. Still, Lincoln considered print "the great invention of the world."[5] He professed, "A capacity and taste for reading gives access to whatever has been discovered by others. It is the key, or one of the keys, to the already solved problems. And not only so; it gives a relish and facility for successfully pursuing the unsolved ones." Following are works that Lincoln studied most. Some impacted him early on. Others slowly ascended in their importance. They were all, to him, vital stepping stones on the path to discovery, which often involved the pursuit of more books. As he once said, "My best friend is the man who'll get me a book I ain't read."[6]

WILLIAM BLACKSTONE'S *COMMENTARIES ON THE LAWS OF ENGLAND*

It is unknown where he first acquired this seminal work. Legend states that Lincoln, while biding time at his New Salem dry goods store in 1832, bought a barrel of odds and ends from a cash-strapped traveler. Upon emptying the purchase, he supposedly came upon the four-volume set. More likely he bought the books at an auction in Springfield while visiting from New Salem. Either way, at age twenty-three, Lincoln started poring over the famous work that defined the principles of modern law.[7]

Since the nation's founding, nearly every lawyer in the United States was familiar with the dense but readable pages of *Commentaries*. Lord Blackstone's lessons were required reading for anyone attempting the bar, and the best lawyers knew the volumes thoroughly. Thomas Jeffer-

Born in 1723, Sir William Blackstone lived to see his *Commentaries* become a major influence upon the leaders of the American Revolution. This fact may have upset him, because Blackstone was a member of Parliament and an avid opponent of American independence.

son considered them the standard texts on common law, though he was uncomfortable with its pro-British tone.[8]

In Volume 1, *Rights of Persons*, Lincoln learned the basic procedures for filing a divorce, dispensing inheritance, and formalizing obligations between employers and their employees. The following volume, *Rights of Things*, taught him how to handle disputes over property, especially land. *Of Private Wrongs* scripted the language and procedures within trial law, while Volume 4, *Of Public Wrongs*, outlined how to defend or prosecute accused criminals. In short, *Commentaries* covered nearly every potentially contentious step of human relations, from cradle to grave.

At first, Lincoln believed his deficient education prevented any chance of practicing law. But as he wallowed in New Salem, increasingly vexed by personal debt and multiple failures in business, he also steadily mastered the volumes. Years later, after becoming an accomplished attorney and candidate for president, Lincoln was approached by a young man wanting to pass the bar. "Get the books, and read, and study them carefully," he said, adding, "Begin with Blackstone's *Commentaries*."[9]

SHAKESPEARE'S DRAMATIC WORKS

"Some of Shakespeare's plays I have never read," Lincoln once admitted, "while others I have gone over perhaps as frequently as any unprofessional reader. Among the latter are *Lear, Richard Third, Henry Eighth, Hamlet,* and especially *Macbeth*. I think nothing equals *Macbeth*."[10]

His first exposure was likely in Indiana, but he began to study in depth at New Salem with the town philosopher **Jack Kelso**, an avid reader of the anguished Bard of Avon. Thereafter, Lincoln maintained a close connection to Shakespeare's works, almost exclusively with the tragedies, an affiliation most prominent during his presidency. His son Robert considered Shakespeare one of Lincoln's favorite escapes. John Hay recalled falling asleep to Lincoln reading him Shakespeare at the **Soldiers' Home** in the troubled summer of 1863. Others admired how he could recite multiple stanzas at any given time. War Department employee David Bates remembered how Lincoln "read to us in the telegraph office. On one occasion, I was his only auditor, and he recited several passages to me with as much interest apparently as if there had been a full house."[11]

When he wasn't reading Shakespeare, Lincoln watched performances. In October 1863, mere days after unleashing the Emancipation Proclamation, Lincoln attended opening night at **Grover's Theater**, where he took in a masterful performance of *Othello*. On several instances, he watched the famed Shakespearean actor James H. Hackett perform the role of Falstaff. Once he had the pleasure of viewing a rendition of *Hamlet* with the celebrated Edwin Booth in the role of the assassin prince.[12]

Lincoln was last seen reading Shakespeare while returning by steamship from City Point, Virginia, after his visit to the recently fallen capital of Richmond. While Lincoln read lines of *Macbeth* to his fellow travelers on the Potomac, 150 miles away Robert E. Lee was discussing terms of surrender for his Army of Northern Virginia. Unbeknownst to everyone onboard, the president had less than a week to live. Given the circumstances, one may wonder whether he recited some of Macbeth's thoughts on death:[13]

> Life's but a walking shadow; a poor player,
> That struts and frets his hour upon the stage,
> And then is heard no more: It is a tale,
> Told by an idiot, full of sound and fury.

Lincoln's personal copy of Shakespeare's works currently resides at the Folger Library in Washington, D.C.

THE BIBLE

Many evangelicals contend that Lincoln was a devout servant of the Testaments. Skeptics often argue that the book played a minor role in his life. In reality, the Bible *did* serve a vital role in Abraham's development, because it helped him learn how to read and write.

Lincoln probably began to flip through the family Bible while a child in Kentucky and started memorizing portions in Indiana. Though both regions were heavily Baptist at the time, Lincoln was not. Still, the Bible was the most widely owned book in the entire nation, and it consequently served as a standard text in basic education. Frontier schools and communities often functioned for decades without bona fide libraries.

Consequently, the Testaments were frequently the only words in print in any given rural log cabin or clapboard farmhouse.[14]

As he aged, he explored texts that were indifferent to Christianity, if not outwardly critical, such as Thomas Paine's *Age of Reason* and Edward Gibbon's *History of Rome*. Few (if any) people recalled him ever reading the Bible while in New Salem, Springfield, or on the legal circuit. This would change years later. After the untimely death of his son William in 1862, Lincoln was frequently seen paging through a Book of Psalms given to him by the American Bible Society. So, too, his language in voice and print became less ethereal and more direct concerning religion. Lincoln made only two obscure religious references in his First Inaugural. In stark contrast, his Second Inaugural, although a fifth as long, contained more than a dozen. Virtually half of the Second Inaugural is priestly in tone. Robert Todd Lincoln remembered, "In the later years of his life, he always had a Bible and a set of Shakespeare very near him, and went to them for relief at all times." But Lincoln remained rather detached when it came to firm doctrines, and he never expressed a belief that Jesus was more than human.[15]

SAMUEL KIRKHAM'S *GRAMMAR IN FAMILIAR LECTURES* (1828)

At age twenty-three, while working at Offutt's dying store in New Salem, Abe told **William Mentor Graham** that he was interested in learning the formalities of grammar. Barely functional in the subject himself, Graham directed him to John Vance's farm six miles distant, depository of the only known area copy of a highly regarded lesson book. Its author, Samuel Kirkham of Maryland, endorsed a rather antiquated style of English. Kirkham also had a flair for interminable narration, as exemplified by the full title of his tutorial: *English Grammar in Familiar Lectures; Accompanied by a Compendium Embracing a New Systematic Order of Parsing a New System of Punctuation, Exercises in False Syntax, and a System of Philosophical Grammar in Notes: To Which Are Added, an Appendix and a Key to the Exercises Designed for the Use of Schools and Private Learners.*

However, on the necessity of his craft, Kirkham was most convincing in his preface: "Grammar is a leading branch of that learning which alone is capable of unfolding and maturing the mental powers, and of elevating

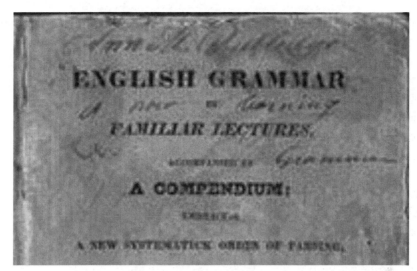

Kirkham's *Grammar* was of the few books Lincoln owned in New Salem, having acquired it outright from John Vance. When his studies were over, Lincoln then gave the book to his friend Ann Rutledge, with the inscription "Ann M. Rutledge is now learning grammer [*sic*]."

man to his proper rank in the scale of intellectual existence; of that learning which lifts the soul from earth, and enables it to hold converse with a thousand worlds." Apparently, Lincoln agreed. He set about memorizing nearly every rule and imposed upon friends and neighbors to test him on the exercises. By his own admission years later, Lincoln studied "imperfectly of course, but so as to speak and write as well as he now does."[16]

Lincoln's grammatical skills improved over the years, but it remained imperfect. Prepositions were particularly challenging, as were punctuations. In nearly all his writings, Lincoln employed commas almost at random. Kirkham also stressed precise spelling; Lincoln did not. Yet there were sections in which the eager pupil clearly excelled—verb use, illustrative adjectives, parsing (i.e., word analysis). Greatest of these strengths involved the chapter "Figures of Speech" and the potential of metaphors. Certainly Lincoln the storyteller knew firsthand the weighty punch of such notions. But Lincoln the speaker, after reading Kirkham, would later dispense them in much stronger doses. A prime example: Five years after studying Kirkham, Lincoln stood before the Young Men's

Lyceum of Springfield to extol the virtues of the Founding Fathers. He concluded, "They were the pillars of the temple of liberty; and now, that they have crumbled away, that temple must fall, unless we, their descendants, supply their places with other pillars. . . . Upon these let the proud fabric of freedom rest." The words "pillar" and "fabric" are the very two examples Kirkham used to illustrate the meaning of metaphor. Kirkham then supplied a quote from Washington Irving, who described the plight of Native Americans: "The proud *pillar* of their independence has been shaken down, and the whole moral *fabric* lies in ruins." Thus, the most memorable words of Lincoln's most revered addresses would involve symbolic imagery, from divided houses to the better angels of our nature, from binding the nation's wounds to a new birth of freedom.

First Six Books of Euclid's *Elements* (English translation, 1848)

After his dismal single term in the US House of Representatives, Lincoln rededicated himself to his law practice. He also returned to another subject long set aside. In his earlier vocation as surveyor, Abraham had tackled the fundamentals of geometry and trigonometry. This time, he went back to their very source.

Often called the Father of Geometry, the ancient Greek mathematician Euclid may not have sired all the principles contained in his *Elements*, but he articulated them with such clarity and completeness that his opus endured as the standard text in the field for more than two thousand years.

At first glance, there would seem no reason for Lincoln to read it in depth. Math was math, not law. But in Euclid's brilliant description of the finite, Lincoln saw infinite worth. Fellow lawyers on the Eighth Judicial Circuit remembered him reading Euclid at every spare moment, often past midnight. By Lincoln's own admission, by about 1850, he had "studied and nearly mastered the Six-books of Euclid." He already had a firm command of public speaking, speech writing, and jurisprudence. What he sought in the *Elements* was its invaluable lessons in logic.[17]

Book I starts with a declaration of "axioms," often translated as "common notions" or, more precisely, self-evident truths. Among these:

"The whole is greater than the part." Herein lies the Aesopian concept of strength in unity, but seen through the eyes of Euclid, the proposition elevates from a moral observation to an irrefutable fact. Other notions addressed equally profound paradigms, including the measurement of equality itself, as stated in the very first axiom: "Things which are equal to the same thing are also equal to one another." If *Elements* did not establish the idea, it certainly strengthened in Lincoln a belief that absolute truths did exist.

An excellent sample of this conviction appears in the fourth of the Great Debates, accompanied by an homage to the Alexandrian. Once again, Lincoln took the position that slavery was irrefutably wrong and accused Stephen Douglas of saying that it was possibly right. To discredit his opponent, Lincoln suggested that Douglas's argument would be like refuting the correct answer to a math problem. "If you have ever studied geometry, you remember that by a course of reasoning Euclid proves that all the angles in a triangle are equal to two right angles. . . . Euclid has shown you how to work it out. Now, if you undertake to disprove that proposition, and to show that it is erroneous, would you prove it to be false by calling Euclid a liar?" The line apparently registered well with the audience of twelve thousand, many of whom erupted in laughter and applauded the equation.[18]

AESOP'S FABLES (1525)

Second cousin Dennis Hanks recalled how thirteen-year-old Abraham had in his possession some dog-eared titles: *Life of Washington*, *Arabian Nights*, and *Aesop's Fables*. When Abe proceeded to read aloud to his cousin and stepmother, an increasingly skeptical Dennis claimed to have said to him, "Abe, them yarns is all lies." Lincoln reportedly answered, "Mighty darn good lies, Denny."[19]

Aesop's Fables was perhaps the most enjoyed of his early readings, and Lincoln would later claim that he could recite the entire text from memory. Part of the attraction may have come from the main characters. Aesop's works were animistic—for example, "The Ant and the Grasshopper," "The Council of Mice," "The Tortoise and the Hare." The appeal stemmed from young Lincoln's own well-established tenderness toward

Born in the seventh century BCE, Aesop was said to be a slave who was eventually set free.

nature. He did not care to hunt, disliked eating wild game, and chastised neighborhood boys for torturing small creatures. One of his earliest essays in school addressed "the wickedness of being cruel to animals."[20]

Not only did the *Fables* nurture Lincoln's faith in thoughtful action, but they also provided a central theme in his political philosophy. He came to share this creed years later and credited its author when he cowrote a campaign circular for the Whig Party in 1843: "That 'union is strength' is a truth that has been known, illustrated and declared, in various ways and forms in all ages of the world. That great fabulist and philosopher, Aesop, illustrated it by his fable of the bundle of sticks; and he whose wisdom surpasses that of all philosophers, has declared that 'a house divided against itself cannot stand.'"[21]

MASON LOCKE WEEMS'S *LIFE OF WASHINGTON* (1808)

Heavily anecdotal, inundated with moral absolutes, and based on flimsy hearsay, Mason Weems's famous "biography" of George Washington was more like hagiography. Washington's biographer William Thayer called it "a mass of absurdities and deliberate false inventions."[22] But its inaccuracy didn't appear to bother preteen Lincoln much. To him, history was not a social science; it was an anthology of stories from which one could extract valuable lessons and admirable ideals.

Weems was nearly of the same mind-set. A bookseller by profession, he set out to write a schoolbook that would simultaneously sow moral messages and reap profits. Peddling customs was common practice, as most early education texts were partially informational and predominantly tutorial, guiding young readers on what were considered proper social values. As such, Weems's Washington chopped down a cherry tree in his youth and then admitted to the deed, knelt to pray as a general at Valley Forge, and preached temperance throughout the whole of his life, all of which Washington never did. The important issue for the author was to take the existing leverage of the national hero and use it to instill patriotism and piety among the young.

Foremost, Weems glorified the Revolution and Washington's role in it, to the point that both the war and the man were one and the same, and all that was good could be found in their union. Whether Lincoln fully believed this cannot be determined, although later in life he did much to perpetuate and celebrate Weems's idyllic vision. In 1842, during a Springfield celebration of Washington's birthday, Lincoln told his receptive audience, "Washington is the mightiest name of earth— long since mightiest in the cause of civil liberty, still mightiest in moral reformation. . . . To add brightness to the sun or glory to the name of Washington is alike impossible." Years later, as he traveled to the nation's capital as president-elect, Lincoln delivered a speech before the New Jersey Senate, describing the book and the subject that inspired him still. Playing to the crowd, he also highlighted the great Revolutionary victory in the Garden State: "In the earliest days of my being able to read, I got hold of a small book . . . Weems's *Life of Washington*. . . . I recollect thinking then, boy even though I was, that there must have been something more than common that these men struggled for. . . . The crossing of the river; the contest with the Hessians; the great hardships endured at that time, all fixed themselves on my memory more than any single revolutionary event."[23]

Perhaps the words of Weems returned to Lincoln once more, in the late autumn of 1863, when he struggled to write a few appropriate remarks

Mason Weems claimed to be the former rector of Mount Vernon Parish. He never held such a post, and no such parish ever existed at Washington's Virginia home.

concerning another American battle. Whether or not it did enter his mind before his trip to Cemetery Hill in southern Pennsylvania, the tone of Weems's following passage does echo what he said there, where "yonder mournful hillocks point the place where many of our brave heroes sleep; perhaps some good angel has whispered that their fall was not in vain."[24]

THE WORKS OF ROBERT BURNS (1834)

Lincoln had a fondness for the greats—Byron, Longfellow, Milton, Poe. Joshua Speed contended that Lincoln could recite more poetry than any other citizen in New Salem. His preference, whom he may have first read as an adolescent in Indiana, was Scotland's favorite son, the lyrical Robert Burns (1759–1796). In some ways, Burns's life rhymed with Lincoln's. Born into a poor rural family, Burns toiled as a farmhand at a young age, and later became a surveyor. Though tall and muscular, he cared little for manual labor. To stimulate his active mind and ward off recurrent depression, Burns began to write and found he had a talent for it.[25]

Yet it is unlikely that Lincoln knew any of these particulars. He was drawn instead to the words themselves, written in raw, fiery, yet musical tones, far more wondrous and ruthless than the modest Lincoln would ever dare to be. As one observer noted, Burns "always wrote at white heat."[26] Dominant among Burns's themes were passion, poverty, and women, and he wrote from experience. Father of three illegitimate children, fond of alcohol, confrontational even with friends, he struggled to keep solvent and sane. But he could write with satirical bite and sincere honesty. Among Lincoln's favorites was a verse titled *Holy Willie's Prayer*. Despite its reverent title, the poem spoke of an obnoxiously pious parishioner, who condemned his flock while lusting after a young girl named Meg.

> O Lord! yestreen, Thou kens, wi' Meg
> Thy pardon I sincerely beg;
> O may't ne'er be a livin' plague
> To my dishonour,
> An' I'll ne'er lift a lawless leg
> Again upon her.

Among Robert Burns's most famous pieces was "Auld Lang Syne" (Scottish for "Old Long Since"), originally a lively dancing and drinking tune.

It may have Burns's relentless drive for justice, and a questioning of the blue blooded, that appealed to Lincoln most. At his very core, Burns was a populist and a patriot. Like a true Whig, he believed the role of government was to honor and serve its citizens, not vice versa. Few things repulsed Burns more than hypocrisy from the social elite, as demonstrated in "Willie's Prayer."

Hooked since youth, Lincoln read Burns for the rest of his days— taking a volume to his law offices, on the Eighth Circuit, and to the White House. During his final year, Lincoln was invited by the Burns Club of Washington to offer a toast to an upcoming celebration of the poet's birth. Lincoln gently declined, responding simply, "I cannot frame a toast to Burns. I can say nothing worthy of his generous heart and transcending genius."[27]

CHAPTER SIX

Animals in Lincoln's World

SUCH A LIST MAY SEEM SUPERFLUOUS, BUT LINCOLN WAS VERY MUCH A product of his time, and his trajectory followed an epochal shift in US history. During his life, Lincoln and the nation converted from a predominantly rural and agricultural being into an increasingly urban entity. One of his first memories involved the sound of wild animals around his childhood home. When Lincoln became an adult, one of the very first pieces of legislation written in his own hand involved determining who held dominion over stray livestock, as humans transitioned from being part of nature to feeling above it. Since creatures were ubiquitous regardless of where he lived, Lincoln's treatment of them reflected his own views on life. Even in cities, fauna were central sources of sound, food, and locomotion, practically inseparable from the day-to-day routine. Through animals, Lincoln learned to navigate his world.[1]

We see this trait among most of the early presidents. Most grew up in the countryside, where bovines and equines were the family trucks and tractors. Many had pets, including during their time in office. Washington had his hunting hounds, including Drunkard, Truelove, and Taster. Ever the international, John Quincy Adams owned silkworms. Confrontational Andrew Jackson raised fighting cocks. Whether it was through the anthropomorphic tales of *Aesop's Fables*, or through an innate reaction to suffering he often witnessed in childhood, Lincoln developed a sensitivity to the suffering of the underdog. As his friend **Joshua Speed** attested, "Lincoln had the tenderest heart for anyone in distress, whether man, beast, or bird."[2]

DOGS

Lincoln lived in a world of mutts, mostly hunting mixes. In his youth, his family occasionally owned stout yellow hounds, or as he would say, "yeller." Purebreds were relatively rare and usually a sign of wealth, such as Rutherford and Lucy Hayes's English mastiff, greyhound, and Newfoundland. Of the breeds that would later grace the White House, some were just becoming a recognized type, including the Airedale terrier (Woodrow Wilson, Warren G. Harding, and Calvin Coolidge would each have one) and the beagle (subjected to Lyndon Johnson's roughhousing). Several breeds did not yet exist, such as the Belgian Malinois (a favorite of Herbert Hoover's), German shepherds (one of many Kennedy pooches), or the golden retriever (of Gerald Ford).[3]

Dogs are our oldest and closest bond in the animal kingdom. Initiated by domestication of wolves starting some fifteen thousand years ago, this relationship flourished because our respective skills greatly aided mutual survival. From protection against other predators to hunting and shepherding, our packs have common cause. When Lincoln was young, his family had dogs to protect the farm and hunt game. In adulthood, Abe found comfort in their companionship. One story, albeit through hearsay, has the twenty-one-year-old driving the family's oxen across a frozen swamp on their way from Indiana to Illinois. When the team broke through the ice, the jolt launched their dog from the wagon and into the swamp. Lincoln jumped into the icy waters and saved him. Once ashore, the dog ran circles around his rescuer in gleeful gratitude. In conveying the tale, Lincoln reportedly said, "I guess I felt about as glad as the dog."[4]

By far the most famous of his canines was the one he had while living on **Eighth and Jackson**. A favorite of Willie and Tad as well, the pooch became a celebrity in his own right when his owner became president-elect. Thereafter, his name effectively became a synonym for the family dog. Apparently Lincoln spoiled Fido as much as he did his children (*Fido* being Latin for "I am loyal"). Opting to leave the sweet but skittish pet behind when heading to Washington—much to the displeasure of his sons—Mr. Lincoln gave specific instructions concerning treatment. Fido's fare was to consist of table scraps, he would be boarded indoors on one of Lincoln's own couches to serve as his bed, and disciplining would be avoided or kept to an absolute minimum. Ultimately, Fido would outlive Mr. Lincoln but not the ire of a town drunk. Sometime after Lincoln's burial, Fido approached an inebriated man who proceeded to mortally wound the trusting animal.[5]

Willie, Tad, and their father still enjoyed the company of another canine while living in the Executive Mansion, a lapdog named Jip. As with Jip and other dogs, as well as cats and other creatures, Lincoln sought the company of animals when under stress. Several friends and acquaintances recalled seeing him caring for pets as he sat in quiet contemplation. White House nurse Rebecca Pomeroy remembered Jip frequently sitting upon the president's lap at the dinner table, getting petted and fed by his otherwise preoccupied owner.[6]

As with other animals, dogs appeared frequently in Lincoln's yarns and analogies. With a nod to places like Fort Sumter, he said US harbor defenses maintained the safety of the nation, "as a bull-dog guards his master's door." Giving advice to a Union officer who had been court-martialed for quarreling over a trivial matter, Lincoln wrote to him saying that it wasn't worth the trouble to contest minor points. "Better to give your path to a dog," penned the president, "than be bitten by him in contesting for the right." When the seemingly interminable 1864–1865 siege of Petersburg began to wear on Ulysses S. Grant and the Army of the Potomac, Lincoln sent a supportive message, telling them all to "hold on with a bull-dog grip, and chew and choke, as much as possible."[7]

HORSES

Being frequently poor, Thomas Lincoln had to settle for horses rather than mules. The latter, being stronger and stouter, typically commanded higher prices on the frontier market. In comparison, a horse was a small but reliable tractor in the fields and an economy sedan on the highway. As such, the modest equine was a practical and necessity investment for the Lincolns and most of their neighbors, and so it would be for the remainder of Abe's life. As a struggling young lawyer touring the Eighth Circuit, and as the US president in a solemn march to Gettysburg National Cemetery, Lincoln went on horseback.[8]

Thoroughly familiar with the species, Lincoln knew how to assess qualities quickly, including how fast it could run—a skill he perfected while living in New Salem. One of the more exciting pastimes in the otherwise mundane village involved breakneck races down the town's main stretch. Lincoln apparently maintained an interest in the sport. Fred DuBois, son of Jesse DuBois who served with Lincoln in the Illinois Legislature, recalled going to the races at the Sangamon County Fair. "Mr. Lincoln and my father and some other friends would get into the family carriage, accompanied always by some of us boys, and drive out to the grounds. Mr. Lincoln was a good judge of horses and he and his companions would often place a small wager on the result of the race."[9]

Among his own steeds were Belle, Old Buck, and Tom. When he rose to the middle class in Springfield, his mounts also served as horsepower for his carriage, when it wasn't in the shop (Lincoln's finances show several payments for surrey repair). While president he was gifted a strong specimen named "Old Abe." Among the best known among them all was a deep cherry veteran of his circuit routes named "Old Bob."

Rev. Henry Brown with "Old Bob," prepared for Lincoln's Springfield funeral process. Library of Congress.

Like Fido, Old Bob outlived his owner. For the funeral procession, he was adorned in black mourning cloth and led behind the hearse by two African American ministers.[10]

By all accounts Lincoln was a caring owner, at times almost to his peril. In 1862, not long after the Lincolns' eleven-year-old son William died, a fire broke out in the White House stables. Guards had to restrain the president when he rushed to try and save the animals. Among the fatally burned was a pony that had belonged to Willie. When Lincoln heard of its fate, he openly wept. Sadly, gruesome deaths among equines were not uncommon at the time. During the Civil War as a whole, somewhere between 1.2 million and 1.5 million horses and mules perished in military service.[11]

Hogs

Far more than red meat, pork was the standard fare for the nation's dinner table. At its apex, the Lincoln family farm in **Perry County, Indiana**, contained over one hundred pigs. In contrast, bovines were valued mostly as wagon engines and dairy machines. Not until the rise of barbed wire in the 1870s, coinciding with the rail access to the prairie west, did cattle become mass-produced and consumed. Up to that point, wood fencing was a structurally difficult, high-maintenance enterprise, usually constructed to keep livestock out of areas rather than in them. This need kept the young Lincoln gainfully employed as a rail splitter, creating barriers around crops. As the idiom went, his final product had to be "horse high, bull strong, and pig tight." In Springfield, well into the 1850s, it was standard practice to have pigs roam as they wished. Landless poor raised them for meat, and their scavenging helped reduce the city of its food trash. At midcentury, there were more than twice as many hogs in central Illinois as horses, mules, and cattle combined.[12]

Consequently, much of the commerce that Lincoln witnessed (and occasionally engaged in) involved swine. Such was the case on young Lincoln's trips to New Orleans, where Midwestern pigs fetched high profits, as the delta was far too warm for hog farms to flourish. On one such foray, Lincoln recalled his employer Denton Offutt concocting a plan to coax the stubborn stock onto the flatboat. "It was in connection with this boat," remembered Abe, "that occurred the ludicrous incident of sewing up the hogs eyes. Offutt bought thirty odd large fat live hogs, but found difficulty in driving them from where he purchased them to the boat." More familiar with the animal, Lincoln knew it was a poor plan: "In their blind condition they could not be driven out of the lot or field they were in. This expedient failing, they were tied and hauled on carts to the boat."[13]

Lincoln would connect this experience with others of a similar nature, in which he witnessed fellow humans beings chained together and hauled away on boats. In 1854, the Kansas-Nebraska Act spurred Lincoln to act against these scenes that so repulsed him. He reentered the political world by launching a series of public attacks against the measure that threatened to expand slavery deep into American territories. During a three-hour speech in Springfield, he appealed to his constituents' experiences and empathy, begging them to recognize the fundamental difference between human beings and livestock.

> It is said that the slaveholder has the same right to take his negroes to Kansas that a freeman has to take his hogs or horses. This would be true if negroes were property in the same sense that hogs or horses are. But is this the case? It is notoriously not so. . . . There are 400,000 free negroes in the United States. . . . These negroes are free, because their owners, in some way and at some time, felt satisfied that the creatures had minds, feeling, souls, family affections, hopes, joys, sorrows—something that made them more than hogs or horses.[14]

Unfortunately for the enslaved, most white Americans at the time continued to view enslaved African Americans as something akin to a domesticated animal—a piece of property, a source of collateral, and bred for labor.

CATTLE, OXEN, AND MILK COWS

At their home at Eighth and Jackson, the Lincolns tended to live on the edge of their means, not frivolously, but making best efforts to present themselves as up and coming. To limit expenses, Mr. Lincoln did most of the exterior chores himself, including milking their cow. She would be the last link to his farming past, a daily reminder of how hard he once had to work just to survive.

Ironically, both his mother, Nancy, and milk cows taught him how painful and fleeting life could be. While the family was living in southern Indiana, a strange illness spread through the Ohio Valley. Livestock died first, then humans. Victims were first hit by "the trembles." Later, their breath turned pungent and smelled of turpentine. Within days came dizziness. If the stricken did not soon recover, they experienced crippling abdominal pain and severe nausea. Next came unconsciousness, then coma, and death.[15]

Nancy Hanks Lincoln suffered such a fate in October 1818. In death she followed her aunt Elizabeth and uncle Thomas Sparrow, the couple having perished just days before from the same disease. It is now known that the affliction came from cows grazing on poisonous white snakeroot, which grew along the wooded peripheries of pasture lands in springtime. Toxins from the plant contaminated the animals' milk, which Nancy ingested. The ensuing infiltration caused the body to stop processing lactic acid, which subsequently built up in the system until she died in agony from lethal metabolic acidosis.[16]

Such were the risks of existence. Milk, water, meat, fowl, and fish could and often did bring illness and death. The majority of lethal illnesses at the time, including typhoid, cholera, and dysentery, were transmitted through food and water. Yet these were also the very sustenance upon which people relied to survive. Throughout his life, Lincoln remained grateful for whatever was available to eat. These same animals helped work the farm, built up credit, transported themselves and their harvest, and moved the family to new and more promising horizons.

There was one beast in the lot that Lincoln knew from experience was of marginal use: the bull. Massive, territorial, dangerous, and useful for only short periods of time, breeder males were otherwise more trouble than they were worth. Unlike most oxen, bull cattle were intolerant of harness work, their meat was as tough and unrelenting as they were, and they tended to be destructively combative. Two in the same pen invited a goring. Thoroughly familiar with their nature, President

Lincoln told a fellow frontiersman why he was reluctant to promote his friend to brigadier: "We already have more generals than we know what to do with." When the visitor persisted, Lincoln reportedly responded, "You are a farmer, I believe, if not, you will understand me. Suppose you have a large cattle yard full of all sorts of cattle, cows, oxen, bulls, and you kept killing and selling and disposing of your cows and oxen, in one way and another—taking good care of your bulls. By and by, you would find that you had nothing but a yard full of old bulls, good for nothing under heaven. Now, it will be just so with the army, if I don't stop making brigadier generals."[17]

GOATS

Nature's mowers, milk jugs, and garbage disposals, goats were valuable albeit ornery pieces of farm equipment. They were also great sources of entertainment for the Lincoln "kids," including father Abraham. It had been some time since children lived in the White House, and an adoring public showered them with gifts. Among the presents were two white goats. Nanny and Nanko, like Willie and Tad, could often come and go as they pleased, and the president found them all a welcome distraction. Once such incident may have been too comedic and ingenious for Dad to punish. Occasionally Tad would harness one of the goats to a table chair and ride his creation like a chariot through the White House. In one instance, Tad and Nanko gleefully invaded a formal event in the grand East Room, bursting through the doorway and doing a hot lap, as hoop-skirted matriarchs scattered out of the way.[18]

As it turned out, the goats served as invaluable companions when Tad lost Willie in 1862. It was not uncommon for Lincoln and Tad to play with Nannie and Nanko on the South Lawn for long periods. The lively animals were evidently therapeutic for the president as well, who simply enjoyed watched them bounce and cavort. One story has Lincoln looking out the window as they frolicked, turning to Mary's assistant and confidant Elizabeth Keckley and saying, "Come here and look at my two goats; see how they sniff the clear air and skip and play in the sunshine . . . whew! What a jump! He feeds on my bounty and jumps for joy. Do you think we could call him a bounty jumper? What jolly fun!"[19]

Mrs. Lincoln found the pets less amusing, largely because of their tendency to chew on the furniture, which in turn caused her to shop for repairs and replacements. Taking their youngest son with her, Mary was on such a trip to the Northeast when Mr. Lincoln sent distressing news: "Tell dear Tad, poor 'Nanny Goat' is lost; and Mrs. Cuthbert [Mary Ann Cuthbert, chief housekeeper] and I are in distress about it. The day you left Nanny was found resting herself, and chewing her little cud, on the middle of Tad's bed. But now she's gone!" Thankfully, the prodigal Nanny returned, though when mother and son were on their travels, the president had to provide updates, including the following:

> *Executive Mansion, Washington, April 28, 1864*
> *Mrs. A. Lincoln, Metropolitan Hotel, New York*
> *"Tell Tad the goats and father are very well—especially the goats."*[20]

WILD ANIMALS

When Abe's mother died, his sister Sarah, suddenly the woman of the house at a mere eleven years of age, was inconsolable. Tradition states that in an effort to ease her sadness, little Abe brought her baby turtles and raccoons. As sweet as his gesture was, it could not stop her weeping. Though he enjoyed fishing and hunting in youth, Lincoln developed a sensitivity to any needless suffering. A childhood schoolmate recalled a brief essay young Abe wrote, in which he chastised fellow boys for tormenting little turtles. At New Salem, gander pulls were a frequent pastime. In fact, there was a run dedicated to such contests down along the Sangamon River near the town mill, where competitors on horseback would charge at a goose hanging from a tree branch. According to the rules of the frontier blood sport, anyone who successfully pulled the gander's greased head from its body took the bird home as his prize. Lincoln evidently shied away from these more violent pastimes.[21]

Joshua Speed recalled riding a country road in the judicial circuit with Lincoln and four others. "There were two young birds by the roadside too young to fly," Speed recounted. "They had been blown from the nest by the storm. The old bird was fluttering about and wailing as mother ever does for her babes. Lincoln stopped, hitched his horse, caught the birds, hunted the nest and placed them in it." The entourage poked fun at him for doing so, but Speed remembered Lincoln responding, "Gentlemen, you may laugh, but I could not have slept well tonight if I had not saved those birds."[22]

In any circumstance, Lincoln could count on a rich litany of animal stories to provide context, levity, or critique—whatever he felt best served his purposes. During the Civil War, a tale from *Aesop's Fables* helped him explain why there were limits to his compromising. When asked to make yet another concession concerning federal defenses, he told "The Lion in Love": When the great cat approached the woodsman to ask for his daughter's hand in marriage, the woodsmen said he would only consent if the lion had his teeth removed, which the lion proceeded to do. When the beast returned to form a union with the woman he loved, the father then said the claws would need to go as well, and the lion agreed. When the once imposing cat came back as a defenseless kitten, the woodsman proceeded to kill him.[23]

CHAPTER SEVEN

Lincoln's Favorite Washington Sanctuaries

LINCOLN FIRST CAME TO THE NATIONAL CAPITAL IN DECEMBER 1847 to take his seat in Congress as the lone Whig representative from Illinois. The city was barely a decade older than he was. Built upon marshland, in summertime the locale offered drenching humidity and clouds of mosquitoes. Winters featured bone-chilling ocean winds and infestations of house mice. In spite of its many detriments, the town grew. Between Lincoln's departure from the House of Representatives and his return twelve years later as president-elect, the District of Columbia's population climbed from around fifty thousand residents to more than seventy-five thousand, 3 percent of whom were enslaved. The ratio had been as high as 12 percent when the nation's capital was a major hub of the lucrative domestic slave trade, and many of the area's private and public construction projects benefited from coerced labor. The numbers declined with the Compromises of 1850, which included the halt of human auctions in the District of Columbia.[1]

Initially known as Federal City, the place was better known as Washington City when Lincoln was president. Despite its growth, and perhaps because of it, the town's infrastructure appeared haphazard and incomplete. Streets alternated between mud and dust. The Capitol dome was little more than a truncated shell (to remain unfinished until 1863). Situated between the White House and Capitol Hill, the Treasury Department was not yet finished. The obelisk Washington Monument stood half done (and would not be completed until 1884). War intensified the city's disheveled state. When Virginia seceded, Confederate lines reached within a mile of the White House. Refugees, soldiers, sailors, office seekers, manufacturers, and profiteers soon stressed Washington to the breaking point, pushing the population to well over one hundred thousand in less than a year.[2]

Overcrowding turned the capital into a human pressure cooker. The year 1863 saw twenty-four thousand arrests, with July averaging a murder every twenty-four hours. By then some five thousand sex workers operated in the district. Sixty-eight defensive forts ringed the city. Inside and out, dozens of makeshift hospitals went up and soon filled with sick, mangled, and dying young men. Business and chaos thrived.[3]

By necessity, and despite a sincere desire to return to Springfield, Lincoln remained within the District of Columbia for the vast majority of his administration, spending far more time in town than most of his predecessors. Because of this circumstance, he actively sought zones of respite within its limits and was rather successful in the enterprise. Following are the most common havens he sought within the crucible.

The Soldiers' Home

Three miles and a thirty-minute carriage ride northwest of the White House stood a quiet country retreat of three hundred acres. Blessed with forested hills and cool breezes, it rested in stark contrast to the continuously agitated Washington below. The federal government purchased the private residence in 1850 to house disabled veterans, many of whom were foreign born with no familial support. Before the Civil War, more than one hundred veterans resided on the premises, most of them in the grand main building that dwarfed the surrounding outbuildings and cottages. On occasion, President James Buchanan visited, setting a precedent that Lincoln would soon follow.[4]

Lincoln first saw the place just days after his inauguration, but the family did not adopt it as their summer home until June 1862. Memories of their recently deceased William, and the nervous hive of activity in the Executive Mansion, encouraged them to seek a change of venue. The pattern was soon set—arrival in late spring, with furniture and servants in tow, and departure back to the White House family quarters in late autumn. In all, Lincoln and his family would spend nearly thirteen months of his presidency at the Soldiers' Asylum, totaling a quarter of his time as head of state.[5]

The First Family occupied the main two-story cottage, once the home of the acreage's former owner. With high ceilings, a voluminous central entranceway, library, and impressive views of the Potomac valley from the back porch, the domicile offered serenity, quietude, and fresh air. There Lincoln received visitors, played chess with friends, often chatted with the officers and men in his guard, and read Shakespeare alone. When necessary, he could attend to the affairs of office without being hounded by civilians and civil servants. Perhaps its most attractive feature for the president was that Mary and Tad loved the place. Removed from Washington's gossip mills, which were never kind to her, Mary achieved a semblance of family normalcy. The immature Tad, who resorted to pranks and tantrums in a plea for attention inside the White House, found a company's worth of older brothers in the president's guards. The soldiers readily adopted him as their mascot, granting him the unofficial rank of third lieutenant. The family of Edwin Stanton also lived in one of the adjacent cottages, growing closer to the First Family with each passing season.

Unfortunately for Lincoln, it would always be an inconsistent refuge. The average day would see him rise around 6:00 a.m., head into the city by 8:00 a.m. or so (usually under close and unwelcome military escort), and return late almost every weeknight with new worries to endure. Even the Soldiers' Home itself gave constant reminders of increasing misery. Just to the northeast of the grounds stood a national cemetery, commemorated in the summer of 1862. By 1863, the graveyard had reached eight thousand Union interments, roughly equal to the entire population of Springfield upon Lincoln's departure. As the president feared, the horrific trials of 1864 would increase the head count dramatically.[6]

TELEGRAPH OFFICE—WAR DEPARTMENT

Union cipher operator David Bates referred to the Telegraph Office as Lincoln's "safe retreat and lounging place, and where he had so often calculated the wavering chances of war and peace." Bates was one of Lincoln's "boys," a small staff of telegraphers that manned Lincoln's de facto

The Main Cottage in 1905. The Soldiers' Home was later a retreat for Presidents Chester A. Arthur and Rutherford B. Hayes, but the refuge would not become a national historic site until the year 2000. Library of Congress.

situation room, and who gave the president something he had always prized most highly—information.[7]

At the beginning of the war, the army monopolized governmental access to telegraphy. But when 1861 ended with no major military successes, even the tolerant Lincoln knew that changes had to come. January 1862 brought a congressional measure to transfer control of the wires from the military to the civilian government. Consequently, the Washington termini for telegraphs were removed from field headquarters and stationed in the War Department building, immediately west of the White House grounds.[8]

Edwin M. Stanton, newly appointed secretary of war, positioned the office right next to his, on the second floor in the building's old library.

This arrangement did not prevent Lincoln from adopting both rooms as his own. Frequently he would walk over from the Executive Mansion (often unescorted), plod up the staircase, and drape his long frock coat over the door of Stanton's office. When things were slow, he would sit at the desk of chief operator Thomas Eckert, prop his feet up, and sift through the stacks of telegrams that had collected over the course of the day. When there were no messages, he would sometimes read aloud from books he had brought along or address voluminous paperwork. Eckert once recalled watching the president diligently working on a draft of the Emancipation Proclamation.[9]

When armies were on the move, Lincoln spent long hours here, often standing over the shoulders of "his boys," waiting impatiently for incoming news. By 1863, the little complex became a twenty-four-hour operation, and the staff increased to a dozen men. Lincoln visited at all hours, but he was routinely patient and grateful. When he set aside days for national prayer and fasting, he knew it physically tested more than a few government employees. On one occasion he jested with his telegraphers, "Gentlemen, this is a fast day, and I am pleased to observe that you are working as fast as you can."[10]

It was here that Lincoln kept abreast of politics as well, checking the results of state and local elections, sending and receiving messages from party supporters, and learning of his own reelection in the early morning of November 9, 1864. He also used the wires to stay in touch with son Robert while he was away at Harvard, and with Mary when she vacationed in New York and New England. Since operators on both ends were privy to all information sent, the telegrams were often rather detached and informal, leading many observers to falsely conclude that the Lincolns were normally distant and cool toward one another.

Lincoln's last visit came on April 14, 1865. He had come to ask Stanton to spare Thomas Eckert for the evening. Stanton refused, stating that Eckert had work to do and that Lincoln himself should consider staying home. Undeterred, Lincoln asked Eckert personally, who conceded to the wishes of the war secretary and politely declined the invitation to see *Our American Cousin*.[11]

GROVER'S THEATER

Lincoln's presidency predated by forty years the rise of spectator sports and movie houses. In his time, the main forms of mass entertainment were public speeches and stage plays. For Lincoln, the former was a professional obligation, and the latter was one of his most cherished escapes. Leonard Grover's Theater on Pennsylvania Avenue was his family's favorite playhouse.

Grover's Theater, also known as the New National, catered to the elite and working class alike, with orchestra boxes at $10 per performance, while second gallery and "colored gallery" seats went for 25 cents. *Hunter and Polkinhorn*, New National Theater.

At the start of Lincoln's presidency, the site was a ghostly shell once known as the National Theater; its charred walls were all that remained from a fire in 1856. A lingering recession and the broiling secession crisis halted nearly all building projects, until the war economically roused a construction spree. Among the resurgent properties was this prime location. On April 22, 1862, investors unveiled Grover's palatial venue, with the Marine Band, comedic actors and actresses, and a packed house.[12]

Common genres for the era's playhouses, including Grover's, were comedic and tragic operas, sappy romances, and lowbrow comedies. Embodying the last was humorist Daniel McLaren Rice, a favorite of Lincoln's, who dressed in a gaudy suit of American flags and told jokes while performing tricks with a trained pig. The duo were truly a pair of hams. Also at Grover's, Mary and Abe watched Irish comedian Barney Williams perform in blackface, mere weeks after the Emancipation Proclamation went into effect.[13]

Otherwise, Shakespeare was standard Grover fare, and it was common for Lincoln to see the Bard's work more than once a week at the venue, including several performances of the esteemed Edwin Booth in the lead roles of Hamlet, Richard III, and the assassin Brutus in *Julius Caesar*. In the spring of 1865, the First Family took in their last performances at the famed theater. March 15 featured Mozart's *The Magic Flute*, and the 21st brought them *La Dame Blanche*, a light opera involving inheritance, young love, and a happy fate. And it was at Grover's that young Tad Lincoln was watching a performance of *Aladdin*, while his father was taking in *Our American Cousin* a few blocks away.[14]

THE NAVY YARD (CORNER OF M AND NINTH STREET SE)

Lincoln often visited unannounced. Willie and Tad were common companions, as were Navy Secretary Gideon Welles or War Secretary Stanton. The more enjoyable visits included the reviewing of troops, testing new weapons, and spending time with Commandant Admiral John Dahlgren. He also attended several macabre and unwelcome funerals, including that of his friend Colonel Elmer Ellsworth on May 24, 1861.[15]

Most calls involved consultations with Dahlgren. Lincoln stopped at the yard on March 9, 1862, when the CSS *Virginia* (a.k.a. *Merrimac*) was in the process of raising Cain and sinking federal ships *Cumberland* and *Congress* at Hampton Roads. Impending was the historic draw between the ironclads *Merrimac* and *Monitor*, but a tie was not yet evident. He shuttled back to the Telegraph Office to read the results.[16]

It was here on April 9, 1865, with their return by steamer from a visit to Grant's encampment in Virginia, that the Lincoln family first heard of Lee's surrender at Appomattox. They were returning from the recently fallen Richmond when cheering throngs at the Navy Yard greeted the First Family and gave them the good news. Less than a week later, the president and Mrs. Lincoln last came to the Navy Yard on Good Friday, 1865, taking a short respite on the ironclad *Montauk* before they headed off that evening for a play at Ford's.[17]

FORD'S THEATRE (TENTH STREET)

Despite producing a great deal of national drama, Washington was not a main stop on the theater circuit. The prestige venues were in New York, Philadelphia, and San Francisco. One exception was Ford's Theatre, a place Lincoln visited at least ten times. Built in 1833, Ford's initially existed as the First Baptist Church of Washington. The church board, unable to afford the massive three-story structure, eventually leased and sold the building to entrepreneur John Thompson Ford in 1861. One board member predicted a dire future to anyone who dared alter the sacred meeting place into a house of entertainment. The premonition seemed to have been fully validated soon after. Lincoln first attended on May 28, 1862, to enjoy a musical concert. However, he did not have another chance to visit the original building. A fire gutted the structure on December 30, 1862, just as Balfe's *Satanella* was about to open.[18]

Completely rebuilt and refurbished, the embellished, lavish venue became the primary locale for the arts in the capital. Housed in towering white walls with ornate gilded trim, and boasting a seating capacity of twenty-four hundred, it reopened on August 27, 1863, and produced an impressive run of 495 performances in two years. Whenever Lincoln came, he occupied the Presidential Box to the right of the stage, which was actually two premier boxes divided by a removable partition. Anyone with enough cash could enjoy the select section, which patrons could attain at a hefty $10 (nearly a month of a private's pay in the Union Army).[19]

In the autumn of 1863, Lincoln and Mary began frequenting the Tenth Street icon. First on their itinerary was *Fanchon, the Cricket* on October 30. That night's event included an announcement of the upcoming program, the "First appearance of the young and distinguished tragedian John Wilkes Booth," adding, "During this engagement all of the celebrated Shakespearean Tragedies will be produced." On November 9, Lincoln watched the young and dashing actor perform in *The Marble Heart*. Five nights later it was *Henry IV* with Lincoln's favorite Shakespearean actor, the celebrated James Henry Hackett, known as the ultimate renderer of Falstaff. Lincoln was so taken by the performance that he watched it again the following evening. Two nights later, it was Hackett again in *The Merry Wives of Windsor*. The following day, the president boarded a train to deliver his "few appropriate remarks" at the new National Cemetery in Gettysburg. Then there were the tragic events of April 14, 1865. Whole forests have been leveled to tell of Lincoln's mortal wounding at John Ford's venue. Arguably, more should be written of how he enjoyed life there.[20]

CAPITOL HILL

On December 11, 1861, Lincoln entered the Senate Chamber to attend the funeral of his dear friend Senator **Edward D. Baker**. Senator Orville Browning commented that "visits of the President to either House of Congress are of rare occurrence. This is the first instance of the kind certainly within the past quarter of a century."[21] Technically this was true, but almost every president before Lincoln had first been a member of Congress, and when they returned, a degree of hospitality usually prevailed. President Lincoln came to the Hill rather frequently, even while it was undergoing extensive renovations (well into 1864, construction crews replaced the building's original shallow domes with far taller and more ornate structures). On February 25, 1861, the president-elect informally met with members of both houses and the Supreme Court. On February 26, he conferred with Republican leaders before the inauguration. Two months later he paid a visit to the Capitol's newest residents, the New York Seventh Infantry Regiment camped inside the building. Later that summer, he arrived to sign bills, including the First Confiscation Act, a small but meaningful step toward emancipating the enslaved whom the Confederacy used in its war effort. Lincoln also personally conferred with Senator Andrew Johnson, among others from time to time, on the strength of Unionism in their respective states.

In many ways the Capitol served as Washington's community center. There were Union Club meetings, floor speeches, US Christian Commission summits, congressmen to visit, and a rapidly growing library from which Lincoln borrowed frequently. He also attended lectures that piqued his interest, including one from abolitionist George Thompson in the House chambers in April 1864, followed a month later by a lecture about the Battle of Gettysburg by one Dr. J. R. Warner. The one thing the president did not do was give the State of the Union address in person. That transaction was done by proxy, a tradition set by Thomas Jefferson, who believed everyone could be saved considerable time and hassle if Congress would just read it themselves. Not until Woodrow Wilson did a president appear in person to go over an annual address in full.[22]

There was one visit Lincoln would have preferred to avoid had the option been open to him. The sixteenth president of the United States was the first to lie in state in the Capitol Rotunda, a position his remains held from April 19 to April 21, 1865.

PART II
THE PUBLIC LINCOLN

CHAPTER EIGHT

Lincoln's Early Jobs and Professions

WHEN VIEWED FROM THE VOCATIONS HE ATTEMPTED, LINCOLN APPEARS to be less a man of destiny and more of a wandering soul. But in his view, choosing one's own line of work was the very definition of the American dream. "There is no permanent class of hired laborers among us," he professed in 1854. "Twenty-five years ago I was a hired laborer. The hired laborer of yesterday labors on his own account today, and will hire others to labor for him tomorrow."[1] Individuals, no matter their ethnicity, had the right to rise as far as their efforts and abilities could take them.

Clearly Lincoln had trouble deciding, though he was certain that the most promising sites were in urbanizing areas to the west. The possibility of high returns on small investments drew many to seek their future where land was cheap and towns were new. The one great difference between his father's generation and that of his own—the elder sought new land, the younger sought new jobs, and Lincoln's vocational search led him in a multitude of directions. It is fair to say that for his early years at least, he was not necessarily trying to capture a specific goal as much as he was trying to escape a life of perpetual manual labor. Below in chronological order are the directions he tried before going into law and politics. As the following illustrates, he was not always successful, but he was rarely idle.

FARMHAND (1815–1831)

"Honest Abe" was not always honest. In a speech before the Wisconsin Agricultural Society on September 30, 1859, he insisted to his listeners,

"No other human occupation opens so wide a field for the profitable and agreeable combination of labor with cultivated thought as agriculture." Embellishing further, he added that farming provided "an exhaustless source of enjoyment." He was undoubtedly playing to the crowd. Most of the audience members were farmers, and at the time most Americans North and South labored directly or indirectly in agriculture. But he never aspired to be one of them.[2]

"I was raised to farm work," he once noted with ambivalence, "which I continued till I was twenty-two." One of his very first memories of childhood was of helping his father plant corn and pumpkin seeds at their Kentucky homestead, only to see their work washed away by rainstorms that very night. Season after season thereafter, he would see interminable hours bring meager harvests for family and friends, and he knew that months of hard work could be obliterated by the whims of nature or commerce. Relocating to better farmland provided modest improvements for the Lincolns, but never enough to convince Abraham to follow in his father's footsteps.[3]

By his late teens in Indiana, Abe began to work for others. But, as was the custom, all wages earned by those under twenty-one had to be handed over to the father. Although Abe relinquished his pay without comment, he may have resented paterfamilias for taking the money, for he never said a kind word about Thomas Lincoln for the rest of his life. The sting of work without pay likely formed the foundation of Lincoln's attitude toward slavery. As historian Gabor Boritt observes, Lincoln rarely mentioned the institution until later years, but when he did, he argued that slavery was unjust, not on the grounds of race, but on the basis that the laborer had to toil without pay.[4]

When the Lincoln family moved to yet another farmstead ten miles southwest of Decatur, Illinois, in 1830, Abe helped his own and other families bust sod, but within a year, and no longer obligated to the family, he was out on his own. In his twenties, Lincoln occasionally helped neighbors with their autumn harvests. Otherwise, he avoided the backbreaking work whenever he could. One of the last times he ever did farm work was in 1834. While canvassing for the Illinois State House, Lincoln came upon thirty men bringing in an autumn harvest.

Rather than interrupt their task with a speech, he simply pitched in and subsequently won their votes.[5]

RAIL SPLITTER (1820–1835)

Congregating under a massive wigwam of canvas and lumber at the May 1860 Republican Convention in Decatur, Illinois, locals increasingly realized their native son stood a fighting chance to win the party's presidential nomination. Their excitement churned the audience of twenty-five hundred partisans into a frenzy. During a spike of ferment, Lincoln's cousin John Hanks marched in with a banner that sent the crowd into deafening delirium. Hanging from a pair of timber fence rails fluttered a proud declaration of hope and glory.[6]

> *Abraham Lincoln, The rail Candidate for President in 1860*
> *Two rails from a Lot of 3,000 made in 1830 by Thos. Hanks and*
> *   Abe Lincoln*
> *Whose Father was the First Pioneer of Macon County*

Watching from the platform, the man of the hour appeared a bit embarrassed by the display. For starters, Lincoln's father was not a founder of Macon County, and it was John Hanks rather than Thomas who helped him split rails. Lincoln himself admitted to the crowd that he probably did not make those particular beams (they were a bit shabby by his standards), but he did confidently attest that he had formed many better ones in his time, and the crowd erupted again. The effect was deep and everlasting. Despite being a successful lawyer, congressman, and nationally known speaker, he would be known ever after as "the Rail Splitter."[7]

Aware of the force of popular opinion, Lincoln embraced the image. Days after the convention, referring to himself in the third person, he described to a campaign biographer his origins as a woodsman. "Abraham, though very young, was large of his age, and had an axe put into his hands at once; and from that time till within his twenty-third year he was almost constantly handling that most useful instrument—less of course, in plowing and harvesting seasons."[8]

Hacking timbers was never a major source of income, but it did occupy much of his youth. The Lincoln homestead in southern Indiana was thoroughly wooded, and nearly every acre had to be claimed and conquered by simple tools and hard labor. Once cleared, fields required strenuous fencing to discourage the deer and livestock from invading the crops. Since nails and lumber were prohibitively expensive (and barbed wire would not be invented for another forty years), the cheapest and most versatile option in forested areas was the timber rail fence. With axe, maul, and wedge, Lincoln cracked away at long trunks of ash, elm, fir, hickory, and poplar, making ten-foot lengths about five inches thick. These coarse lengths would then be constructed in long rows, often stretching for hundreds of yards.[9]

By most accounts, the exceptionally strong teenage Lincoln took a measure of pride in his ability to fell and divide solid timbers. The practice continued into his twenties, when he assisted his extended family in establishing farms in Macon County, the place from which the celebrated campaign rails were said to have come. He also helped build some of the pens and fencing in his adopted home of New Salem in the 1830s. But by the time John Hanks dubbed him a rail splitter in 1860, Lincoln had not done such work for nearly a quarter century.

FERRYMAN (1826–1827)

When the teenage Lincoln lived in southwest Indiana, his immediate surroundings were quite provincial. In the state's southern reaches along Pigeon Creek, population densities rarely exceeded ten people per square mile. Meanwhile, a mere fifteen miles farther south, the mighty Ohio River hosted flotillas of merchants, gamblers, miners, livestock dealers, and (on occasion) enslaved human beings. Drawn by curiosity as much as opportunity, Lincoln, his second cousin Dennis Hanks, and neighbor Squire Hall began to chop and sell cordwood to the passing steamers in the summer of 1826, establishing their ad hoc enterprise near where the Anderson River emptied south into the Ohio. It was here that Lincoln would take a job as ferryman, earn his first dollar, and experience his first run-in with the law.

Anderson River required ferry service for those wishing to traverse its hundred-foot breadth, and local entrepreneur James Taylor obliged. The task of shuttling travelers and traders, often at all hours of the day and night, may have inspired him to hire Lincoln as an assistant in 1827. Eighteen-year-old Abe was soon living at the Taylor home and working the crossing for $6 per month.[10]

In his spare time, Abe constructed a small rowing scow, which he would use to transport foot passengers for a few cents per trip, saving them and himself the hassle of taking the cumbersome ferry on each passing. On one occasion, two frantic men approached him and said they had missed their steamer, which at that very moment was paddling its way near them and down the Ohio. Abruptly loading his newfound passengers onto his little rowboat, Lincoln made fast time with the oars and completed their connection to the passing boat. Grateful for his service, the two men boarded the steamer, turned to their young rescuer, and each tossed him a silver half dollar. Lincoln could hardly believe it.

In 1939, marking where Lincoln shuttled travelers 112 years before, Indiana established Lincoln Ferry Park. The scenic enclave still stands, and it includes a portion of the original farmland of his employer, James Taylor.

Never before had he received such a reward for such short work. He would later recall how suddenly "the world seemed wider and fairer."[11] Sadly, the moment would not last.

Later that spring, after expanding this little side service to other passengers, Lincoln earned the contempt of two brothers, who brought him before a justice of the peace in Lewisport, Kentucky. His accusers claimed the young Lincoln had violated their licensed monopoly on ferrying in the area, and they were seeking punishment. A nervous and intimidated Lincoln admitted that he had taken passengers from the shore to passing riverboats and that he was ignorant of the law. But, he added, technically he never went from bank to bank, and thus was not ferrying across the river. The judge, one Samuel Pate, either was impressed by the argument or chose to follow the letter of the law. Regardless, he let Lincoln go.[12]

FLATBOAT PILOT (1828–1829, 1831)

Lincoln became a voyageur at age nineteen. An acquaintance of the family, James Gentry, hired him to accompany his son Allen on a cargo run to New Orleans. Lincoln had never trekked more than fifty miles from home. This trip would traverse twelve hundred miles. Nor had he ever seen a major city. With forty-five thousand residents, New Orleans was fourteen times larger than the entire population of Spencer County. Yet on this great voyage, Lincoln nearly died.[13]

Making their way down the Father of Waters, Allen and Abe occasionally stopped to trade along the "Sugar Coast," or lower Louisiana area of the Mississippi, where 90 percent of the nation's sugarcane grew. The succulent and expensive delicacy, along with tobacco and cotton, could be traded for Indiana corn and hams. While moored on the river one night near Baton Rouge, the two young boys, in Lincoln's words, "were attacked by seven negroes with intent to kill and rob them." After a brief and violent fight, in which the two young travelers "were hurt some in the melee," they managed to cut their line and float away.[14]

Once they reached New Orleans and sold the balance of their cargo, they stayed only a few days. What they did and where they went is unknown. Also uncertain is whether Lincoln, when observing slaves being bought and sold in the city, ever said a line often credited to him: "If I ever get a chance to hit this thing, I'll hit it hard." In truth, neither Gentry nor Lincoln took notes, kept a journal, or wrote home during the trip.

What is certain is that Lincoln took a paid steamboat ride back to Indiana, perhaps the first in his life. Though the entire journey lasted only about two months, he had turned a year older in the interim, and arguably, he saw the world for the first time.[15]

It would be two years before Lincoln attempted the trip again. He had ample incentive to go. In the miserable spring of 1831, after the Lincoln family had moved to Illinois, they endured several crippling bouts of fever, along with one of the worst winters on record. When entrepreneur Denton Offutt offered to hire Abraham, second cousin John Hanks, and stepbrother John Johnston to help him take a flatboat of cargo southward, the trio readily accepted. The destination was again New Orleans, and they started from a place that was new to Lincoln—a growing entity called Sangamon County, home to bright new communities such as New Salem and Springfield. It was the latter destination where Lincoln and his cohorts met up with Offutt, only to learn that Offutt had not procured the flatboat as promised, so they all proceeded to make one. Felling trees and slicing them into beams and planks at William Kirkpatrick's mill just northwest on the adjacent Prairie Creek, the men assembled a shallow draft vessel of about sixty feet in length. "We finished making and launching the boat in about four weeks," recalled Lincoln. "We loaded the boat with barrel pork, corn, and live hogs, and left Sangamontown." At that moment, Lincoln considered himself a "friendless, uneducated, penniless boy, working on a flat boat—at $10 a month."[16]

Soon after their journey began, it came to a teetering stop. On April 19, 1831, the boat became stuck atop a milldam in New Salem. Several townspeople came down to the river, where they saw the tall and gangly twenty-two-year-old hired hand, dressed in rolled-up blue jeans, a blue-and-white-striped cotton shirt, and a buckeye chip hat atop his thatch of black locks, busily trying to save pigs and grain from sinking into the rushing waters. The crew managed to get the vessel moving again, and a month later, they reached their destination, minus Hanks, who debarked in St. Louis and returned to his family in Illinois. This time, Lincoln may have found New Orleans more enjoyable, for he stayed about a month, along with Offutt. The two had never met before this trip, but by its end Offutt was fully impressed by the amiable and dependable Abraham. On their return northward, Offutt provided this unique individual a job in New Salem.[17]

STORE CLERK (SEPTEMBER 1831–APRIL 1832)

At age twenty-two, on his second return from New Orleans, Lincoln headed directly to where his little flatboat briefly became lodged. There he would lodge himself in late July 1831, "a piece of floating driftwood," as he would describe himself, coming to rest in the town where he would live for six pivotal years.[18]

Fellow settler Denton Offutt, said to be energetic, talkative, and by nature an optimist, evidently thought enough of New Salem that he proceeded to build a store there, on the town's eastern ridge overlooking the Sangamon. He also believed that the moderate river would soon bring considerable riverboat traffic to this small but growing town. Nearly all one hundred inhabitants felt the same. By September 1831, Offutt's simple shop was up and running. The building was average size for the area, just fourteen by sixteen feet. Abe was to tend the place with a coworker three years his junior, Tennessee-born William "Slicky Bill" Greene. They would also share the rustic sleeping arrangements in the back, often just a single cot. At the time, having one's own bed was a privilege that few enjoyed. Wages for each employee consisted of about $15 per month (approximately $420 in 2021).[19]

Stocked with sacks of seed and coffee, rows of fresh eggs, bags of salt and sugar, saddles, and sundries, the enterprise also furnished barrels of whiskey, one of the establishment's more popular products. For Lincoln, the most valuable commodity was camaraderie. Stores were often social centers for young men, who gathered to talk of politics, of residents new and old, and of earthy blood sports like hunting, fishing, and gander pulls. Offutt's was no different. The shop also became a popular hangout for a handful of local toughs known as the Clary's Grove Boys. The little gang had taken a quick liking to Lincoln. Popular is the story of Lincoln wrestling their leader, **Jack Armstrong**. There is much conjecture and perhaps too much attention paid to this famous scrap. Some accounts have Armstrong cheating to win and Lincoln forgiving him for the indiscretion. Others have Lincoln winning, while still others have the contest ending in a draw. Ultimately, the encounter was just one of many where Lincoln could, and did, establish himself as strong in social, mental, and physical character.

For such a frequented shop, it took in very little revenue, but it did help Lincoln become one of the central features of the community. By March of the following year, his newfound popularity led him to announce his candidacy for the Illinois legislature. Those plans, and his work at Offutt's, would be interrupted by events outside his control. The first involved a scheme to tame the Sangamon River, followed by a federal fight against the Sauk and Fox people.[20]

STEAMBOAT OPERATOR (1832)

In the spring of 1832, Lincoln volunteered for a project to prove that the Sangamon could be traversed by steamship, a feat never before attempted. Had the venture succeeded, it might have enabled one of the area's seedling towns to become the next Louisville or St. Louis. The announcement came in the January pages of the *Sangamo Journal*. Entrepreneur Vincent Bogue was going to hire the two-story, 150-ton steamer *Talisman*, load it full of cargo in Cincinnati, sail it down to St. Louis, and then chug up the Illinois River to the mouth of the Sangamon. Bogue declared he would then need "ten or twelve men, having axes with long handles under the direction of some experienced man." A man with experience was Lincoln, who claimed to know more of the river than anyone, and who had a little practice at chopping wood.[21]

Once underway, the voyage ran cold and slow. It was mid-March, and ice floes blocked the route. After the crew broke those apart, the axe work began—almost incessantly. Branches and brush hung low over the banks, clawing at the 136-foot-long, 48-foot-wide craft, doing a fair bit of damage to its stacks and rails. Floating debris and submerged trunks also imperiled the vessel. The many wild intrusions only solidified Lincoln's ideas for internal improvements. Just days before this little adventure, Lincoln published his very first political platform, calling for government help in clearing waterways so that the natural arteries of the nation could pump lifeblood into young economies.[22]

Further bolstering his spirit, and that of the whole crew, were the growing clusters of heartened onlookers. Running along the riverbank, waving and shouting, some of them had never seen a steamship. The passing vessel, churning and billowing, gave proof of progress. On March 24, ten days after its Sangamon journey began, the *Talisman* reached its destination of Portland Landing, six miles past New Salem and just six miles overland to Springfield. To celebrate the great occasion, citizens held a grand ball at the Springfield courthouse, and Lincoln likely attended.[23]

The euphoria was short lived. Within a week, the Sangamon turned shallow from lack of rain. Falling levels meant that the steamer could be trapped, perhaps for months. With fellow New Salemite J. Rowan Herndon at the pilot's wheel and Lincoln in assistance, the two helped the beleaguered boat make a hasty retreat to the deeper Illinois River. They nearly came to grief at New Salem, getting stuck at the milldam, the very same that caught Lincoln's flatboat three years previous. With little time to spare, part of the dam was dismantled to let the boat through. Nature, it appeared, still commanded the Sangamon.[24]

SOLDIER (APRIL–JULY 1832)

Mere days after the *Talisman*'s setback, approximately fifteen hundred Sauk men, women, and children, along with members of the Fox and Kickapoo tribes, began to do something few Native Americans were attempting at the time. They were heading east. Crossing the Mississippi from the territory of Iowa into Illinois, the Sauk were under the guidance of Black Hawk, an aging warrior born before the American Revolution, who fought on the side of the British in the War of 1812. By 1832 he was ready to lead another campaign to reclaim lost ground. In response, Illinois governor John Reynolds ordered sixteen hundred state militia to assemble and repel what he called an "invasion." From sizeable Sangamon County, Reynolds set the quota of volunteers at 350. Among those in New Salem who answered the call were Jack Armstrong, "Slicky Bill" Greene, and Abraham Lincoln.[25]

Despite his genial nature, or perhaps because of it, Lincoln was elected captain by his fellow volunteers, an event he would later recall as one of the greatest honors of his life. His company of approximately sixty men became part of the Thirty-First Illinois Militia Regiment. Their mission—chase down and subdue Black Hawk. Their performance—less than stellar. Within a week, discipline began to fall apart. Minimal rations, long marches, and a soggy April made for irritable conscripts. Unaccustomed to taking orders, especially from a twenty-three-year-old raconteur, the company made poor time and no contact with the Sauk. Furthermore, several in the ranks began to view the entire affair as a goose chase of a few score Natives who posed no personal threat to them. Lincoln himself would come to view his own involvement in the war as more humbling than heroic. "I had a good many bloody experiences with the mosquitoes," he remembered, "and although I never fainted from loss of blood, I can truly say I was often very hungry."[26]

He did witness, however, the graphic potential of armed conflict. Twice, Lincoln and his men came upon mutilated corpses. On the evening of May 15, his company encountered the aftermath of a deadly skirmish near Sycamore Creek in north-central Illinois, where the bodies of a dozen volunteers lay prostrate. Atop their heads were fleshy crimson patches where their hair used to be.[27] The sight of maimed bodies did little to inspire Lincoln's temporary charges to stay in the field. In turn, professional soldiers viewed these locals with contempt. Colonel Zachary Taylor admitted, "The more I see of the militia, the less confidence I have of their effecting anything of importance."[28]

For Lincoln, however, there evidently existed a desire to remain, in part because his prospects back in New Salem were even less compelling. When his thirty days of service were up, he reenlisted, first as a private for twenty days, then as a scout for thirty more, and he provided his own weapon and horse. Coming close on several occasions to engaging in battle, he always missed out. When the war finally came to an end in August at the Battle of Bad Axe, resulting in the death or capture of most of Black Hawk's remaining band, Lincoln had already been mustered out and was back in New Salem. While he did not celebrate his involvement in the war, refusing to maintain the complimentary title of captain, he did establish connections with prominent individuals he met in the service, including **John Todd Stuart, Orville Browning,** and **Edward Baker,** who would later play critical roles in leading Lincoln to brighter pastures.[29]

STORE OWNER (SEPTEMBER 1832–APRIL 1833)

The journey back from the war took Lincoln longer than expected. Someone stole his horse. He returned with less than two weeks to go before the August elections, and with little time to renew his stump speaking, he never caught up. In the contest, he managed to win 277 out of 300 votes in the immediate area, but his relative anonymity elsewhere in the county sentenced him to an eighth-place finish out of thirteen candidates, one of the worst showings of his **election record**. With two more years until the next election, the Offutt store having failed in his absence, and no other promising options for work, Lincoln cautiously stepped into the realm of self-employment—and fell headlong into a chasm of debt.

It seemed like a wise move at the time, to take part ownership of a store on the south side of Main Street with neighbor William Berry. They were both poor, and they obtained the establishment purely on credit, several hundred dollars' worth in promissory notes at double-digit interest. But Berry was a minister's son, with an advanced education, having gone to Illinois College in Jacksonville. He had also served under Lincoln as a corporal in the Black Hawk War. New Salem was still growing, and though it was no more than twenty families in total, it was just as large as a village named Chicago to the north and almost as populated as Springfield to the south.[30]

After just a few months of modest business, Lincoln and Berry seized an opportunity. Reuben Radford's shop across the street was newer and larger than theirs, but it had recently been "renovated" by the Clary's Grove gang. Reuben either said or did something to earn their ire, and they responded by trashing the place. In turn, he decided to sell out to William Greene, Lincoln's ex-workmate at Offutt's. Greene then sold the fixer-upper to Lincoln and Berry at a steep $650, again mostly on credit. Soon this second locale offered not only the staples of bulk flour, salt, and seed but also selections of hats, shoes, and yards of cloth. The following

March, Berry took out a tavern license, allowing the store to also offer lodging, meals, and alcohol. There were reasons to be optimistic.[31]

Perhaps it was the tough competition from the Hill-McNeil store right next door, or possibly Berry's alleged drinking problem. The marginal traffic on the shallow Sangamon probably did not help. Whatever the cause, the hopeful partnership "winked out" before it completed its first year.[32]

With his current prospects, Lincoln could subsist, but he could do almost nothing about the many debts he and Berry had accrued. He would soon take a second job, and then a third; yet even these barely addressed the interest he owed. In January 1835, Berry made matters worse by dying. At that point, Lincoln owed more than $1,200, what he satirically named the "national debt," though he was only barely exaggerating. At the time, the ultra-frugal Andrew Jackson administration had whittled the federal debt down to $28,000, the lowest in US history. Despite the considerable stress of a high balance, Lincoln evidently never held grudges against his creditors. It would take nearly a decade to pay off the entire balance, but he reimbursed every cent, plus interest.[33]

POSTMASTER (MAY 1833–MAY 1836)

The United States Postal Service was born before the nation itself. In response to royal British censorship of their dissenting newspapers, rebellious colonials formed their own ad hoc letter service in 1774. In July of the following year, the Second Continental Congress took over the operation; however, the price of missives was not cheap. At times during the ensuing Revolution, US rates were forty times higher than the empire's, but with their first postmaster general Benjamin Franklin at the helm, many patriots remained committed.[34]

By the 1830s, local post offices would be the main (and often only) contact between US citizens and their federal government, and the service was quite limited. Payment was primarily cash on delivery, and the charge was by sheets and distance rather than by weight. For example, sending a single-page letter locally cost 6¼ cents. Sending it four hundred miles cost four times more. Federal adhesive postage stamps first appeared during the James K. Polk administration in 1847, and these would not be widely available until the following decade. One's "post office" was often just a rented room in a shop, inn, or tavern. Free-standing mail centers were not commonplace until the end of the nineteenth century.[35]

Just how Lincoln became postmaster of New Salem is not entirely clear. The job required an appointment from the executive branch. Andrew Jackson's administration was vehemently Democrat and committed to the spoils system, while Lincoln was a known Whig. Tradition states that local women did not care for the existing postmaster, alleged misogynist Samuel

In his First Inaugural Address, Lincoln vowed that he would defend, among other things, the Postal Service, declaring, "The mails, unless repelled, will continue to be furnished in all parts of the Union." Library of Congress.

Hill, and they petitioned the government to appoint the affable Lincoln. More than likely, Lincoln's own hypothesis is closer to the truth. He surmised that the lowly stipend of $50 per annum made the position "too insignificant to make his politics an objection." However, the job's perks did appeal to him. All his personal mail came free of charge. In addition, his office became the only receiving point for all incoming newspapers, as they were delivered by government mail rather than through private carriers. While he waited for customers to pick up their latest issue, he could read each periodical to his heart's content, receiving a wealth of knowledge on a pauper's income. In the process, he also became better informed of local and national issues than nearly everyone else in the area. The work was also relatively easy. Deliveries only came twice a week, and the volume was low. He could usually carry what he needed in his hat, though door-to-door service was not required. Collecting payment was his chief concern, and even then, he sometimes waived fees (a practice called "franking") when the recipients were strapped. He was, however, quite zealous about keeping a clear record of accounts in his ledger. In a larger sense, his work as postmaster, and the next job he acquired, enabled him to become one of the most visible and informed residents of Sangamon County, attributes that inspired Lincoln to run for a higher, elected public office.[36]

SURVEYOR (JANUARY 1834–NOVEMBER 1836)
Between the time of Lincoln's birth and his twenty-fourth year, Illinois had transformed from a territory to a state, from three thousand registered residents to a population of nearly three hundred thousand. This rapid growth in farmers, speculators, renters, and squatters led to an intense demand for clear lines of land ownership. Not surprisingly, surveyors were often overwhelmed with job orders, as was Sangamon County's head surveyor John Calhoun. To lighten the burden, Calhoun hired Lincoln, who desperately needed the income, in late 1833. To prepare, the understudy claimed that he simply "procured a compass and chain, studied Flint, and Gibson a little, and went at it." The process was more complicated than that.[37]

The "Flint" Lincoln mentioned was Abel Flint's *A System of Geometry and Trigonometry with a Treatise on Surveying in Which the Principals of Rectangular Surveying without Plotting Are Explained.* Its companion piece was Robert Gibson's equally wordy *A Treatise on Practical Surveying Which Is Demonstrated from Its First Principles Wherein Everything That Is Useful and Curious in That Art Is Fully Considered and Explained.* Lincoln had virtually no previous training in higher mathematics, and the tomes were almost as cumbersome as their titles, but he needed to master them. Each book focused on geometry (to calculate lengths, area, and irregular shapes) and trigonometry (to formulate distances, elevations, and locations). He attacked the volumes with the same zeal he employed with almost every new text, reading them again and again, often aloud, through long hours of intense study.

Then, in his words, Lincoln "went at it," a geomatrician on horseback, plodding into the wilderness, armed with the tools of the trade—stakes, compass, plumb lines, Jacob staff, pencils, and paper. The pay was substantial, about $6 to $12 per assignment, but the work was often exhausting. Frequently he encountered bogs, bugs, hunger, rain, fields of wrathful underbrush, unmerciful heat, bitter cold, and the occasional wild beast. Adding to the challenge was the conundrum of English measurement. If only the Founding Fathers had adopted the French invention of metric, with its comprehendible increments of ten, or the octal (base-8) approach that several European intellectuals advocated because it was so easy to divide. Instead, American surveyors had to wrestle with the archaic, imperial measures of feet, rods, furlongs, and acres. Fortunately, Lincoln and others possessed the invaluable "Gunter's Chain." Developed by Oxford mathematician Edmund Gunter in the 1600s, it consisted of one hundred metal links, each a rod of eight inches and connected by rings. Durable, transportable, with a total length of sixty-six feet, known as "a chain," it could calculate quirky English distances. For instance, a furlong was simply a quarter chain. An acre equaled ten chains square. Eighty chains in a straight line was a mile.[38]

Lincoln's first known survey was on a cold January 14, 1834. The stake-out was for Russell Godbey, who had purchased a piece of property just north of New Salem, or as Lincoln figured, "West half of the Northeast quarter of Section 30 in Township 19 North of Range 6 West." Later that year, Abe platted his first major road project, leading a team of four to lay out a path from Musick's Ferry through New Salem toward Jacksonville, a distance of nearly twenty-seven miles.[39]

The surveys continued, but he was not fond of the enterprise. He considered the job practical but temporary. It "procured bread, and kept body and soul together," and allowed him to travel on a wider arc than normal, fostering working relationships with some of the more influential elements in Sangamon County, including land owners, investors, bankers, and lawmakers.[40]

When Election Day came in August 1834, Lincoln's connections finally paid off, and he won a seat in the Ninth Legislature of the Illinois House of Representatives. He would continue his work as a surveyor, eventually platting out the new Illinois towns of Albany, Bath, Huron, and Petersburg, among others. He also maintained his position as town postmaster. Despite his triple income, the industrious twenty-six-year-old was still poor, and he longed for a greater source of revenue, one that would allow him to pay off the "national debt." Though painfully aware of his limited education, Lincoln dedicated himself in full to the study of law, in hopes that one day he could pass the bar and finally leave the slow road of mere subsistence.

CHAPTER NINE

Lincoln's Election Record

MOST PRESIDENTIAL HISTORIANS DEEM LINCOLN THE GREATEST US chief executive to date, but his contemporaries viewed him as quite human and not always their best political choice. In Lincoln's twelve runs for elected office, he received the most votes in just five of those contests and attained a majority of votes only twice—in his race for the US House in 1846 and in his decisive win in the 1864 presidential campaign. Coincidentally, in neither of those instances did he run as a Republican. The party did not yet exist in 1846 during his congressional bid, and he was part of the conglomerated National Union Party in 1864, running as he did with Tennessee Democrat Andrew Johnson in an attempt to reach as many voters as possible.

Reflective of his uniqueness, Lincoln also lived his public life in the minority—he was never a Democrat. Illinois may be known as the Land of Lincoln, but from 1828 to 1856, the state always went Democratic in presidential elections. It would be understandable for a rural lad like Abe to side with the rough-hewn Jacksonians, but his open admiration for poets, mathematicians, philosophers, and statesmen placed his heart firmly in the Whig realm. In 1860, the Democrats were unquestionably the largest, oldest, and most organized faction in the United States. Were it not for the Party of Jackson splitting over the issue of slavery in 1860, and the exodus of Southern Democrats from the House and Senate in 1861, the newborn Republicans would have stood little to no chance of winning the presidency (let alone Congress) in the ensuing elections.

Also significant is how undemocratic the nation was in the Lincoln era. Partisan newspapers, divided families, and raucous caucuses were a matter of course. At his birth, no state permitted female suffrage. When he first held office, Pennsylvania removed the right of African American male voting from its constitution. During his presidential bid, only one slave state (Rhode Island) enfranchised free blacks, along with just four "free soil" states (Maine, Massachusetts, New Hampshire, and Vermont). Secret balloting would not occur in the United States until the late nineteenth century. In a nation of, by, and for the people, representation existed indirectly, if at all.[1]

In the races listed in this chapter, the winners of the seats are marked with an asterisk (*).

1832 Illinois House of Representatives

Candidate	Party	Votes
Edmund Dick Taylor	Democrat	1,127*
John Todd Stuart	Whig	991*
Achilles Morris	Democrat	945*
Peter Cartwright	Democrat	815*
A. G. Herndon	Democrat	806
William Carpenter	Democrat	774
John Dawson	Democrat	717
Abraham Lincoln	Whig	657
T. M. Neale	Whig	593
Richard Quinton	Democrat	485
Zachary Peter	Whig	216
Edward Robinson	Whig	169
William Kirkpatrick	Democrat	44

Just twenty-three years old and newly arrived from his limited work in the Black Hawk War, Lincoln issued *A Communication to the People of Sangamon County*, likely in the form of a handbill to his literate constituents. Declaring his candidacy for the assembly, he promoted "the

Democrat Edmund "Dick" Taylor received the highest number of votes in the 1832 contest. A shrewd businessman, he supported Whig internal improvement projects. In 1862, thirty years after his victory over Lincoln et al., he met with President Lincoln to propose federal paper currency that would be legal for all debts private and public. Taylor would thus come to be known as the "Father of Greenbacks."

public utility of internal improvements; that the poorest and most thinly populated countries would be greatly benefitted by the opening of good roads, and in the clearing of navigable stream." Concerning the fledgling concept of public education, he avowed, "I view it as the most important subject which we as a people can be engaged in. That every man may receive at least, a moderate education, and thereby be enabled to read the histories of his own and other countries, by which he may duly appreciate the value of our free institutions."[2]

When the ballots were tallied in the first week of August, Lincoln received an impressive 277 out of 300 votes among his fellow New Salem residents, a strong showing considering that he had been living in the village for just six months. But across Sangamon County, he took only 657 from 8,339 ballots, or around 7 percent. It was a large field, with thirteen candidates vying for just four positions. Lincoln's soon-to-be mentor John Todd Stuart was the lone Whig elected; the other three were Democrats, who enjoyed the support of a predominantly rural area more interested in small government than Lincoln's relative modernity. Overall, the state stayed heavily Democratic, riding the coattails of a domineering presidential incumbent Andrew Jackson, who won Illinois handily on his way to a landslide reelection over Lincoln's Whig hero Henry Clay.[3]

1834 Illinois House of Representatives

Candidate	Party	Votes
John Dawson	Democrat	1,390*
Abraham Lincoln	Whig	1,376*
William Carpenter	Democrat	1,170*
John Todd Stuart	Whig	1,164*
Richard Quinton	Democrat	1,038
Andrew McCormick	Whig	694
William Alvey	Whig	613
T. M. Neale	Whig	514
S. J. Campbell	Democrat	192
James Shepherd	Democrat	154
James Baker	Whig	130
John Durley	Whig	92
William Kendall	Whig	42

Elections for Illinois state offices took place in their usual time slot, the first week of August. A New Salem neighbor remembered Lincoln stopping by while he and a team of others were busy harvesting wheat. Reportedly Lincoln lent a hand and showed such exceptional skill with a scythe that the men collectively decided to vote for him. Frequently helpful to others, as well as highly visible as a surveyor and postman, Lincoln also benefited from public support from his mentors Democrat **Bowling Green** and Whig **John Todd Stuart**. The final tabulation revealed the young man had garnered broad appeal even outside New Salem. Lincoln more than doubled his vote total from the previous election, joining incumbent Stuart as the other Whig representative from Sangamon.[4]

1836 Illinois House of Representatives

Candidate	Party	Votes
Abraham Lincoln	Whig	1,716*
William F. Elkin	Whig	1,694*
Ninian Edwards	Whig	1,659*

Candidate	Party	Votes
John Dawson	Whig	1,641*
Dan Stone	Whig	1,438*
Robert L. Wilson	Whig	1,353*
Andrew McCormick	Whig	1,306*
John Calhoun	Democrat	1,278
J. M. Early	Democrat	1,194
Richard Quinton	Democrat	1,137
Thomas Wynne	Democrat	972
Aaron Vandaveer	Democrat	922
Uriah Mann	Democrat	913
George Power	Democrat	905
James Baker	Whig	101
J. L. Thompson	Democrat	38
T. Young	Whig	12

Evident above is Sangamon County's rapid shift from a Democratic enclave to a Whig stronghold. This would be the session of Sangamon's "Long Nine," with the growing county granted seven House seats plus its regular two senatorial positions, all of them filled by men six feet in height or taller. Expressing the shift toward urban power, all seven representatives from the county were Whigs, including the converted John Dawson.[5]

1838 ILLINOIS HOUSE OF REPRESENTATIVES

Candidate	Party	Votes
Abraham Lincoln	Whig	1,803*
Ninian Edwards	Whig	1,779*
Edward D. Baker	Whig	1,745*
John Calhoun	Democrat	1,711*
William Elkin	Whig	1,688*
John Dawson	Whig	1,614*
Andrew McCormick	Whig	1,569*

Candidate	Party	Votes
Thomas Vance		1,537
Moses Anderson	Democrat	1,506
Harry Riggin	Democrat	1,318
Davis Robinson	Democrat	1,167
Francis Reegnier		1,069
Wharton Ransdell	Democrat	228
William Hacknay	Democrat	198
James Baker	Democrat	182

By now Lincoln had become a leading figure in the assembly. Consequently, he devoted more time campaigning for others, including his new law partner John Todd Stuart for US Congress. Running against Stuart was the Democrats' "Little Giant" Stephen Douglas, an individual Lincoln first met when the two worked in the Illinois House. The fight between Stuart and Douglas became just that, an actual fight. On more than one occasion, the towering Stuart and the intense Douglas actually came to blows. Biographer Benjamin Thomas notes that Lincoln advised simply ignoring the "Little Giant." Said Lincoln sardonically, "Isn't that the best mode of treating so small a matter?" Yet Stuart could not contain himself. During a debate in Springfield, the otherwise venerable Whig grabbed Douglas by the neck, to which Douglas responded by sinking his incisors deep into Stuart's hand. Lincoln and fellow partygoers won their positions by safe margins, but the Stuart/Douglas brawl came down to the wire. Out of more than thirty-six thousand ballots cast in the district, Stuart won by just thirty-six votes. However, by winning, Lincoln's senior law partner spent a decreasing amount of time on their practice, which eventually led to the pair parting ways.[6]

1840 ILLINOIS HOUSE OF REPRESENTATIVES

Candidate	Party	Votes
James M. Bradford	Whig	1,859*
James M. Brown	Whig	1,857*

Candidate	Party	Votes
John Darnielle	Whig	1,852*
Josiah Francis	Whig	1,846*
Abraham Lincoln	Whig	1,844*
John Calhoun	Democrat	1,266
Jesse B. Thomas Jr.	Democrat	1,241
James Barrett	Democrat	1,211
John Cooper	Democrat	1,175
Moses Anderson	Democrat	1,174

Though technically finishing fifth and last among the available slots, Lincoln and his well-organized Whig companions had essentially orchestrated a five-way tie. By this time it was clear, to Lincoln at least, that his stature in the House and party had reached its apex and may have been on the wane. Courtship with Mary Todd, a growing law practice, and the promise of achieving middle-class status pulled him away from politics for the time being. Far from settling down, Lincoln started several new journeys at once—a full-time professional career in law, a committed relationship with Mary, and the prospect of fatherhood. In addition, he began these quests while in his mid-thirties, a decade later than was customary, yet very much in keeping with *his* internal clock. With the exception of his physical height, Abe tended to bloom late in life.[7]

1846 US HOUSE OF REPRESENTATIVES

Candidate	Party	Votes
Abraham Lincoln	Whig	6,340
Peter Cartwright	Democrat	4,829
Elihu Walcott	Liberty	247

As the above races for the state house attest, Lincoln's party had successfully built a Whig island in a vast Democratic sea. Consequently, his Illinois Seventh District became a virtual Whig lock in its US Congressional race. But the prize of that rare US House seat had to be shared among the party loyal, lest they split into factions and lose the post. A gentlemen's agreement led to a rotational system, whereby Whig candidates would run, win, serve one term, then step aside. In 1844, Lincoln reached the short list to go to Washington, but the nomination and election went to his close friend **Edward Baker**.

Lincoln received the nod in 1846, though victory was not assured. While Lincoln toured central Illinois as surveyor and lawyer serving scores of clients, his Democratic opponent, Peter Cartwright, had already crisscrossed much of Illinois and the Ohio River Valley as a Baptist preacher during the Second Great Awakening, personally converting thousands and connecting with an evangelical base. Yet compared to the flexible Lincoln, Cartwright spoke vehemently against alcohol, which his fellow Democrats found hard to swallow. Lincoln also benefited from being the least committed of the candidates on the topic of slavery. Cartwright, despite his Jacksonian connections, railed against the institution, and Elihu Walcott's Liberty Party held the singular plank of abolitionism. Lincoln still won, but, as was standard for the time, his congressional session would not convene for nearly a year. In the interim, the thrill of victory quickly wore thin. "Being elected to Congress," he confessed to his friend Joshua Speed, "has not pleased me as much as I expected."[8]

For the 1848 race, Lincoln dutifully deferred, and the Whig hierarchy nominated his old law partner Stephen T. Logan. But international events conspired against the Whigs of Sangamon. Border disputes with Mexico bred a war that Lincoln and the Whigs openly opposed. The two-year conflict not only bred a groundswell of nationalism and xenophobia but also netted the United States an overwhelming military victory, half of Mexico's land, a gold rush, and a gateway to Asia. Consequently, Logan lost to the Democrats in an extremely close vote, and Lincoln had good reason to believe his political life was over. Upon Lincoln's return to Springfield, he admitted, "I was losing interest in politics."[9]

1855 US Senate

In this race, fifty-one legislator votes were needed to win.

Candidate	Position	1st Round	9th Round	10th Round
Abraham Lincoln	State Rep.	44 votes	15 votes	0 votes
James Shields	Incumbent	41 votes	n/a	0 votes
Lyman Trumball	State Rep.	5 votes	35 votes	51 votes
Joel Matteson	Illinois Governor	1 vote	47 votes	47 votes

The 1855 contest involved the Senate seat of incumbent James Shields. Born in Ireland, he became state auditor of Illinois, during which Representative A. Lincoln criticized his service. Shields then challenged Lincoln to a duel. When reason prevailed, the two became amicable. Shields later became US senator for three different states and a Union general in the Civil War.

One shocking, unforeseen event pulled Lincoln back into the political spotlight: the otherwise innocuously named Kansas-Nebraska Act of 1854. Shepherded through the Senate by Stephen Douglas, it dissolved the 1820 Missouri Compromise Line dividing free-soil and slave lands, shattered existing political parties into "Pro-" and "Anti-Nebraska" factions, formed initially hard-line abolitionist cells across the Northern landscape (soon to call themselves Republicans), and called for "popular sovereignty" whereby residents pouring into these regions could decide to spread human slavery into the Northwest. To this day, the act remains one of the most incendiary congressional creations in US history.

Its passage so consumed Lincoln that his associates saw him become withdrawn, deeply contemplative, a vessel of potential energy. When his district again elected him to the state assembly, he resigned the post. The US Senate was his goal, and he quietly solicited support from nearly anyone with political leverage—sitting and former officials, judges, lawyers, clients, friends old and new, and advised them to be careful about their work. To his friend Elihu Washburne, he cautioned, "Don't let anyone know I have written you this; for there may be those opposed to me, nearer about you than you think. Very truly yours &c A. LINCOLN."[10]

When Douglas returned home to publicly defend his role in creating the law, Lincoln began following him across the state, telling crowds he would rebut every speech Douglas made, and often drew thousands in the endeavor. At Springfield, Lincoln railed to a mass of listeners, "For the spread of slavery, I cannot but hate. I hate it because of the monstrous injustice of slavery itself. I hate it because it deprives our republican example of its just influence in the world—enables the enemies of free institutions, with plausibility, to taunt us has hypocrites." Days later at Peoria, an invigorated Abe punctuated his point: slavery was stuck for the time being in the Southern states, but it should never spread another inch: "On the general question of domestic-slavery, I wish to MAKE and to KEEP the distinction between the EXISTING institution, and the EXTENSION of it, so broad, and so clear, that no honest man can misunderstand me, and no dishonest one, successfully misrepresent me" (all caps in original).[11]

Per the law at the time, state legislatures rather than all enfranchised white males selected US senators. With meticulous scrutiny, Lincoln gathered the name of every Illinois representative and senator, researched where they stood on the Nebraska spectrum, and wrote clandestinely to their respective circles of support, pushing for the seat. To Washburne he calculated, "I cannot doubt but I have more committals than any other one man. Your District comes up tolerably well for me; but not unanimously by any means. . . . Tell Norton that Mr. Strunk and Mr. Wheeler come out plump for me. . . . I understand myself as having 26 committals; and I do not think any other one man has ten—may be mistaken though."[12]

As it turned out, Lincoln was mistaken. Old Democrats refused to help him, as did pro-Nebraska Whigs and Southern apologists. He nearly received enough votes on the first balloting but lost ground thereafter. Finally, rather than seeing the pro-Nebraska governor win, the defeated Lincoln tossed his support to a tacitly anti-Nebraska Democrat in Lyman Trumball. Adding salt to his wounds, the Illinois Assembly seat Lincoln had relinquished went to a pro-Nebraska Democrat, one Jonathan Daniel.[13]

1856 REPUBLICAN NOMINATION FOR VICE PRESIDENT

Candidate	Position	Votes
William Lewis Dayton	Former US Senator	523
Abraham Lincoln	Former US Representative	110
Nathaniel Banks	Governor of Massachusetts	46
David Wilmot	Former US Representative	43
Charles Sumner	US Senator	35
Jacob Collamer	US Senator	15
John Alsop King	Former US Representative	9
Samuel Pomeroy	Former Massachusetts Representative	8
Thomas Ford	Former Governor of Illinois	7
Henry Charles Carey	Economist	3
Cassius M. Clay	Former Kentucky Representative	3

The fact that Lincoln could garner second place reflected his growing stature among Republicans at their Philadelphia convention. His runner-up position is even more impressive considering who stood below him in the count. While the VP nomination went to accomplished William Dayton, a former US senator and associate justice on New Jersey's Supreme Court, the rest of the field included Nathaniel Banks, former governor of Massachusetts and future major general in the Union Army. Also in the running was congressional powerhouse David Wilmot, proposer of the Wilmot Proviso that unsuccessfully attempted to keep slavery out of all territories gained through the Mexican War. A veteran of that same war, Cassius Clay received far less support than the moderate Dayton and Lincoln, because of his vehement abolitionism in Kentucky and the US Congress. A former owner himself, Clay twice survived assassination attempts, both times personally fighting off his would-be murderers. For Clay's courage and commitment, Lincoln would later name him minister to Russia, a role in which Clay managed to convince the authoritarian Romanovs to support the Union cause. Arguably more famous than all of them was radical Republican Charles Sumner, who received just 35 votes to Lincoln's 110. The heralded defender of abolitionism was still recovering from when Preston Brooks nearly beat him to death on the Senate floor after Sumner chastised the brutality of slavery and Brooks's familial ties to it.[14] There were also five other candidates in this election, who received fewer than three votes.

1858 US Senate
Fifty-one legislator votes were needed to win this election.

Candidate	Party	Votes
Stephen A. Douglas	Democrat	54
Abraham Lincoln	Republican	46

Lincoln's near victory for US Senate in 1855, his impressive showing at the 1856 Republican National Convention, his growing prestige as an attorney and speechmaker, and his careful distancing from radical abolitionists made Lincoln the leading hope to topple the South-soothing Stephen Douglas from his perch in the nation's upper house. For Lincoln personally, it was the bellicose Kansas-Nebraska Act that stoked his political ambitions white hot. Since its inception, the offense galled him. In August 1855, Lincoln wrote to his dear friend Joshua Speed, "I look upon that enactment not as a *law*, but as *violence* from the beginning. . . . The slave-breeders and slave-traders, are a small, odious, detested class, among you; and yet in politics, they dictate the course of all of you, and are as completely your masters, as you are the masters of your own negroes." In 1856, he delivered anti-Nebraska speeches across Illinois and into Michigan and wrote personal letters to friends on how the law threatened the very foundation of democracy, and he ran in 1858 virtually on this one singular issue.[15]

The contest spawned seven Great Debates, which deepened the sincere loathing between the candidates, and splayed the question of the epoch before the people in print and in homes across the country. The actual election fell upon a few score men, as it always had for every senatorial seat from the nation's birth and well beyond Lincoln's lifetime. On November 2, 1858, the Illinois legislators met, and the Democrats held firm. On receiving the news, the *Rock Island Argus*, which would go on to consistently oppose President Lincoln, declared in its headlines, "Glorious Democratic Victory! Black Republicanism Wiped Out! Illinois Redeemed!" In contrast, Whig and Republican papers like the *Chicago Tribune* voiced dark disappointment, even surprise. It was one thing to foresee a Douglas victory in a historically Democratic state, but it was quite another for the free-soil land to marry itself to a slavery-friendly future.[16]

For all his life, whether a contest took place in court, legislation, games, or elections, Lincoln took wins and losses generally in stride, but losing this race hurt him. At least he could console himself for making a stand, he wrote a friend, even if slavery would likely endure and expand for the foreseeable future. "Though I now sink out of view, and shall be forgotten, I believe I have made some marks which will tell for the cause of liberty long after I am gone." His supporters were less conciliatory.

"Street fights are not as numerous as expected," reported the *Illinois State Journal*, but "by sundown, however, city prison is nearly full."[17]

1860 US PRESIDENCY

Candidate	Party	Electoral Votes
Abraham Lincoln	Republican	180
John C. Breckenridge	Democrat	72
John Bell	Union	39
Stephen A. Douglas	Democrat	12

This was and remains the most controversial election in US history, one that sparked a war that cost approximately 700,000 American lives. So divisive was the immediate result that weeks after its conclusion, a South Carolina convention declared independence from the United States and began seizing federal property within its borders. Before Lincoln's inauguration, six other state conventions rejected the electoral outcome and professed separation from the Union. Alabama's ordinance of secession echoed others by proclaiming in its opening sentence, "Whereas, the election of Abraham Lincoln and Hannibal Hamlin to the offices of president and vice-president of the United States of America . . . is a political wrong of so insulting and menacing a character as to justify the people of the State of Alabama in the adoption of prompt and decided measures for their future peace and security." Contrary to the Alabama convention's assertions, and similar vexations from other Southern delegations, the Lincoln/Hamlin ticket was far from abolitionist, and the North was hardly a unified front. In Lincoln's own Springfield, the vote was nearly evenly split between Lincoln and Douglas, with Sangamon County as a whole going against their native son. Illinois itself barely went to Lincoln, with 51 percent voting for him, while Douglas took 47 percent, mostly from the southern and rural areas of the state.[18]

All four horses in the race faced ridicule, libel, slander, and threats. To frighten voters into supporting pro-slavery vice president John Breckenridge, Texas papers falsely claimed that a series of slave uprisings were sweeping across the state. Supporters of centrist John Bell predicted that a Breckenridge victory would spell open warfare and the end of the Union. Spurious stories spoke of voter fraud, rising militias, and deathly ill candidates. Partisans fabricated poll numbers to show their man with insurmountable leads. Popular was the rumor that Lincoln was black, and it hardly mattered in the South, because he wasn't allowed on a single ballot. Sadly, one Georgia newspaper was rather prophetic in what may have seemed hyperbolic at the time: "Let the consequences be what they may—whether the Potomac is crimsoned in human gore, and Pennsylvania Avenue is paved ten fathoms deep in mangled bodies . . . the South will never submit to such humiliation and degradation as the inauguration of Abraham Lincoln."[19]

However "undemocratic" Lincoln's election may have seemed among the South's volatile patriarchs, he did receive the constitutional requirement of an electoral majority. In addition, over 1,865,000 citizens voted for him, with Douglas in second on the popular vote with slightly over 1,380,000. Four months later, in forming their own government, the Provisional Confederate Congress elected their chief executive by deciding the winner among themselves, selecting former US senator Jefferson Davis with a grand total of fifty votes.[20]

1864 US PRESIDENCY

Candidate	Party	Electoral Votes
Abraham Lincoln	National Union	212
George B. McClellan	Democrat	21

By the summer of 1864, the promising results of Vicksburg and Gettysburg faded into disillusion. In their recent spring campaign, the Army of the Potomac endured a string of bloody draws in the Wilderness, Cold Harbor, and Spotsylvania, only to become stuck in a rigidifying siege of Richmond and Petersburg. Western Theater gains remained largely in place, albeit shored by expanding and contentious occupation. Emancipation proved as severely divisive as Lincoln had feared. The national debt in blood and money continued to skyrocket. There came a point in which Lincoln believed he would not win renomination let alone reelection.

Peace Democrats and conservative Republicans decided to support *homme fatale* George B. McClellan for president, believing he could negotiate an end to the war and strictly limit emancipation. On the other end of the spectrum, radical Republicans in the Senate publicly lauded Treasury Secretary Salmon P. Chase as their preferred candidate, though Chase unconvincingly declared ignorance. Far more overt in opposition, the ousted Union general John C. Frémont painted himself as the true warrior for emancipation and military. Even Frederick Douglass began to doubt Lincoln's ability to endure, fearing that the president might compromise minority rights in favor of Confederate surrender.[21]

The situation had become so grim that on August 23, 1864, Lincoln informed his cabinet, "This morning, as for some days past, it seems exceedingly probable that this Administration will not be re-elected. Then it will be my duty to so co-operate with the President elect, as to save the Union between the election and the inauguration; as he will have secured his election on such ground that he cannot possibly save it afterwards." Just the day before, William Seward's adviser and erstwhile journalist Thurlow Weed informed the secretary of state, "I told Mr. Lincoln that his re-election was an impossibility, I also told him that the information would soon come to him through other channels. . . . Nobody here doubts it; nor do I see anybody from other States who authorizes the slightest hope of success."[22]

Most vexing was McClellan's official nomination to the Democratic ticket in late August, providing a viable candidate for pro-military voters, anti-emancipationists, lifelong Democrats, and peace campaigners. But then a string of events suddenly shifted the winds in Lincoln's favor. Days after the Democratic Convention, Union forces broke the Southern stronghold on Atlanta and overtook the critical city. Later that September, General Philip Sheridan's forces began to take back the Shenandoah Valley. The naval blockade, strengthened by the recent capture of Mobile Bay, showed concrete signs of strangling the Southern economy and its tenuous currency beyond recovery. Further, while some among the Army of the Potomac's old guard were still sentimental about "Little Mac," most Union troops served in the Western Theater outside of his command. Though Lincoln still worried about losing the soldier vote, the election demonstrated that the vast majority in blue were committed to see the war to its fruition, and many had become converts to emancipation.[23]

In the end, the electoral vote became a landslide; Lincoln took 212 delegates to McClellan's 21. The popular vote, however, was far closer, with around 55 percent backing the incumbent. Back in Springfield, the tally was even closer: Lincoln edged Little Mac by only ten votes among the townsmen, and as he had in 1860, Old Abe lost the popular vote in his home county of Sangamon.[24]

CHAPTER TEN

In the State House

Lincoln's Most Significant Actions as an Illinois Legislator

THE TOPIC IS WORTHY OF EXPLORATION FOR MANY REASONS, INCLUDING the fact that the phrase "all politics is local" was a concrete fact in early nineteenth-century America. At the time, there was no such thing as a federal income tax, no Federal Reserve System, a miniscule military, few public works, no national parks, and federal welfare programs were still a century away. Public policy was born and raised in state legislatures.

In addition, it is easy to forget that "Lawyer Lincoln" was a politician two years before he was a lawyer. Billy Herndon later said of his mentor and law partner, "Politics were his life and newspapers his food, merely using the law as a stepping stone to a political life and it was in this field that he seemed to be happy." Gibson Harris, who had studied in the office of Lincoln and Herndon, observed, "He took up the law as a means of livelihood, but his heart was in politics . . . he reveled in it, as a fish does in water, as a bird disports itself on the sustaining air." A political animal for certain, Lincoln still lost his first bid for the state house in 1832. Then again, he was only twenty-four at the time and barely known outside New Salem.[1]

When a slightly older, wiser, and better-traveled Lincoln won in 1834, he represented Sangamon County modestly, but he resembled Illinois uncannily. Both the man and the state were young, tall, and awkward.

During his four short terms, they would grow enormously (the state's population nearly tripling during that short span of time), and arguably, they grew far too quickly. A massive miscalculation, detailed below, beset Lincoln and Illinois for years. From then on, politics remained the first true love of his life, but he learned to curb his passions, up to and including trial separations from public office. Opportunities would come, but he would treat them with far more prudence than he practiced while in the state house.

A WAVE OF INTERNAL IMPROVEMENTS

Lincoln possessed a Hamiltonian belief in commerce and a Jeffersonian faith in the common person, and as biographer Gabor Boritt finds, the man dared to dream big. As if allergic to the past, Lincoln labored to cover Illinois with railroads, pikes, and waterways. Many people shared (though few matched) this enthusiasm for internal improvements. In Lincoln's very first term, the vast majority of legislative proposals concerned private and public transportation projects. One of Lincoln's very first bills that passed involved permitting construction of a private toll bridge across Salt Creek in Sangamon County (which happened to financially benefit a friend of his). When it came to whether private business or public coffers should bear the burden of construction, his approach bordered on socialism. In a frontier region, Lincoln surmised that no private corporation was yet wealthy enough to build the major arteries that Illinois's economy needed.[2]

The most ambitious of these enterprises became known as "The System," a network of canals and rail lines connecting communities with each other and the rest of the world. Chief among these was the Illinois and Michigan Canal, a behemoth one-hundred-mile trench attaching the Illinois and Chicago Rivers, thereby linking the Mississippi to Lake Michigan, and thus the Gulf of Mexico to the Atlantic, with Illinois as the middleman. Equally audacious was the System's rail portion, with an inaugural Northern Cross slicing though the state west to east, and an Illinois Central traversing north to south, with multiple spurs latching onto nearby towns. Along with road construction and river improve-

Flagship of the ambitious internal improvements program during Lincoln's legislative tenure, the Illinois and Michigan Canal survived many setbacks and delays, and it contributed to Chicago's rise from obscurity into a major transportation hub. Portions of the canal can still be seen today. Library of Congress.

ments, the entire endeavor involved nearly $20 million in appropriations (or approximately $550 million in 2021), practically all of it borrowed.[3]

This approach conflicted directly with existing convictions in Washington. Andrew Jackson and his conservative Democrats were so passionately opposed to almost any form of federal spending that in early 1835, the national debt came extremely close to zero. Among many things he hated, Jackson also loathed the Bank of the United States, with its questionable fusion of private and public enterprise that tended to favor the inherently wealthy. Yet it was another of Jackson's many revulsions that doomed Illinois to a lifetime of debt. By vetoing the re-charter of the Bank of the United States, and consequently shrinking its thousands of lines of credit to borrowers large and small, Jackson helped push a young and overly optimistic international economy into freefall. The resulting Panic of 1837 lasted seven years, left untold numbers jobless and penniless, and ground the System to a halt. Frantic themselves, members of the Illinois House voted a multitude of times to end their infusions of credit and cash into the System, with Lincoln voting in opposition every time. Once he had made up his mind, there was no turning back. In the end, the much-heralded Illinois and Michigan Canal did not open until 1848, multitudes of banks and businesses failed altogether, and most of Illinois remained provincial and indebted for decades.[4]

LAND SPECULATION

Illinois had been a state for less than twenty years. Consequently, most of the acreage within was federally owned. With an eye toward his infrastructure dreams, Lincoln wanted to finance most projects through land sales. He proposed buying five hundred thousand acres from Washington for $1.25 per acre (about $35 in 2021), to be sold by the state to its citizens at a modest profit. Failing that, he lobbied the US Congress to give Illinois 20 percent of all federal sales of land within Illinois.[5]

Revealing his ability to play many angles, Lincoln appealed to pinchpenny Jacksonians with this lessening of government holdings and subsequent move to private property. He also tried to convince Congress that it was in their best interests to lighten the enormous workload of its Land Office. To his Whig constituents, Honest Abe pitched his ideas as governmental support for the struggling yeoman. Unfortunately for the visionary of New Salem, most of his colleagues and virtually all of Washington ignored his inquiries. This was an especially harsh blow for Lincoln and his internal improvement allies, because they were betting on this federal-to-state land arrangement to pay for their breakneck construction of canals and railroads already underway.[6]

Decades later, President Lincoln would exorcise Jackson's tight-fisted land policies by signing the **Homestead, Land-Grant, and Pacific Railway Acts of 1862**, which sold, granted right-of-way, or transferred some 350 million acres (approximately three times the size of Montana) to state and private hands.

CREATING A NEW STATE CAPITAL

The evolution of the United States may seem to be a steady westward progression, like a sun streaming across the continent. In reality, European, African, and Asian relocation spread more like mold, with a spore here and there. For Illinois, germination began on the southwest border. The territory's first capital was the hamlet of Kaskaskia, at the mouth of its eponymous river that flowed into the Mississippi. In 1820, the state legislature moved operations to Vandalia one hundred miles to the northeast, and the choice proved to be a cautionary tale to haphazard planning.[7]

At first glance, Vandalia (population one thousand) seemed a rational choice for a seat of government. Located in the state's southern third, where the majority of Illinois's fifty-five thousand residents lived, the town was about to become the western terminus of the National Road, the first great east–west pike of the United States. Vandalia also possessed over a dozen stores, a church, a newspaper (moderate Democrat), a few taverns, multiple log and clapboard homes, and a two-story brick state house along the west side of the town square. But the state house itself was hastily constructed, it leaked often, and its walls were already bowing precariously outward. The town also experienced frequent sweeps of disease, killing off or driving away large portions of the populace. A new building for the follow session was not much larger, and its wet plaster sickened a fair share of assemblymen.[8]

Heading the charge for yet another new capital were the lanky "Long Nine," senators and representatives of Sangamon County, thus nicknamed because they all stood six feet tall or taller. Sangamon itself towered above the rest, being the largest of Illinois's counties by far, with the most assemblymen (two senators and seven representatives), and geographically twice as large as Rhode Island. Though Democrats held the majority, the Whiggish Nine possessed leverage, advancing a bill for a new state center when others resisted.

After a largely ceremonial first tally, where twenty different towns received at least one vote, Springfield soon emerged as the clear front-runner, with the Stay-in-Vandalia faction finding themselves tied with Peoria in a distant second. By the fourth round of voting, Springfield was a lock. Vexed and beaten, those for Vandalia mocked the new lowland capital as "Swamp-field" and openly hoped that the following legislative session would overturn the decision. To celebrate their achievement, the Long Nine invited the whole legislative body to nearby Ebenezer Capp's tavern, where the jovial contingent consumed cigars, oysters, and sweets galore, including over eighty bottles of champagne. Alas, visions of a new metropolis have yet to fully materialize. To this day, Springfield is just the sixth-largest city in Illinois, and no burg other than Chicago currently numbers more than 250,000.[9]

OPPOSING ILLINOIS HOUSE RESOLUTION TO CONDEMN ABOLITIONISM (JANUARY 12, 1837)

In the early 1800s, humans owning and trafficking humans served as the historical rule rather than the exception. Much of Greece and Rome—civilizations the Founding Fathers greatly admired—were built upon enormous amounts of coerced labor. The very concept of race and race-based slavery originated in England's Caribbean colonies in the mid-1600s, precepts quickly adopted by European societies stationed in the Americas. Despite the Northwest Ordinance of 1787 and the 1818 Illinois Constitution forbidding slavery within its borders, the state continued the practice in various guises thereafter, especially in its southern counties near the slave lands of Missouri and Kentucky. In some Illinois locales, one in ten residents were enslaved. By 1820, nearly one thousand Illinoisans were African Americans owned and laboring against their will. As late as 1824, a referendum asked whether there should be a convention to establish Illinois as a slave state. The vote was close, with 44.6 percent in favor of such a convention.[10]

Locally and nationally, overt opposition to the institution was miniscule. In 1837, William Lloyd Garrison's *Liberator* had been in print for only six years. Frederick Douglass was an unknown enslaved teenager. Harriet Beecher Stowe's *Uncle Tom's Cabin* was still fifteen years away. Yet Illinois's governor, the Kentucky-born Joseph Duncan (plus a multitude of Southern politicians), pushed for national condemnation of abolitionism altogether, hoping to crush any movement before it germinated.

After minimal debate, the Democrat-led Illinois House voted over-whelmingly in support of the measure, with seventy-seven voting "aye." In a relatively silent but public display of protest, Lincoln was one of only six assemblymen who voted in opposition. Most of Lincoln's white constit-uents dreaded a sudden freeing of America's millions in bondage because it could mean that blacks would be free to live and work among them. So virulent was this tribal fear that when a white mob shot and killed abolitionist Elijah Parish Lovejoy in Alton, Illinois, in the same year that Lincoln cast his losing vote, no one was ever convicted of the murder.[11]

As time would demonstrate, Lincoln acted quickly in defense of industrial growth, but he bided his time when addressing abuses of labor.

MILD SUPPORT OF PUBLIC EDUCATION

When Lincoln became a candidate for president, landed gentry had good reason to paint him as a radical. Among many insurgent concepts he espoused, along with practically giving away federal land to citizens and viewing African Americans as humans, was his advocacy of public educa-tion. For the well-to-to, the idea of using tax-payer dollars—which came primarily from land sales—and using those monies to teach the rabble's children for free, verged on inviting a revolution of the masses. This very fear led Southern state legislatures to forbid the enslaved to learn how to read and write and oppose poor white access to the tools of self-reliance and self-awareness.[12]

In his unsuccessful 1832 bid, Lincoln told the voters of Sangamon County, "I desire to see the time when education, and by its means, morality, sobriety, enterprise and industry, shall become much more general than at present." Yet as a legislator, most of his backing was little more than lip service. He never served on the Education Committee, and he may have believed the modest-fee system operated fine without public funding. By his second term, Sangamon County boasted over fifty private schools—far more than any other Illinois county—educating thousands of young minds each year. In his second-to-last term, Lincoln pushed for state testing of prospective teachers, his own childhood experiences teaching him that adults frequently took on titles that they did not earn.[13]

Partitioning Sangamon County (1839)

At its height, the county of Sangamon encompassed more land than the state of Rhode Island. In the evolution of most US territories, states, and counties, there came a time when the growing populations within created opportunities to segment the lands even further and, in doing so, allow one party or another to gain representatives, senators, and a slurry of other political offices in the process. In 1839, Lincoln helped push through a bill that carved the area into four counties, with Dane, Logan, and Menard joining old Sangamon.[14]

Stumping for Tippecanoe (1840)

Lincoln was a complicated man, and few events illustrate this fact better than his support for William Henry Harrison in the 1840 presidential election. Abe enthusiastically welcomed the Whig nomination of the famed Indian fighter and viewed the attachment of Virginian slave owner John Tyler as a balanced, winning combination. With the same methodical calculation he used when contesting bills and offices, Lincoln wrote to his colleague John Todd Stuart, "I believe we will carry the ticket. The chance of doing so appears to me 25 percent better than it did for you to beat [Stephen] Douglas [whom Stuart defeated in a run for the US House in 1838]."[15]

Meanwhile, Lincoln was running for his fourth and final appearance in the state assembly and, in doing so, canvassed for Harrison more than for himself. Armed with party platforms and campaign biographies, Lincoln strongly toed the party line, depicting the Democrat Van Buren as an urbane, out-of-touch member of the elite, as opposed to the supposedly hard-drinking, cabin-born war hero Harrison. In reality, it was Van Buren who was born into modest means, a kind and bookish young boy in an immigrant family who worked in their small Kinderhook tavern. Harrison, by contrast, came from one of the most powerful and prosperous clans in Old Dominion, only later adopting the Midwest and a frontier mythos as part of his political persona. In the rural, conservative southern counties of Illinois, Lincoln highlighted Van Buren's previous support for granting the vote to New York's property-owning African Americans, while he sidestepped Harrison's support for slavery north of the Ohio River. The Whig Party also blamed Van Buren for the disastrous Panic of 1837, though the greater blame rested on Whig overspeculation and Andrew Jackson culling the credit-lending Bank of the United States.[16]

In the end, Illinois still went to the Democrats, with Van Buren netting 47,443 votes to Harrison's 45,576. At the national level, the popular vote was nearly as close, with Harrison gaining nearly 1.3 million votes to Van Buren's more than 1.1 million, but the electoral count was a blowout, 234 to 60. Unfortunately for Lincoln and the Northern Whigs, not to mention Harrison, Old Tippecanoe's stint in office lasted barely a month, leading to a Tyler presidency and sectional fights that would endure for decades.[17]

CHAPTER ELEVEN

Lawyer Lincoln

Notable Cases Won and Lost

YOUNG AND LIVING IN SOUTHERN INDIANA, LINCOLN HAD FEW PLEA-
sures at his disposal other than reading, but he did partake in one of the
area's most popular pastimes, and that was court hopping. Staged in rustic
log buildings and modest clapboard courthouses, jurisprudence provided
a semi-annual dose of high drama and low comedy for the otherwise
grinding life of frontier America. These traveling legal shows brought
forth a community's dirty laundry, to be scrubbed and wrung by some
of the more famous names in the state, and it was common practice for
the populace to gather the kids, pack a picnic, and make a holiday of the
proceedings. Lincoln first attended such an event in Boonville, Indiana,
when he was just a teenager. He walked or rode the dozen miles from
the family farm near Gentryville to watch the sessions. While intrigued
by the legal choreography, he was not yet inspired to become a lawyer.
Painfully aware of his educational limitations, he assumed such a career
was beyond his reach.[1]

Ten years later in New Salem, armed with a handful of law books, he
had a change of heart. Lincoln also had the guidance of Springfield attorney **John Todd Stuart**, who permitted the eager student to read from his
law library. After four years of study (when most law apprentices required
only two), Lincoln took the Illinois bar in 1836. No record has yet been

found concerning how well he fared. The only thing certain is that it was an oral examination (Massachusetts was the first state to have a written bar exam, in 1855) and that Lincoln passed its few basic questions. Soon after, he moved to Springfield to ply his new trade.[2]

When it came to disputes, Lincoln the attorney preferred litigation, and he often presided as a mediator. Otherwise, most of his work involved the rather tedious administration of private and public commerce—bills of sale, deeds, wills, mortgages, leases, contracts, and the like. On occasion, he found himself in courtrooms, which ranged from rented taverns to, on one occasion, the Supreme Court of the United States. Following are the more notable of his performances in chronological order.

THE PEOPLE V. TRUETT (1838)
Lincoln's First Murder Trial

Politics by nature are divisive, a prime example being Lincoln's first case involving homicide. In a race for the Land Office Register in Galena, Illinois, a Dr. Jacob Early voiced his disapproval when rival Democrat Henry Truett won the nomination. Reacting to Dr. Early's public displeasure, Truett confronted Early in the Spottswood Rural Hotel in Springfield. A scuffle ensued, wherein the doctor tried to administer a dose of swinging chair to Truett's head. In response, Truett pulled a pistol and shot him dead.

The affair produced a slurry of media coverage. Truett's defense team consisted of several prominent lawyers, the least experienced being Lincoln, but his co-counselors thought enough of the neophyte to let him play a prominent role in the litigation. It was an emotionally difficult assignment for the green twenty-nine-year-old. Lincoln personally knew both the accused and the deceased. He was also aware that a guilty verdict could result in the death penalty. The group decided to place their hopes on an argument of self-defense. Emphasizing the physical differences between Dr. Early (tall and burly) and their client (short and spindly), they contended that Pruett had reason to fear for his own life. The strategy worked, and the jury acquitted the accused. Lincoln's team received Truett's eternal thanks, plus several hundred dollars in legal fees.[3]

GRABLE V. MARGRAVE (1840–1842)
Legal Precedent and Women's Rights

In 1839, a twenty-year-old Melissa Jane Margrave and thirty-seven-year-old William Grable consensually engaged in physical relations. Nine months later a baby arrived, but in the interim Grable had married another woman. Legally, Miss Margrave's options were limited. Illinois law provided few avenues for a woman to bring suit against a man, and even fewer chances to secure child support under any circumstance. As was common in such matters, Margrave chose to have a male relative file on her behalf. In Gallatin County Circuit Court, her father, Thomas, claimed William Grable seduced his "workforce": under the law, unwed daughters were technically servants of their fathers until they left home. At the time, Illinois relied heavily on English common law, where edicts on seduction had been in place since the 1600s. As such, the circuit court ruled against the randy Grable, but it fined him a meager $300 in damages plus costs. Regardless, Grable filed an appeal, and *Grable v. Margrave* went to the Illinois Supreme Court.

To strengthen the Margraves's chances, their attorney Samuel Marshall hired Lincoln to represent the family. Over his entire career Lincoln tried only nine such seduction cases, most often on the side of the woman (and always with male relatives filing on the female's behalf). But Lincoln knew English law exceptionally well, thanks to his intense study of **Blackstone's** *Commentaries*, the standard text on US and British jurisprudence. In defense, Lincoln argued that not only was the original verdict correct in compensating Mr. Margrave for lost services, but further punishment was also in order. Citing three previous English rulings on seductions, Lincoln demonstrated that, under common law, seducers could be punished for publicly shaming their victims. The Supreme Court agreed, unanimously.

The final verdict of *Grable v. Margrave* accomplished something few of Lincoln's five thousand cases ever did—it helped establish a precedent in US law. The decision also advanced the legal rights of women in Illinois. In victory, Lincoln was rather modest, and all he asked for in payment from fellow attorney Samuel Marshall was $5 and a two-year subscription to Marshall's newspaper, the Shawneetown *Illinois Republican*.[4]

RE: *BRYANT ET AL. V. MATSON* (1847)
The Matson Slave Case

It may be enticing to envision Lincoln as naturally fixated with slavery, motivated since birth to hasten its eradication. In truth, the institution was an afterthought throughout most of his life. He rarely spoke of it until he was in forties and encountered it personally even less. As a lawyer, he never defended a slave in court, largely because the opportunity never surfaced. In a quarter century of legal practice, only twenty-four of his cases involved African Americans (most of whom were never enslaved), and the litigations usually involved debt or contract disputes.[5]

In one instance Lincoln was asked, and agreed, to serve as counsel for a slave owner who was suing to regain a family of escapees. In 1845, Robert Matson took several of his enslaved from his Kentucky farmland into free-soil Illinois, where they worked a farm he owned in Coles County. In the summer of 1847, Matson prepared to take his "property" Jane Bryant and four of her children back to Kentucky. Mrs. Bryant responded by taking her children into the Illinois countryside, finding refuge with abolitionists.

Harboring fugitive slaves violated the US Constitution, and on those grounds the local sheriff captured and incarcerated the Bryants. In addition, Matson sued their protectors for stealing his chattel. Matson's lead counsel retained Abe Lincoln, who was about to depart for Washington to take his seat as a member of the House. Meanwhile, the individuals who harbored the Bryants filed a countersuit, because Illinois law forbade slavery.

The state law seemed clear. Article VI of the Illinois Constitution proclaimed, "No person bound to labour in any other state shall be hired to labour in this state." The price of violation was steep. All human property in the state was to be immediately relinquished and emancipated. But there were loopholes. The law did not apply to the transfer of slaves across Illinois into another slave state. Also, to be residents in Illinois, African Americans needed a "certificate of freedom" assuring they were not a fugitive. In addition, people of color were required to attain a $1,000 bond as security, on the promise that they would always be lawful and financially solvent.[6]

In defending his slaver client, Lincoln argued that Matson brought his chattel into Illinois as seasonal, temporary laborers. In other words, the enslaved were in transit, and Matson had no motive or intent to keep them in extended residence. The court found Lincoln's argument spurious, because at that point the Bryant family had been in Illinois for two years. Not only did Lincoln lose the case, but his client also skipped town without paying his fee.[7]

For the enslaved Bryants, victory proved bittersweet. They were emancipated, but they could not stay in Illinois. In 1848, the American Colonization Society helped secure passage for Jane and her children to Liberia. Without means to support themselves, and living thousands of miles from anyone they knew, the family soon descended into abject poverty. As for Lincoln's attitude on the whole matter, he remained silent. As was his habit for nearly all cases he tried, he did not leave any account of his personal feelings on the outcome.[8]

LEWIS, FOR USE OF LONGWORTH V. LEWIS (1849)
Arguing before the US Supreme Court

Lincoln had just completed his term in the Thirtieth Congress and remained in D.C. to view the inauguration of Zachary Taylor. A few days after the swearing in, he would be sworn in himself, as an attorney before the US Supreme Court, Chief Justice Roger B. Taney presiding. It would be the one and only case Lincoln ever argued before that esteemed body.

At the time, the Supreme Court held its sessions in a grand semicircular room directly beneath the old Senate Chamber (and would not have its own building until 1935). The case itself was of no great significance, other than accurately reflecting just how far Lincoln had ascended as a lawyer and just how complex his current vocation could be. The official docket title read *William Lewis, who sues for the use of Nicholas Longworth, Plaintiff v. Thomas Lewis, Administrator de bonis non of Moses Broadwell, Deceased.* Tangled therein were issues of appeal, breach of contract, ejectment from land, inheritance, interstate litigation, and statutes of limitation. Origins of the problem went back thirty years to Illinois, where one William Lewis bought 390 acres in Ohio from a Moses Broadwell. Unfortunately, Broadwell did not own one hundred of those acres, and he

Dissenting against the majority, and siding with Lincoln, was Associate Justice John McLean. McLean would sharply disagree with his fellow judges in a future case, opposing the Court's majority decision in the infamous Dred Scott Case of 1856.

further complicated matters by dying. Meanwhile, the real owner of the disputed acreage ejected Lewis from his land. Nearly twenty years after that, Lewis sued Broadwell's estate for damages. An administrator of the estate retained Logan and Lincoln, pleading that a statute of limitations had passed, thereby making the lawsuit null and void.

The case reached the Supreme Court because there was a question as to whether an 1827 ejectment law in Illinois (which had no limitations for out-of-state lawsuits) should be applied, or whether an 1837 amendment (which set a time limit of sixteen years) was the standing rule.

In effect, Lincoln proposed that the clock had started in 1827, and with the amendment in 1837, William Lewis's sixteen-year window to sue had long since closed. To bolster his argument, he cited similar cases in Connecticut, Illinois, Massachusetts, New York, and Vermont, but to no avail. The Court sided against his client, stating that the 1837 law was the one currently in place, and thus Mr. Lewis filed suit with a good ten years to spare. Lincoln would tangle with Justice Taney again, right after the chief justice would swear him in as the sixteenth president of the United States.[9]

OLDHAM AND HEMINGWAY V. LINCOLN ET AL. (1853–1854)
Lincoln the Defendant
Of Mary Todd's many relatives, her brother Levi may have been the least likable. Mrs. Lincoln's biographer Jean Baker considers him "the family

failure," and to Mary especially he appeared callous, selfish, and lazy. Even so, Mary and her husband were shocked to learn that dear Levi, in a dubious ploy for money, convinced his recently deceased father's business partners to sue Mr. Lincoln for fraud.[10]

Allegedly, Lincoln had done some legal work for the cotton manufacturing company by collecting a debt for them, and he supposedly never forwarded the money. The amount they claimed Lincoln defrauded was a hefty $472.54 (more than $15,000 in 2019). The potential cost to Lincoln's legal and social standing, however, could hardly be calculated.[11]

It was neither the first nor the last time Lincoln would be named a litigant, undergoing the experience at least thirty-two times in his life.[12] But this instance was particularly offensive to him, and he expressed his emotions in a rare show of anger. "I find it difficult to suppress my indignation towards those who have got up this claim against me," he wrote to his legal representative in Kentucky. "I would really be glad to hear Mr. Hemingway [one of Robert Todd's old business partners] explain how he was induced to *swear* he *believed* the claim to be just!"[13]

Lincoln knew he would win the case, likely on technicalities and/or lack of evidence. But the inference of his guilt was more than he could bear. To make matters worse, Levi appeared willing to try his hand at extortion. In the official complaint, he had the partners mention that Lincoln and others were in line to receive $1,500 in Lexington property from the estate of the deceased Robert Todd, a subtle ruse to suggest that Levi and friends were open to a settlement in lieu of a potentially embarrassing trial.[14]

As the accusations mounted, Lincoln's temper grew. His accusers disclosed virtually no evidence. Writing to his attorney in Lexington, Lincoln fumed, "If they will name the man or men of whom, they say, I have collected money for them, I will disprove it." He later added that, from his memory, neither he nor any of his partnerships did any work for the company. "This matter," the otherwise steady Lincoln growled, "harasses my feelings a good deal." As quickly as it erupted, the case died. Two days before Lincoln's forty-fifth birthday, Hemingway and his associates suddenly dropped the suit.[15]

ILLINOIS CENTRAL RAILROAD COMPANY v. COUNTY OF MCLEAN (1853–1855)

In Support of Big Business

He may have been a man of the people, but by the 1850s, Lincoln was also a lawyer for large corporations. Of all the clients he ever had, the most common was the Illinois Central Railroad. He served the transportation company in more than fifty cases and took home tens of thousands of dollars in retainers and fees. By far the most lucrative case he ever tried involved service to the Illinois Central, and yet he had to sue the company to get paid.[16]

It all began as an economic stimulus plan. To spur development, the Illinois Legislature gave the corporation a tax exemption lasting six years (in lieu of 7 percent of company earnings thereafter) to build a north–south line across the state. The ensuing construction brought the Illinois Central to McLean County. Though grateful for gaining access to rail service, the county nonetheless taxed the Illinois Central on the property held within its boundaries. The company sued, with Lincoln as their chief attorney.[17]

The case reached the Illinois Supreme Court, where the county argued that the state had no right to dictate local taxation. In response (and a reflection of his political philosophy), Lincoln defended the state's constitutional ability, and virtual obligation, to serve as the overriding voice on laws affecting the whole of Illinois, including statewide tax exemptions. Ironically, two of the attorneys for McLean County were Lincoln's old law partners John Todd Stuart and Stephen T. Logan. In the end, the court sided with Lincoln, the company, and the state.[18]

Normally, Lincoln's fees were modest—$5 here, $20 there. On major cases for large corporations or wealthy property owners, he occasionally charged a few hundred. In his victory against McLean County, he coolly requested $5,000, more than he normally made for an entire year. Perhaps not surprisingly, the company balked, refusing to grant even half the amount. In turn, Lincoln sued.[19]

In yet another strange twist, *Lincoln v. the Illinois Central Railroad* took place in the McLean County Circuit Court. In litigation, Lincoln made the compelling point that by preventing McLean County from taxing the company, he also prevented every other county government from doing the same. By his calculations, he had spared the corporation hundreds of thousands in potential losses.[20]

Though the court ruled in his favor, Lincoln did not receive payment until August 1857, four years into the ordeal, and only then because McLean County threatened the Illinois Central with noncompliance and started to seize its assets. With belated cash in hand, Lincoln promptly gave half the money to his junior partner Billy Herndon and loaned the other half to political ally Norman Judd.[21]

MCCORMICK V. MANNY AND CO. (1855)
The McCormick Reaper and Stanton's Cold Shoulder

From 1776 to the day Lincoln became an attorney, US courts ruled on fewer than twenty patent cases. During his twenty-five-year law career, over four hundred such cases reached the courts, including one that should have been the biggest of Lincoln's career. Yet, in the course of events, the prairie lawyer found himself almost completely marginalized by fellow counselors and was left out of the final proceedings.[22]

The issue revolved around a grain harvester designed and sold by John H. Manny and Associates, a design that the famous Cyrus McCormick considered a near copy of his own revolutionary reaper. Immediately, McCormick's jealous competitors threw their weight, and a good deal of funding, behind Manny. On both sides, prominent lawyers from the East rushed to be a part of the fight, with Peter H. Watson, a patent lawyer from Washington, leading the defense. Manny's team reasoned that since both manufacturers were based out of Illinois, and the trial would likely take place in Chicago, it would behoove them to secure the assistance of an attorney from the state. Unable to attain their first choice, they went after Lincoln. Watson personally traveled to Lincoln's home at **Eighth and Jackson** to offer a substantial $400 retainer.[23]

Fresh from a defeat in his first bid for the US Senate, Lincoln pursued the case with uncommon focus. Keeping in close contact with his fellow attorneys, and with a personal fascination with technology and mechanization, he reviewed the latest details on patent law, researched the fundamentals of the suit, and traveled two hundred miles to see the

Manny plant for himself. "I went out to Rockford," he informed Watson, "and spent half a day, examining and studying Manny's Machine."[24]

While digging through the details, he became somewhat bewildered that his colleagues were not forwarding him any information. He then learned, by way of the media rather than his colleagues, that the trial had been moved to Cincinnati in September. Uninvited, Lincoln made the trek anyway, on a two-day journey of more than five hundred miles. His arrival only brought more confusion, as his three fellow lawyers coldly ignored him and did not let him take part in the trial. Reportedly, one of them referred to the weary Lincoln as nothing more than "a long, lank creature from Illinois, wearing a dirty linen duster for a coat." The assessment was a bit harsh, even if it did come from the venerated Pittsburgh attorney Edwin M. Stanton.[25]

Taken aback, Lincoln tried to salvage his trip by turning it into an ad hoc vacation. He spent several days touring the city and its wealthier neighborhoods, and spent his nights at the home of Mary's cousins Mr. and Mrs. William Dickson. Unable to shrug off the disappointment of the trial, he left for Springfield after less than a week. Thanking his hostess for her kindness, he nonetheless confessed, "I never expect to be in Cincinnati again. I have nothing against the city, but things have so happened here as to make it undesirable for me ever to return."[26]

Contrary to his expectations, Lincoln did return to Cincinnati on a political trip in 1859, where he addressed local Republicans, including a young lawyer named Rutherford B. Hayes. In 1861, he visited yet again, as president-elect on his way to Washington.

HURD ET AL. V. ROCK ISLAND BRIDGE COMPANY (1857)
The Profitable *Effie Afton* Case

Rivers were the highways and interstates of early America, allowing cheap transport of people and goods to wherever the waters flowed. Unfortunately, goods and people could only travel as fast and as far as nature permitted. Replacing these slow, twisting, and often clogged arteries in the 1850s were the more direct and impulsive railways, churning and boiling in earnest above and beyond the temperamental rivers. By necessity, rail bridges began to span rivers with increased frequency, planting their bulky legs into the water and creating narrow paths through which boats had to maneuver.

In the spring of 1856, the side-wheeler *Effie Afton* approached the very first bridge across the Mississippi. Although an impressive 230 feet long and 35 feet wide, holding 200 passengers and 350 tons of cargo, the northbound steamer looked rather modest compared to the bridge. At more than 1,500 feet in length, the span stood on five massive foundations of stone and iron, with an impressive 286-foot turntable near its center to allow taller ships to pass.

Unfortunately, the *Effie Afton* grazed a foundation on its portside, causing the ship to turn across the current. The force of the river then listed the vessel to a forty-five-degree angle, consequently toppling stoves on board and setting the craft on fire. Fortunately, the flames spread slowly at first, allowing everyone on board to reach safety on neighboring boats and the bridge. But a second fire eventually broke out, setting the bridge itself on fire, which consequently burned and collapsed onto the ship, sending a tangled mass of girders, cargo, a wrecked hull, and screaming livestock floating downstream. Not surprisingly, boat and bridge owners fought each other over who was responsible, and the former sued the latter for $200,000 in damages.[27]

The case was, in many respects, symbolic of a much larger fight over which cities would rule the growing country—the old, established river towns like St. Louis, or the new and booming rail hubs like Chicago. Their respective city newspapers paid close attention to the proceedings, bringing a spot of fame to the teams of lawyers involved. Leading the defense at the US Circuit Court in Chicago were the bridge company's chief attorney Norman Judd and the established A. Lincoln. A series of continuances and the gathering of evidence delayed a decision for several months. Lincoln used the time to visit the site personally, talk to witnesses, and take a steamer beneath the remaining bridge several times to test the waters. His ensuing argument, that the bridge posed no "material obstruction," rested on hours of testimony from engineers, navigators, drawbridge operators, and the passengers themselves. The plaintiffs countered with their own flood of testimonies, arguing that the bridge's bulky design stirred the waters to the point that no predictable flow existed that ships could consistently navigate.

In the end, three of twelve jurors believed the *Effie Afton* lawyers, but that was far from the unanimous vote required in federal common law. The judge dismissed the case on a hung jury, and Lincoln received $400 plus expenses for his trouble.[28]

Far more important, this was one of the first major federal cases in Lincoln's career, and one of the few he took part in that established a strong legal precedent. In the transportation war between riverboats and railways, the latter was beginning to enjoy a growing legal leverage.[29]

THE PEOPLE V. WILLIAM ARMSTRONG (1857–1858)
The Almanac Case

Two boys, falsely accused of murdering a deputy, appeared doomed to the hangman's noose by a damning testimony. A star witness for the prosecution claimed that he saw the boys commit the crime by the light of a high, shining moon. When all hope seemed lost, defense attorney Abe Lincoln produced a dog-eared almanac and proved the witness to be liar. The almanac clearly indicated that on the night of the murder, the moon hung low and dim. No one could have seen more than a few feet in such darkness. The innocent boys walked free.

Stirring was this climactic scene of the 1939 film *Young Lincoln*, starring a fresh-faced Henry Fonda. Moderately successful, the movie did much to solidify the popular perception that, as a person and a lawyer, Lincoln relied primarily on an innate sense of justice and an unbending faith in folksy common sense. Meant to glorify Lincoln's greatness, the film arguably belittled his intellect, his effort, and the professional skill he brought to the actual Almanac Case, the most famous trial of his long career. Far from young and idealist, he was nearly fifty at the time, and a twenty-year veteran of his practice.

As for the circumstances, the night in question was August 29, 1857, following a religious camp meeting in Mason County, Illinois. About a mile away from the services, as was common during revivals, whiskey vendors and gamblers offered other pleasures to the gathering crowds.

Among those in attendance were area boys William Duff Armstrong, James Norris, and James Metzker, who, in the course of drinking heavily, started to fight each other. In the melee, Metzker got the worst of it and rode his horse off into the night, severely injured. It was a Saturday. By Tuesday, he was dead from severe head trauma.[30]

Norris and Armstrong were arrested and charged with murder. They subsequently received the assistance of three lawyers, none of whom were Lincoln. Norris was sentenced to eight years for the lesser charge of manslaughter, while Armstrong attained a change of venue to neighboring Cass County. It was then that Hannah Armstrong, mother of William, asked for Lincoln's help. The family had known Lincoln since his New Salem days, and they were quite close to him. She was the widow of his old friend **Jack Armstrong** of the long-ago Clary's Grove Boys, and Lincoln had stayed with the family on several occasions. As a favor to her, Lincoln took on the case.

Duff remained in custody from November to May of the next year, until the Cass County Circuit Court reconvened. During the ensuing trial, Lincoln selected a relatively young jury (average age, twenty-eight) in hopes that they would be more sympathetic to the twenty-five-year-old Armstrong. He indeed dismantled a witness's "moonlight" testimony by producing an almanac to disprove its possibility. But he also brought forth a doctor who stated that the fatal blow came to the back of the head, whereas Armstrong allegedly struck Metzker from the front. There was also some question as to whether Metzker suffered his fatal head injury after falling from his horse during his escape.[31]

Lincoln followed with an intensely sentimental summation, where he reminisced about the Armstrongs and their kindness to him in youth, and his memories of holding an infant William in his arms. He also had the legal savvy to have the jury know, via instructions from the judge, that Armstrong could only be found guilty if he and Norris had clearly acted "in concert" against the victim, and if the lethal blows came unquestionably from Armstrong. Faced with such narrow parameters for judgment, a weak prosecution, and Lincoln's skillful approach, the jury ruled in favor of Armstrong. As he promised, Lincoln refused payment for his services.[32]

CHAPTER TWELVE

Most Common Types
of Lincoln's Legal Cases

LINCOLN WAS PRESIDENT FOR A LITTLE OVER FOUR YEARS. HE WAS A lawyer for more than twenty-five. In his role as an attorney, it may be popular to picture him as a frontier lawyer of, by, and for the people, picking his fights and opting for the underdog. A few of Lincoln's contemporaries established this image and after his death portrayed his legal career in glowing terms. Yet during their time with Lincoln on the circuit and in the courtrooms, few of his associates bothered to mention him in their letters or diaries. He was one of the boys, highly competent, but not evidently bound for professional fame or greatness, certainly not in the caliber of a David Davis or a Stephen Douglas, let alone a Daniel Webster or Henry Clay. His venues were primarily the county courthouses of Illinois's Eighth Circuit dotting the east-central portion of the state. Twice a year, for two to three months, Lincoln and his associates traveled the area's rugged roads in buggies and on horse-back, itinerate and workmanlike.[1]

And the man was prolific, being involved in over five thousand litigations in his career. In notes that Lincoln wrote for a law lecture, penned sometime in the 1850s, he modestly claimed, "I am not an accomplished lawyer. I find quite as much material for a lecture in those points where I have failed, as in those wherein I have been moderately successful. The leading rule for the lawyer, as for the man of every other calling, is diligence." Rather than aiming for the pivotal or dramatic,

Lincoln simply took virtually any opportunity to work, and much of it involved procedures and documents necessary to build a community and keep it running. Around 96 percent of his business was in civil and chancery issues, compared to less than 4 percent involving criminal cases, and most of those were misdemeanors. And jurisprudence was a central part of public life at the time. What is known about Lincoln's father, for example, is traced primarily through the paper trail of the American legal system—his bills of sale, land deeds, mortgages, jury records, and so on.[2]

Concerning income, Lincoln's four-year stint as a junior partner with **John Todd Stuart** netted him around $800 per annum, and slightly higher amounts with **Stephen T. Logan**, firmly planting him economically and socially into Springfield's middle class. Being senior partner with **Billy Herndon** proved far more lucrative. In the sixteen years before his presidency, Lincoln's increasingly bigger cases gave him yearly incomes between $3,000 and $5,000. Following are the most common forms of work that enabled Lincoln to establish that level of income and create the social and political network that slowly established him as a viable candidate for higher office.[3]

ASSUMPSIT (1,240)

In an era of handshake deals and verbal arrangements, assumpsit was a catch-all court action, applying to any agreement that was not officially under sealed contract. Plaintiffs filed whenever they wanted repayment plus damages. Reflecting the lack of codified relationships and documented transactions on the frontier, assumpsit was by far the most frequent form of legal action in antebellum Illinois.

In his early years of practice, Lincoln was tasked with a multitude of these cases, while his senior partners pursued more lucrative lawsuits. Most assumpsit issues were less than glamorous. For example, the 1838 tussle of *Sugg v. Morris* involved one Joel Sugg suing a Joshua Morris because Morris did not pay him for caring for a mess of hogs. Lincoln defended Morris, who claimed that Sugg owed him far more money than he ever earned. The court sided with the pig-tending Sugg, and Lincoln's client lost a grand total of $35.26.[4]

Nonpayment of gambling debts (including wagers on the outcomes of presidential elections), death of livestock in shipment, broken marriage agreements, shoddy carpentry, loss of rent—Lincoln often saw several such cases in the course of a day. Thus, he rarely had time or incentive to become emotionally invested, even when he was a plaintiff himself, as in the 1855 suit of *Lincoln v. Brown*. Played out before the justice of the peace of Christian County, the affair involved a matter of legal fees owed to Lincoln from a previous case. Lincoln had successfully defended Mr. Samuel Brown when the latter was accused of assault with a deadly weapon—namely, chasing trespassers out of his watermelon patch by shooting his gun several times. When Brown refused to pay him, Lincoln sued and won a mere $6.22.[5]

DEBT (667)

Business lived and died on credit. In the volatile spurts of expansionist nineteenth-century America, investor optimism often ran high, as did risk. Lincoln himself attained his short-lived shops in New Salem almost wholly on credit. When they "winked out," he was up to his long neck in debt. "Money" in the modern sense—Federal Reserve notes—would not emerge until the Legal Tender Act of 1862. Before then, balances were often paid in relatively rare gold US coins, trade, barter, and ad hoc forms of local paper money, such as promissory notes, IOUs, contracts, and other proxies. Lincoln was often a creditor, and, like other citizens in a commercial society, he found himself simultaneously owing and awaiting payments. Credit was often easy to attain, but pricey. Standard interest rates were around 10 percent, and usually due in six months. For farmers especially, foreclosures would loom in the aftermath of blight, drought, flood, and/or storms. Debts could include farm mortgages, uncollected rent, and delivery of everything from seed corn to sows.[6]

Lincoln's first partner Stuart did not wish to bother with debts, but their sheer volume provided a steady source of revenue, so he handed the cases to his younger associate. In Lincoln's first year of practice, all but twenty-six of his ninety-one cases were related in some way to debt. Still a junior partner under Logan, he continued to take on nearly every debtor case that came into the firm. The overdue notes normally involved amounts between $100 and $200, and usually Lincoln represented the plaintiff looking for payment, plus damages.

Though he could certainly sympathize with the man down on his luck, Lincoln found little incentive (and little luck) defending the person in the red. In any given year, he could expect to lose these defense cases over 90 percent of the time. Otherwise, it was generally easy work—most legal books contained standard forms to follow. Usually, Lincoln encouraged mediation, because he could often get paid just as much with less time and effort. In nearly four hundred instances he successfully convinced parties to settle out of court. For his services, Abraham commonly received $5 to $20 for the more modest contests. Nonetheless, debt cases were where many a borrower learned to detest lawyers.[7]

FORECLOSURE MORTGAGE (219)
The phrase "dead pledge" was used often in the wilderness of Illinois, and although it may sound like a form of frontier justice, the term is far more litigious in its original French—*mortgage*. Almost half of all Lincoln's cases involved some form of debt, and over two hundred addressed real estate collateral on defaulted loans.

One case was notable for a few reasons. In 1858, a man whose name was synonymous with financial prowess loaned a Mr. Langenbahn $250 to purchase a pair of mules. Mr. Rothschild and his client likely knew that mules were often a wise investment. Mules were the diesels of their time, far sturdier, stronger, and possessing greater endurance than horses. Though often costing twice as much and unable to breed, they were also far less susceptible to disease, lived longer, and could work nearly twice as many years. Used to pull plows, market wagons, and canal boats and turn mill axles, mules were also highly valued by the military for their ability to endure hardships and lug artillery. Langenbahn's venture evidently did not pay well, and he defaulted on Rothschild, so Rothschild sued and won. Ordered to pay $280.55 in twenty days or the court would sell the mules, the defendant ponied up. The proceeding's notable feature? Lincoln served as judge, just one of reportedly 320 incidents where he worked in such capacity.[8]

Bill in Chancery (148)

US law is thoroughly based on English common law, but there are situations in which that venerated jurisprudence lacks specific guidelines, especially in cases involving promissory notes and land. Chancery is relatively flexible and expedient, and it used to apply commonsense justice over the exact letter of common law. Approximately 20 percent of Lincoln's cases occurred in chancery court, and many of those fell under the catch-all phrase of "bill in chancery."

Intending to simplify the process of redress, chancery bills could still become quite complicated. Just as they are in the twenty-first century, nineteenth-century transactions in land and loans were often split and sold again, creating a tangle of owners, renters, lenders, and debtors. Billy Herndon experienced this personally when he loaned $2,000 to Joseph Ledlie, an occasional client who dealt in real estate. Such an advance was exceptionally large, equivalent to approximately $63,000 in 2021, but Ledlie had recently won a settlement worth more than twice that amount, thanks to his lawyers Herndon and Lincoln. But Ledlie failed to pay Billy back the $2,000, just as he had defaulted on other loans in Sangamon County. Meanwhile, Ledlie continued to buy and sell land, which irked Herndon to the point that he retained his own law partner to sue the meddling Ledlie and prevent him from gaining more real estate until the note was honored. Evidently the parties settled out of court (Lincoln preferred mediation over court appearances anyway), and the judge dismissed the case.[9]

Divorce (145)

Mary and Abe's marriage was far from perfect, but it was certainly not as catastrophic as so often portrayed. Compared to the divorces Abraham saw as a lawyer, his marital relationship seemed nearly idyllic.

As a legal option, divorce was nearly impossible in the early years of the United States. Dissolution of a marriage often required the approval of the state legislature. Only gradually did courts claim jurisdiction. When Illinois became a state in 1818, it allowed court-ordered divorce only in situations of adultery, bigamy, or "impotence" (parlance for infertility). Desertion became allowable grounds in 1825. Two years later, a spouse could file if their partner was a heavy drinker or frequently abusive. By 1845, in Lincoln's eighth year of practice, a marriage could be dissolved if one of the members committed a felony.[10]

When Lincoln took on these cases, he usually backed women, and he usually won, though "winning" was relative. Divorce for women often meant a loss of social standing and personal security. Rarely was alimony awarded. All too common were cases of adultery, alcoholism, battery, abandonment, venereal disease, and even drug addiction.

In 1842, the partnership of Lincoln and Logan defended one Ailsey Bancom, mother of seven children. She had been married twenty-three years to John Bancom, who she contended had become a drunk, provided no material or emotional support, and eventually threatened to kill her. Mr. Bancom never showed up to testify, so the court ruled in her favor. Caroline Beerup in 1853 asked Lincoln and Herndon to help her separate from Stephen Beerup, who had physically tortured her and committed adultery before leaving her for the gold rush in California. The court granted a divorce and gave her full custody of her six kids. In 1860, Lincoln helped Nancy Clarkson secure a divorce from husband John Clarkson, who had committed adultery, deserted the family, and had just been convicted of raping their daughter.[11]

As a consequence of what he had seen time and again, Lincoln was not averse to ending marriages. There was one bond, however, that he believed was indissoluble. "A husband and wife may be divorced and go out of the presence and beyond the reach of each other," he said in his First Inaugural Address, "but the different parts of our country can not do this."

CHAPTER THIRTEEN

On the Hill

Lincoln's Most Significant Actions as a US Representative

LINCOLN AND FAMILY LEFT FOR WASHINGTON IN LATE OCTOBER 1847, journeying by steamboat, stagecoach, and rail. After several stops along the way, they arrived on December 2, two days before he was to take his seat. It was customary for Congress to convene nearly a year after elections, providing time for representatives and senators to settle affairs at home before their journey, which for some involved a trek of more than a thousand miles across an expanding country.

One of Lincoln's first official acts was to draw lots for where he would sit. By choice he selected the Whig section. By luck he drew a spot on the last row, a position rather emblematic of his status. Farther ahead of him sat the likes of Alexander Stephens and Robert Toombs—future founding fathers of the Confederacy (though Stephens's eloquence and integrity on the floor at times moved Lincoln to tears). Also on the Whig side sat the revered John Quincy Adams, the august eighty-year-old still a political force. Across the aisle sat Andrew Johnson of Tennessee and future secessionist Robert Barnwell Rhett. There was also the soon-to-be famous Pennsylvanian David Wilmot, who for many reasons despised Rhett and his fellow Southerners, the majority of whom owned human beings and wanted to expand the nation's slaveholdings. Over in the regal Senate, the conservative, pro-military, pro-expansionist Democrats ruled. In the lower chamber, the Whigs held a narrow majority. Their edge, however, did not ensure unity, and it was the speed of slavery's growth more than any other issue that divided the Whig House.[1]

As we will see, US Representative Lincoln bore little resemblance to the flexible assemblyman and attorney back in Illinois. Biographers and admirers often minimize his stint in Congress because he repeatedly did two things that run counter to his intrepid legacy—he gambled, and he lost. Yet arguably his days in the chamber also mark his finest as a human being. Lincoln stood firmly against his fellow citizens and their insatiable appetites for foreign lands and forced labor. Before, he occasionally spoke against such greed. Now, he would act.

OPPOSING THE MEXICAN WAR

Lincoln's congressional term began on December 6. Within two weeks, the young representative from Illinois was already on record accusing President James K. Polk of being a land-hungry despot, eager to take all of Mexico and more. From the House floor, Lincoln presented his biting "Spot Resolution," demanding from the commander-in-chief evidence that the United States had in fact been invaded, and where exactly American blood had been spilled in that alleged invasion. Polk of course felt no need to respond, nor could he. The border between the newly annexed Texas and sovereign Mexico remained vague, and if there was an aggressor, it wasn't the Mexican populace.[2]

Lincoln knew he risked alienating much of his fellow countrymen, which included law partner Billy Herndon. When Herndon criticized him for his antiwar position, Lincoln penned the famous response, "Allow the President to invade a neighboring nation, whenever he shall deem it necessary to repel an invasion, and you will allow him to do so whenever he may choose." Despite the criticisms, and there were many, Lincoln took the floor again the following month to say that the conflict had gone on long enough. Polk and the war hawks, Lincoln argued, were threatening to turn the American republic into a despotic empire.[3]

> The war has gone on some twenty months; for the expenses of which, together with an inconsiderable old score, the President now claims about one half of the Mexican territory . . . the other half is already

inhabited, as I understand it, tolerably densely for the nature of the country; and all its lands, or all that are valuable, already appropriated as private property. How then are we to make anything out of these lands with this encumbrance on them? . . . I suppose no one will say we should kill the people, or drive them out, or make slaves of them, or even confiscate their property.[4]

Despite his freshman status, Lincoln's comments did possess some gravity. He not only spoke for many Northerners who feared an unending expansion of Southern slavery but also served on the War Department Expenditures Committee. He hesitated to deny funding for the war, but he essentially accused Polk of being both power hungry and feeble minded. "As I have before said, he knows not where he is. He is a bewildered, confounded, and miserably perplexed man." Lincoln consequently voted against any measure that deemed the conquest "just and necessary." He also promoted every resolution from outside communities calling for a quick end to hostilities, including the printing of a Quaker peace pamphlet at government expense. Once more, he vehemently denied the right

Eleventh president of the United States James K. Polk was the eighth chief executive to have owned human beings, yet only the third to oversee territorial expansion of the country during his tenure, the others being Thomas Jefferson with the Louisiana Purchase and John Quincy Adams in purchasing Florida. Library of Congress.

of slavery to expand into this new territory. In an August 24, 1855, letter to his friend Joshua Speed, Lincoln recalled, "When I was in Washington I voted for the Wilmot Proviso as good as forty times."[5]

In the end, the war proved extremely lucrative for the United States. The area of land alone acquired in the Treaty of Guadalupe Hidalgo exceeded the total area of Britain, France, Italy, and Spain combined. Millions of acres of grazing land, gold and silver rushes, logging and croplands, and a golden gateway to Asia turned the United States into a continental power. Because of these gains, for all intents and purposes, Lincoln could assume that his political career was over, but he never expressed regret for his opposition. The overexpansion of the Union, he rightly predicted, would bring it perilously close to breaking apart.

TRYING TO END SLAVERY IN WASHINGTON, D.C.

The younger Lincoln definitely was aware of race and slavery, but aside from his brief visits to New Orleans, he witnessed little of it directly. Such was the case for most congressional members raised on free soil. For them, the institution was more of a troubling intangible than an everyday, concrete reality. This distance closed dramatically when they lived and worked in the nation's capital. In that Southern city surrounded by slave states, one in nine Washington residents were enslaved. Nearly one in four people in the city were free African Americans, many of whom once lived in bondage.[6]

Back in Illinois, Lincoln occasionally dealt with questions of chattel slavery in court, but in his first month in Congress, he endorsed a statement from D.C. residents calling for a repeal of slavery in the District, as well as another resolution from an Indiana county in support. Locals then requested the ending of at least the slave trade within the city, which sparked even greater conflict within the House. One particular incident hit close to home quite literally when, on January 14, 1849, individuals seized an African American worker at the **Sprigg boarding home** where the Lincoln family resided. When an irate colleague presented a measure to immediately end the practice of D.C. slavery, Lincoln actually opposed it, deeming the bill too extreme to achieve majority support, but he then announced intentions to introduce a bill of his own, one that would free all children born to enslaved women after January 1, 1850, and compensate all cooperating slave owners for their losses. Ultimately Lincoln withdrew his proposal; yet he as well as his enemies continued to view Washington as ground zero. So long as human bondage endured in the heart of the national government, it would course through the nation's bloodstream.[7]

Congressman Lincoln backtracked on the subject truly only once. In April 1848, approximately eighty enslaved people escaped a steamboat docked on the Potomac, and they were summarily captured and imprisoned. House fights over the issue turned so volatile that Lincoln voted to table further debate. He would, however, as president, finally achieve victory. On April 16, 1862, well before he even considered the Emancipation Proclamation, Lincoln signed into law the District of Columbia Emancipation Act. On paper, the law read like the schematics of a pressure valve, gifting Unionist slaveholders $300 compensation for each human they surrendered and $100 to every freed person who emigrated outside the United States. To those whom the law liberated, the day marked the end of generations of forced labor, and the chance to direct their own lives for the foreseeable future.[8]

SUPPORT FOR INTERNAL IMPROVEMENTS

On the same day Lincoln refused to table discussions on ending slavery in D.C., he also voted in favor of a resolution affirming federal authority to build harbors. Promoting the general welfare and providing for the common defense of a more perfect Union, the measure was of course in keeping with his Whig commitment of public works; it was also a harbinger of what was to transpire in the first days of his presidency. If the Civil War didn't begin at Fort Sumter, it likely would have started at another of the nation's twenty coastal bastions, constructed as they were by federal dollars for the purpose of protecting the whole of the country.

On June 20, 1848, Lincoln took the floor and chastised Polk for vetoing a substantial internal improvements bill; he also rebuked the recent Democratic National Convention for opposing federal improvements altogether. "The question of improvements is verging to a final crisis," he said, "and the friends of the policy must now battle, and battle manfully, or surrender all." Lincoln added that if their concern revolved around spending government funds, Polk and company might want to reconsider waging war against its neighbors, "as relates to the present embarrassed state of the Treasury in consequence of the Mexican war."[9]

PRAISING THE REVOLUTIONS OF 1848

Historians increasingly see the American Civil War not as a lone event but part of a global conflict. In the accelerating Industrial Revolution of the middle nineteenth century, those who earned their income—the growing middle and working classes—began to openly revolt against those who inherited their wealth (namely, the royal houses). As skills steadily replaced land as the basis of power, and the cities grew in place of the noble estates, labor moved against the landlords.[10]

Arguably the first fissures began in the Caribbean, with the successful Haitian rebellion against France ending in 1804, followed by popular movements against the dying Spanish Empire across Central and South America. In East Asia, a series of horrific wars in China cost millions of lives, as urbanites and the peasant poor fought or fled the decaying Manchu Dynasty, while in Japan the long feudal rule of the shoguns crumbled under the weight of progressives and modernists. In Europe, 1848 unleashed revolution after revolution against royalist governments that refused to acknowledge that a new day had come.

Congress and Lincoln first voiced public support for the democratic movements in Europe in April 1848, congratulating the people of France for their overthrow of King Louis Philippe. Upon his return from Washington, Lincoln participated in a public display of support with the people of Hungary and their attempt to split away from the Austrian Empire. On September 6, 1849, Lincoln and a group of like-minded colleagues, including Simeon Francis and Judge David Davis, crafted "Resolutions of Sympathy with the Cause of Hungarian Freedom," with the statement, "the Government of the United States should acknowledge the Independence of Hungary as a Nation of freemen." Regrettably for the engineers, poets, mechanics, and playwrights, the good wishes of Lincoln and company meant little when pitted against conservative armies.[11]

For Lajos Kossuth's arrival in the
United States in 1852, artists wrote
plays and ballads in his honor.
In 1990, the federal government
placed a bust of Kossuth in the US
Capitol Rotunda to commemorate
the fall of Soviet communism and
the rise of political freedom in
Europe.[12] Library of Congress.

Yet Lincoln remained committed to the ideal that inheritance should
never overrule merit. One such example involved the arrival in the States
of Lajos Kossuth, who led Hungary in an unsuccessful bid to rend his
country from the Austrian Empire. After a brief but prosperous period
of independence, Hungary collapsed under the weight of the Hapsburg
military, leading Kossuth to escape to Britain and the United States. In
both places, progressives gave him warm and massive welcomes, while
conservatives feared the example he set as a revolutionary. Southern
whites were especially unnerved by his freeing of Hungary's serfs. So
widespread was his celebrity in the North that some one hundred thousand people came out to great him at his arrival in New York. Kossuth
then spoke at a number of high-profile events, including a joint session
of the US Congress. The Magyar was in fact only the second such international to do so, behind the legendary Marquis de Lafayette.[13]

Praising the erudite emancipationist, during Kossuth's visit, Lincoln
and his like-minded Springfieldians spoke publicly on Hungary's right to
independence, as well as acclaiming "the patriotic efforts of the Irish, the
Germans and the French, who have unsuccessfully fought to establish in

their several governments the supremacy of the people." Though cautious on the idea of direct intervention, Lincoln and his associates crafted a resolution that condoned "interfering in favor of any people who may be struggling for liberty in any part of the world, when a proper occasion shall arrive." A decade later, Lincoln and others came to the conclusion that the time had arrived to actively support four million of their own fellow countrymen in their long and bloody struggle to be free.[14]

CAMPAIGNING FOR ZACHARY TAYLOR IN THE 1848 ELECTION

Lincoln wasn't so much a supporter of General Taylor as he was an animated opponent of virtually any Democrat, including their nominee for the 1848 race: Michigan's Democratic senator Lewis Cass. While Taylor's political views were largely mysterious, having never run for office—or possibly even voted before—Cass was an adamant and aggressive expansionist, whereas Lincoln firmly opposed such imperial designs. Lincoln's natural choice would have been his idealized Henry Clay, but Clay's election record was less than ideal, having lost bids for the presidency in 1824, 1832, 1840, and 1844. Lincoln also knew that he and Clay had doomed themselves by adamantly, though nobly, opposing the Mexican War. As a military hero of that conflict, Taylor presented a figure that could win back nationalists and defeat the Democrats. "Our only chance is with Taylor," Lincoln wrote to a constituent back in Illinois. "I go for him, not because I think he would make a better president than Clay, but because I think he would make a better one than Polk, or Cass, or Buchanan, or any such creatures, one of whom is sure to be elected, if he is not."[15]

Lincoln canvassed for a man he hardly knew, though he was aware that Taylor vowed to use the veto sparingly, a position most promising for free-soil advocates and legislators supporting internal improvements. Lincoln attended the Whig National Convention in Philadelphia, visited vice presidential nominee Millard Fillmore in New York, wrote to friends across the country, and spoke at meetings of Washington, D.C.'s "Rough and Ready Club." He also conducted a speaking tour across Massachusetts on behalf of the nominee, in New Bedford, Boston, Cambridge, Dorchester, Lowell, Worcester, and elsewhere, sharing the stage at times with former New York governor William H. Seward and others.[16]

Ironically, the greatest threat to a Whig victory involved a split among the Democrats, when Northerners backed former president Martin Van Buren on a free-soil platform. Lincoln and others successfully argued that Van Buren was as unelectable as Clay, and the only way to stop the extension of American slavery was through Taylor, a man who owned many human beings. Ultimately Taylor won, narrowly. Key victories in Massachusetts, Pennsylvania, and New York enabled him to take the executive position, despite losing much of the South and the entirety of the Midwest.[17]

Admission of Wisconsin into the Union

On May 11, 1848, Lincoln added his approval for the formation of the country's thirtieth state, but he did so with reservations. Speaking to the House, he criticized federal doubling of land prices within the new state. At their current rates, acreages were dreams still achievable for the region's more modest farmers and waves of new immigrants. Raising the prices might fill the state's coffers in the short run, but at the expense of the common man. In this seemingly minor point, Lincoln was actually inching toward one of the most radical planks of the future Republican Party—affordable land for the masses.[18] So divisive was this issue that when it finally appeared as a bill during James Buchanan's presidency, all save one Northern congressmen voted for it, and all but one Southern legislators opposed it. In deference to his conservative base, the Democratic president vetoed the bill.[19]

Wisconsin would go on to serve Lincoln well, electing him to the White House in 1860 and providing over ninety thousand troops in the ensuing Civil War. In turn, Congress and Lincoln enacted the 1862 Homestead Act, granting citizens over 350,000 acres in Wisconsin by the end of the war alone, and mandating that none of those lands could ever contain enslaved people.[20]

The Funeral for John Quincy Adams

On February 21, 1848, with Lincoln in attendance, members of the House watched in shock as fellow representative John Quincy Adams collapsed as he rose to speak. A brain hemorrhage felled the statesman, and though he rallied briefly as he convalesced in the House Speaker's office, he would die in that very room two days later. Officials formed a committee to plan the funeral. Lincoln was among thirty people chosen. The assignment was far from a formality, though Lincoln himself played a minor role. Adams's stature exceeded that of any political figure living, being a former US senator, minister to Russia, ambassador to the Netherlands, secretary of state, president, and finally a representative for a phenomenal nine terms.

The day of the funeral, February 26, began with salutary cannon fire at dawn. Much of the House chambers, as well as homes and public buildings across the city, were draped in black. A choir sang from the gallery, speeches tried to encompass his monumental achievements, and a preacher struggled to relate with the skeptic in Adams. At the conclusion, bearers carried his casket into cool winter air and through throngs of mourners. In the procession were members of Congress, the Supreme Court, the cabinet (including Polk), and members of the military. More fitting to the man who favored intellect over politics, also in attendance were scholars, college students, artisans, and members of literary clubs.[21]

Washington would not see a display of such sincere loss and mourning until Lincoln's death seventeen years later. As with Lincoln's body, Adams's did not come to final rest for some time. His first interment was in the Congressional Cemetery, followed by a brief respite in Hancock Cemetery (named after the father of Declaration of Independence signatory John Hancock) in Quincy, Massachusetts. When his wife Louisa died in 1852, the couple was laid to rest in the family crypt with the First Parish Church across the road from the Hancock gravesite.[22]

Chapter Fourteen

Worst Days in the Presidency

At the time of Lincoln's inauguration, the collective mood could hardly be described as optimistic. Yet there wasn't an aura of doom either. Ceremonies instead expressed excitement and anticipation because the future, as always, was yet unknown.

Of course, we cannot help but see this moment differently, having copious evidence of Lincoln's tomorrows while he had none. What was obvious to him, and those close to him, was that he abhorred violence. Even in his rustic youth, Abe disdained the blood sports and cruelty to animals that otherwise served as entertainment on the frontier. His service in the Black Hawk War resembled the later experiences of one Samuel Clemens in a Missouri militia outfit, as both men discovered an inability to embrace armed combat, preferring instead the weapons of logic, law, and wit. Witnessing suffering and death deeply hurt Lincoln, which explains why he worked incessantly to escape the stark realities of pioneer life for the more controlled and comfortable world of the middle class.

Yet suffering and death would find him, as it did suddenly and unexpectedly for countless individuals about to be directly impacted by the Civil War. As we look through the medium of photography, we cannot help but notice how he aged so dramatically during his presidency. As the days and nights outlined below testify, the war took nearly two years to reach full fury, but the Lincoln family started to lose loved ones early and often. In that regard, Lincoln himself exemplified the average American. As painful as the war proved to be on a national level, it was the personal, unexpected traumas that most affected the individual.

FRIDAY, MAY 24, 1861

A young Elmer Ellsworth first entered Lincoln's world as a law apprentice in the Lincoln-Herndon office of August 1860. Originally from New York State, he made his way to Chicago and then to Springfield. Lincoln instantly took a liking to him, calling Elmer "the greatest little man I ever met."[1] William Herndon noted that the excitable youngster had passion for justice but little patience for the minutiae of legal work. Coming on board in the midst of the 1860 presidential campaign, Ellsworth eagerly supported his mentor, forming a Zouave-clad company of Wide-Awakes to parade for their favorite candidate, much to the pleasure of Republican onlookers. Southern Democrats, in stark contrast, interpreted such gatherings as paramilitary operations.

Fairly, Ellsworth had an affection for all things military. He hoped in vain for an appointment to West Point. At age fifteen he even formed a military drill team. Acting as bodyguard, Ellsworth escorted Lincoln to the polls on November 6, and accompanied him to Washington with Ward Hill Lamon on February 11 the following year. Once inside the national capital, Lincoln tried to get him a military appointment, either in administration or in the field. "Ever since the beginning of our acquaintance," Lincoln wrote to his disciple, "I have valued you highly as a person[al] friend, and at the same time, have had a very high estimate of your military talent." The fall of Sumter sent Ellsworth racing to New York to form a regiment consisting predominantly of firefighters, known appropriately as the Eleventh New York Fire Zouaves in their flashy uniforms.[2]

Sometime during the month of May, a Confederate national flag appeared atop the Marshall House Hotel in Alexandria, Virginia, within sight of observers across the Potomac. The banner became something more than a sign of singular protest when the State of Virginia declared secession from the Union on May 23. The following day, Ellsworth, a handful of his men from the Eleventh New York, and Edward House of the *New York Tribune* entered the hotel with the intent of removing the offending ensign. In the process, the hotel's owner, James W. Watson, murdered Ellsworth with a shotgun blast.

Lincoln was in the White House library on the second floor when the news came. He tried to maintain composure, to no avail, and he began to audibly weep. The president greeted the body as it arrived in the Navy Yard and arranged that his fallen ward lay in state in the East Room of the Executive Mansion. He later said, "The event was so unexpected, and the recital so touching, that it quite unmanned me."[3]

Monday, October 21, 1861

About twenty miles northwest of Washington, near the town of Leesburg, Virginia, four small boats began to shuttle green Union troops—a few dozen at a time—west across the Potomac. Their target was a Confederate encampment of no particular military importance but a symbolic embarrassment to federal authority. Arriving while skirmishing was already underway, the operation's commanding officer Colonel **Edward D. Baker** brought his experience in the Black Hawk War and the Mexican War, an ability to inspire others, and an enormous amount of self-confidence. Baker was also a seasoned politician and a dear friend of the president.[4]

In a fight that would come to be known as the Battle of Ball's Bluff, Baker had difficulty orchestrating an effective assault. Evidently, he also gave little attention to his precarious, narrow exit route, should things go poorly (ever since his days as a young lawyer, he was known for his disdain for details). When fortunes turned against his piecemeal advance, and Baker desperately tried to rally his men, a bullet pierced his chest and killed him instantly. His fleeing troops overloaded their watercraft, and others desperately tied to swim the river span, while Confederate shells and snipers raked the boats and bobbing men. News of the horrific rout reached Washington a few hours later. The following day, the flow of the Potomac brought confirmation of the bitter defeat, as it sent wreckage and corpses floating through the heart of the city.

Upon hearing the news of Baker's death, Lincoln became inconsolable and wept for days. He attended the funeral at General James W. Webb's home, barely able to speak without crying. Young Willie Lincoln wrote a poem to commemorate his father's lost friend.[5]

Thursday, February 20, 1862

Known for being an unhealthy place, the Federal City became positively septic with the onset of the Civil War. Transforming into a vast network

William "Willie" Lincoln was arguably the brightest of their four sons, inquisitive, introspective, and well read even at the age of eleven. Library of Congress.

of Union encampments, batteries, and fortresses, as well as a destination for desperate refugees, the capital saw its population nearly triple in a year. Confined within this hyper-urbanizing space, viruses and bacteria flourished, and among the war's leading killers of civilians and combatants was typhoid. In the armed forces alone, approximately 65,000 Federals and Confederates succumbed to the disease, a toll greater than the battles of First and Second Manassas, Shiloh, Fredericksburg, Chancellorsville, Gettysburg, Chickamauga, Stones River, the Wilderness, Cold Harbor, and Spotsylvania combined. And it was likely typhoid that struck Lincoln's two youngest sons in early February 1862.[6]

On the war front, Federal progress in Kentucky, Missouri, and coastal North Carolina greatly bolstered Union morale and hopes for an end to the war. Patriotic euphoria burst forth from sudden victories at Forts Henry and Donelson in Tennessee. Conquest of the Confederate strongholds unlocked the waterways of the Cumberland and the Tennessee, netted well over ten thousand Confederate soldiers, and laid the transportation hub of Nashville ready for capture. All of this came just days before the much-anticipated celebration of George Washington's birthday. Yet the Lincolns could not bring themselves to celebrate, as they tried to nurse their young boys back to health.

Tad rallied and recovered, but eleven-year-old Willie struggled. After a steady decline, his heart stopped beating around five o'clock on the afternoon of February 20. "Nicolay, my boy is gone—he is actually gone." Lincoln broke down after informing his secretary what had just happened. His mother later said, "The idolized one is not with us, he has fulfilled his mission and we are left destitute."[7]

At once the Executive Mansion became a funeral home. After an embalming on the premises, Willie rested in state in the ovular Green Room on the main floor. Funeral services were done four days after death in the grand East Room, normally the site of regal assemblies and state dinners. Bouquets of azaleas, camellias, and mignonettes adorned the body along with wreaths of evergreens. As was the custom, Mary began to wear black and would continue to do so for over a year. Holidays, anniversaries, and even battlefield victories were not celebrated in the White House or on the grounds. Stationery from the Executive Mansion appeared with black bordering. While allergic to religious dogmatism, Lincoln appeared to undergo a spiritual intensification after Willie's death. Words of heaven and providence entered into his speech and writing with greater frequency. He appeared to develop an intensifying sense of fatalism.[8]

Mary held at least eight séances in the Executive Mansion. That the First Lady summoned spiritualists to communicate with her dead son was nothing remarkably unique in American society. First Lady Jane Pierce did the same when she lost her young son in a train accident months before entering the White House.[9]

For Lincoln, letters of condolence poured in, including one from an unexpected source.

> You have been a kind true friend to me in the midst of the great cares and difficulties by which we have been surrounded during the past few months—your confidence has upheld me when I should otherwise have felt weak. I wish now only to assure you and your family that I have felt the deepest sympathy in your affliction. George B. McClellan.[10]

TUESDAY, DECEMBER 16, 1862

As if the horror of Fredericksburg was not bad enough, along the "Dare Line" of the Rappahannock, halfway between Washington and Richmond, Union general Ambrose Burnside launched a series of attacks on December 13, resulting in nearly ten thousand Federal dead and wounded. So traumatized by the slaughter he had wrought, Burnside contemplated leading one last, desperate charge himself. Only the winter's early nightfall ended the suicidal attacks. It would be the second bloodiest day in US military history up to that point, outdone only by a previous battle along the Antietam. Upon learning what had happened, Lincoln uttered his now famous lament: "If there is a worse place than Hell, I am in it."[11]

The military failure inspired abolitionists in the Senate to try and remove from the cabinet Lincoln's right-hand man William H. Seward, whom they viewed as soft on slavery and the Confederacy. The radicals were possibly looking to replace the president himself in favor of their man Salmon P. Chase. When Lincoln learned of the plot, he confided in Senator Orville Browning, "What do these men want? They wish to get rid of me, and I am sometimes half disposed to gratify them. . . . Since I heard last night of the proceedings of the caucus I have been more distressed than by any event of my life." Lincoln was not one to exaggerate, but the slaughter along the Rappahannock, paired with the apparent collapsing of his political party (if not his administration), led him to tell Browning, "We are now on the brink of destruction. It appears to me that the Almighty is against us, and I can hardly see a ray of hope." Later that evening, Lincoln received two documents that confirmed his darkest fears, one being a resignation letter from Assistant Secretary of State Frederick Seward, the other a notice of departure from William H. Seward himself.[12]

Treasury Secretary Salmon P. Chase, darling of the abolitionist wing of the Republican Party, possessed an exceptional intellect along with a strong ambitious streak. Lincoln benefited greatly from the former and tolerated the latter. Library of Congress.

But three days later, having mentally rallied from the initial shock, Lincoln conducted one of his most celebrated strokes of statecraft. He invited the radicals to meet with him at the White House. Without telling them, he also invited Chase and the rest the cabinet, excepting Seward. Showing his authority, Lincoln informed them in so many words that he was aware of their designs. He added that he was very much in control of his office and that Seward never acted without his full consent. When asked directly whether they still supported Seward's removal, the majority said no. Embarrassed, disarmed, the senators eventually left empty handed, but not Lincoln. The following day, Chase gave his boss a letter of resignation, which Lincoln deftly pocketed. Back in control, Lincoln told Seward to remain in town and in the cabinet. Recalling his farm days on horseback, he said, "I can ride now. I've got a pumpkin in each end of my bag."[13]

WEDNESDAY, MAY 6, 1863

Lincoln had reason to be optimistic when he visited the Army of the Potomac along the Rappahannock in early April 1863. Despite more than two years of stalemate and the recent horrors of Fredericksburg,

"Fighting Joe" Hooker was now at the helm, a general more capable and aggressive than the recently transferred Burnside. Warmer days dried the spring mud into firm roads. His Army of the Potomac had reached a new peak strength of 133,000 men, more than twice the size that Lee was able to muster. Hooker also formed a cavalry corps, giving his massive force a dynamic strike capability it had preciously lacked. Moreover, he had a plan of attack, and it was sound. Rather than launching the same suicidal frontal assaults that Burnside had used, Hooker would employ 10,000 mounted troopers to throw a series of glancing jabs. With Lee's main force preoccupied, 40,000 infantry troops would cross the river unopposed farther north and launch a vicious blow from behind. Lee would have to respond to this larger attack or be trapped against the river. If and when the Confederates turned to face this emerging blow, Hooker would then release the remainder of his gargantuan force from behind the jabbing cavalry, crossing the Rappahannock to crush the rebels and perhaps the rebellion itself.

"My plans are perfect," Hooker boasted, "and when I start to carry them out may God have mercy on General Lee, for I will have none."[14]

The result was far worse than could have been imagined. Reading Hooker's feint, Lee divided his smaller force into three, pulling a large segment westward under Thomas Stonewall Jackson in reserve. That very force surprised and routed Hooker's wing coming in from the north. Hooker's following direct attack never fully materialized. Concussed himself from an artillery salvo that nearly killed him, Hooker ordered a full-scale retreat.

Chancellorsville is often called Lee's masterpiece, but the artist himself believed it to be a terrible failure. While his countrymen celebrated, Lee admitted, "I on the contrary, was more depressed . . . our loss was severe, and again we had gained not an inch of ground and the enemy could not be pursued." He also lost Stonewall Jackson, mortally wounded by his own troops in a nighttime reconnoiter.[15]

That all mattered little to the Union war effort. They had endured two years of horrifically bloody repulses, with no progress. The enemy stood unmoved and seemingly would remain so forever, not fifty miles from Washington. On May 6, when hearing of Hooker's collapse, Republican senator Charles Sumner found Navy Secretary Gideon Welles and exclaimed, "Lost, lost, all is lost!" Journalist Noah Brooks, near Lincoln when he heard the news, said the commander-in-chief's face suddenly lost all color. "Had a thunderbolt fallen upon the President he could not have been more overwhelmed." Edwin Stanton believed the period to be one of the Union's darkest moments. General George Gordon Meade heard the president say the defeat was "more serious and injurious than any previous act of the war." Bewildered, pacing the floor of the War Department as if caged, Lincoln could only bring himself to say, "My God! My God! What will the country say? What will the country say?"[16]

TUESDAY, JULY 14, 1863

Finally the Army of Northern Virginia was out in the open, unable to hide behind the protection of a river, dense forests, or the cradle of the Shenandoah. The Army of the Potomac had rushed overland fast enough to catch the Confederates before they could get to Baltimore, Philadelphia, or even Harrisburg. Just south of Gettysburg, George Gordon Meade found high ground and waited, reversing the roles of Fredericksburg. In anticipation, Lincoln practically lived at the Telegraph Office awaiting intelligence, which came in agonizingly small amounts. Only a pair of telegraph lines connected the War Department with southern Pennsylvania, and they often went dead. Adding to his worries, the First Lady was the victim of a carriage ride accident on July 2, thrown from her vehicle at high speed when the driver lost control of the horses.[17]

On the morning of July 4, the wires brought news of a three-day battle in which Meade's force repelled several large assaults, with the enemy pulling back soon after. Lincoln sent accolades as well as encouragement to pursue in earnest. Then days passed, with no indication that Meade was going to counterattack. Lincoln's vexation grew by the hour. If Gettysburg was a victory, then where were the hordes of prisoners and captured artillery? Why didn't Meade unleash his reserves, including an entire corps of twelve thousand men with hardly a scratch on them? The time to strike was now, Lincoln insisted, while the Confederates were bloodied, beleaguered, and backed against the rain-swollen Potomac. Those close to Lincoln stated they had never seen him so furious. "They will be ready to fight a magnificent battle," fumed the commander-in-chief, "when there is no enemy there to fight."[18]

In the interim, the glorious news of Vicksburg's capture had Lincoln believing the end of the conflict could be just days away. He was in the Telegraph Office when Meade sent word of a "triumph"—the Army of the Potomac had driven the rebels "from our soil." "Will our generals never get that idea out of their heads?" Lincoln vented to his secretary John Hay. "The whole country is our soil." On July 14, setting rage to paper, the president censured his commander: "I do not believe you appreciate the magnitude of the misfortune of Lee's escape. He was within your easy grasp, and to have closed upon him would, in connection with our other late successes, have ended the war. As it is, the war will be prolonged indefinitely. . . . Your golden opportunity is gone, and I am distressed immeasurably because of it."[19]

Ultimately Lincoln decided against publicly chastising Meade. Better to do what he had done after the bloodbaths of Shiloh and Antietam and present them as victories to the public. He neatly folded the letter and slipped it into an envelope, upon which he wrote, "To Gen. Meade, never sent or signed." Oldest son Robert Lincoln, General-in-Chief Henry Halleck, Navy Secretary Gideon Welles, and nearly everyone who came in contact with Lincoln during the second week in July agreed with Salmon P. Chase when the treasury secretary said of his president, "He was more grieved and indignant than I have ever seen him."[20]

SUNDAY, SEPTEMBER 20, 1863

A messenger aroused Lincoln from a late night's sleep at the **Soldiers' Home**. The Union Army in north Georgia had just been routed along Chickamauga Creek and was in full retreat back to nearby Chattanooga. The president immediately returned to town, entered the Telegraph Office, and transmitted words of encouragement to Major General William Rosecrans, but the sentiment was not entirely sincere. In the early hours of September 21, he entered Hay's bedroom lamenting, "Rosecrans has been whipped, as I feared."[21]

The extent of the rout could hardly be exaggerated. Confederate losses were greater, but they could rightly claim a major victory. The

Union lost seventeen hundred killed, nearly ten thousand wounded, and thousands more missing or captured—one out of five men engaged. Lincoln had reason to believe his otherwise capable commander Rose-crans was physically and mentally spent, so he relieved "Old Rosie" of his duties.[22]

Normally Lincoln spared Mary military details. She was already quite familiar with the realities of warfare, visiting the hospitals around Wash-ington as she often did. But with Chickamauga, he shared his miseries with her—while she was in New York. "The result is we are worsted," he telegraphed her. "We, after the main fighting was over, yielded the ground, thus leaving considerable of our artillery and wounded to fall into the enemies' hands, for which we got nothing in turn. We lost, in general officers, one killed, and three or four wounded . . . including your brother-in-law." So distraught was Lincoln over the entire setback that he later begged Mary to return as quickly as she could, telling her, "I really wish to see you."[23]

FRIDAY, APRIL 14, 1865

The day begins bathed in warm spring sunshine. Whereas the night before produced fireworks, bonfires, clanging church bells, and boisterous parties, today there are just birdsongs to break the quiet. In Charleston, South Carolina, four years to the day of its surrender, Fort Sumter hosts a multitude of Unionists in a re-hoisting of Old Glory. Among those in attendance are several thousand formerly enslaved people, the abolition-ist William Lloyd Garrison, and the fort's former commander Major General Robert Anderson. Farther north, Lincoln enjoys breakfast with his son Robert, who has just returned from Appomattox. Afterward, he takes a brief carriage ride with the victorious General Grant. Congress-men greet them upon their return, effusing praise for the pending end of the war. An uncommonly relaxed cabinet meeting follows, in which Grant shares details of their latest collective successes. Afterward, Lin-coln relaxes with a late private lunch with Mary.[24]

Before an evening at **Ford's Theatre**, the First Couple partake of a leisurely ride down to the water's edge, to the **Navy Yard** for a look at ironclads fresh from victory at Fort Fisher, North Carolina, one of the very last Confederate defenses in operation. After they return home, Mr. Lincoln entertains visitors (and mostly himself) by reading several chapters aloud from the humorist Petroleum V. Nasby's "Letters."[25]

Hours later, it matters little to the audience and cast of *Our American Cousin* that the president and First Lady are tardy, a fact made abundantly clear by their cheers and salutations. A tired but appreciative Lincoln extends his hand from the President's Box in appreciation, and then rests back into the upholstered rocking chair with a clear view of the stage. As the comedy continues, Lincoln appears to be in the spirit of the production, laughing several times at the bantering dialogue. He may have been laughing when the shot came.[26]

The following makes for difficult consideration. Lincoln likely felt nothing. If he did, it was an intense blast of warm air and searing, driving heat at the base of his skull near his left ear, followed by a rapid, heavy hammer blow to the same region. The .44-caliber soft lead bullet is a thick slug, and as it cracks the occipital lobe, its girth and slow velocity drag fragments of bone and strands of hair into the wound, spreading the damage to an ever-widening corridor before coming to a stop behind Lincoln's right eye.

One of the first army doctors to arrive on the scene is Dr. Charles Leale, who proceeds to probe the diagonal track with his finger in an attempt to remove the projectile. Unable to find the object, Leale removes his finger and, in doing so, frees a blood clot. The ensuing release of fluid reduces pressure upon Lincoln's brain stem (a.k.a. medulla oblongata), the section of the brain that conducts cardiopulmonary functions. As a result, the president's body begins to resuscitate, though his cerebral tissue is too severely damaged for him to regain consciousness. The army surgeons have seen many similar brain injuries on the battlefield. They know the victim will soon die.[27]

Chapter Fifteen

Best Days in the Presidency

FEW WERE THE TIMES THAT COULD BE CONSIDERED "GOOD" DURING Lincoln's presidency. He lost weight, slept poorly, and drove himself to exhaustion. A man who just a few years before could even find joy in the poor food, rustic accommodations, and rutted travels of a circuit ride could barely tolerate existence in the largest mansion in the United States. At best there were happy moments, such as lively dinner conversation with William H. Seward, sharing a story with the troops, attending a play downtown, or observing the comical antics of his mischievous young sons. Days became somewhat better as the war progressed. The death toll mounted, but his confidence in overall victory slowly found traction by the middle of his second year in office.

Even in the best of times—in fact, especially during those times—Lincoln habitually expressed gratitude and encouraged the nation to do the same. Even after military successes, he called for thanksgiving days, for fasting, prayer, and contemplation—he shied from celebration. Throughout his life, Lincoln simultaneously lived in the moment and worked toward the long view. Yet on occasion these paradoxical characteristics came together, when an event would transpire in which he could feel the warmth of the sun and see a brighter future. Following in chronological order are some of those rare fusions during his presidency.

SATURDAY, FEBRUARY 15, 1862

While the war in the East was producing little more than camp pandemics for the Lincoln administration, something was about to implode in their favor beyond the Alleghenies. There were three gateways that led deep into the heart of the Confederacy—the Mississippi, Tennessee, and Cumberland Rivers. In early February, the Union Army and Navy were smashing through defenses along two of them and were about to crack the lone remaining citadel along the third. The inertia was so decisive that on February 15, 1862, President Lincoln enjoyed the rare privilege of officially congratulating officers and men midway through a decisive victory. Nine days previous, Union gunboats and land forces under Andrew Foote and U. S. Grant, respectively, had forced the evacuation of Fort Henry along the Tennessee. Immediately thereafter, the same offensive bottled up more than thirteen thousand secessionist combatants in Fort Donelson guarding the Cumberland. In any other similar circumstance, Lincoln would have deferred his accolades. As it turned out, this campaign produced an outcome that exceeded his wildest hopes.[1]

In a desperate bid to hold their position, nearly 17,500 Confederates poured into Fort Donelson, the nearby town of Dover, and the three miles of trenches and rifle pits sunk into the surrounding hills. Last to arrive was a brigade under General John B. Floyd, a man of no military experience beyond a few embarrassing defeats in northwest Virginia. Fortunately for the Union, Floyd was also the senior officer at the fort.[2]

As Union artillery, gunboats, and 27,500 troops began to descend upon Donelson, Floyd opted to abandon the fort rather than be caught in a siege. On the morning of February 15, just as Lincoln was sending

Vicksburg, Mississippi. The Union Army and Navy dedicated months to the capture of the Confederate Gibraltar. Thereafter, Federals occupied the area for the remainder of the war. Library of Congress.

his congratulatory message, Floyd ordered a mad dash south along the river. Initially, Floyd's breakout succeeded, so well in fact that he suddenly believed he could defeat Grant's legions altogether. So he ordered his men back into the defenses just as Grant's men were breaking through the outer parapets. The following day, Floyd managed to escape with a few thousand enterprising associates, leaving the rest to defeat and seizure.[3]

Grant estimated his men netted more than 14,600 prisoners. In the course of ten days, the South lost more men to capture than it had in all previous engagements of the war combined, more than all the casualties Robert E. Lee would later suffer at Chancellorsville, more than three times all the Confederate dead at Gettysburg. In an even greater blow, the Confederacy would begin to lose city after city along those river routes, first Nashville, then Memphis, and Chattanooga, never to regain them again.[4]

TUESDAY, FEBRUARY 25, 1862

In September 1861, Lincoln received a message from Illinois governor Richard Yates that the war was already gutting the state financially—$3,533,511.02, to be exact (or more than $111,000,000 in 2021). Other states loyal to the Union expressed similar hardships. By Christmas 1861, the national government itself was nearly bankrupt. Exacerbating the problem, citizens hoarded gold and silver. Daily federal expenditures reached the millions of dollars. Lincoln lamented that "the bottom is out of the tub."[5]

To get capital moving again, Secretary of the Treasury Salmon P. Chase called for the federal government to issue paper currency. Paper money already existed, in the form of notes from state and city banks, railroad companies, and even community businesses. In times of peace, the system worked because most transactions were local. The US Constitution allowed Congress to mint coins, but it gave no such power to print money. Doing so would be unconstitutional, or at least an abuse of power, some argued. Lawmakers also feared a public rejection of any new scrip. Non-interest bearing, unbacked by gold or silver, US notes could become as worthless as the paper on which they were printed. At least the Confederate version could be exchanged for its value in silver, albeit two years after the Union and Confederacy agreed to a treaty of peace and separation, if and when that happened. But Chase and other advocates had a plan to make the thin scrip viable. With a few exceptions, citizens, businesses, and the government itself had to accept the money "for all debts public and private." Consequently, holders of said notes could turn around and spend it themselves, and those on the receiving end could not reject it.[6]

Lincoln signed the bill into law just hours after congressional passage, but he may have done so absentmindedly. Just five days previous to this, his eleven-year-old son Willie had perished, most likely from typhoid, and both Mary and their youngest son Tad were still desperately ill. In addition, tensions with European powers were reaching a breaking point, and although there had been some progress in the Western Theater, stalemate endured in the East. Yet, with that signature, Lincoln helped save the Union economically. In short order, the US Treasury issued $150 million in notes, and an initially hesitant public began to favor the light, convenient form of exchange; businesses slowly recovered and capital flowed again. The currency, dubbed "greenbacks," would become the life-blood of the federal economy, a currency so stable that Southern civilians soon preferred it to their own, and so powerful that it would become the symbol of American capitalism thereafter.[7]

WEDNESDAY, JULY 2, 1862

Military fortunes lagged, but when it came to momentous legislation, the president was on a winning streak. On May 20, he signed into law a Homestead Act. In the works for decades, backed by progressive Whigs, Republicans, and European socialists, the bill provided government land in the Midwest to homesteaders at an affordable price. Strongly opposed by Democrats and, understandably, Native Americans, passage simultaneously garnered votes and fueled rapid expansion into the Dakotas, Missouri, Minnesota, and Michigan. On July 1, Lincoln endorsed the Pacific Railway Act, a coup for the North. The federal government had long debated supporting construction of a transcontinental rail line connecting San Francisco to the East. The only question involved the point of origin. White Southerners pointed to New Orleans, one of the largest cities in the nation. Northerners wanted to link their region to the Pacific gateway. When secession came, so did the Union Pacific Railroad to Omaha.[8]

Then, on July 2, the president quietly unleashed a movement that embodied his most cherished ideals. At that moment, he signed the document without comment, but he had been talking about education, engineering, and the applied sciences since he first took to the stump back in New Salem.

Prior to the Civil War, there were essentially two engineering colleges in the country—namely, West Point and the Virginia Military Institute. Students went not for military opportunities (of which there were almost none at the time) but to learn how to construct internal improvements. A career in the military meant frontier duty, meager pay, and little chance for promotion. A career as an engineer meant designing the Industrial Revolution in the cities. The 1862 Land-Grant Act (introduced by Congressman Justin Morrill of Vermont) offered a fundamental change in the access and application of higher learning. States would receive federal land, hundreds of thousands of acres each, to use or sell as they saw fit. In return, each state had to establish a college for the agricultural and mechanical sciences, an alma mater for the modern age. What Lincoln had tried to promote as a country politician, he set into overdrive as president.[9]

TUESDAY, JULY 7, 1863

The day began with office work and angst. Frustrated by the limited gains at Gettysburg, awaiting news on whether General George Meade had yet bagged the fleeing Army of Northern Virginia, Lincoln pored over maps of the Vicksburg military situation with Treasury Secretary Salmon P. Chase and others. For months, the Union Army had tried charging, trenching, tunneling, flanking, and shelling its way into the citadel, the last effective Confederate stronghold on the Mississippi River, only to fail every time with heavy casualties.

At that moment, with telegram in hand, Navy Secretary Gideon Welles entered the room and informed Lincoln that Vicksburg had fallen to U. S. Grant—on the Fourth of July, no less. At first Lincoln simply placed the maps down on the table and announced he would head over to the **Telegraph Office** to forward the information to General Meade. It was as if, being so accustomed to hearing of crushing setbacks, Lincoln's mind couldn't quite process what it had just heard. "He seized his hat," Welles observed, "but suddenly stopped, his countenance beaming with joy. He caught my hand, and throwing his arms around me, exclaimed, 'I cannot, in words, tell you my joy over this result, It is great, Mr. Welles, it is great!'" Walking together over to the War Department, Lincoln added, "This . . . will inspire me."[10]

As specifics came in, Lincoln had even more reason to celebrate. Grant had captured over thirty thousand prisoners and more than 170 artillery pieces, six times George Meade's catch at Gettysburg. Nearby Port Hudson fell soon after, contributing five thousand more prisoners, and giving the Union control over the length of the Mississippi.[11]

When the news reached the capitals of Europe, along with reports of Lee's apparent defeat in Pennsylvania, international lines of credit to the Confederate rapidly evaporated. Across the South, currency inflation spiked, as did military desertions. In losing Vicksburg, the Confederacy also lost connection to Arkansas, much of Louisiana, and Texas. In the North, the dollar surged in strength, and the growing Midwest could once again trade with the world.[12]

MONDAY, MAY 9, 1864

To the Civil War student, the Battle of the Wilderness evokes images of dense undergrowth, enemies and allies unseen, screaming wounded consumed by brush fire, and horrific body counts. Military historiography commonly treats the engagement as a costly stalemate, a dire prelude to the remaining war in the Eastern Theater, with its series of bloody engagements and prolonged sieges. But in Lincoln's universe, telegraph wires and newsprint offered a very different picture. When U. S. Grant, fresh from successes in the Western Theater, began the spring campaign with a big push against the Army of Northern Virginia, Lincoln, Stanton, and others hoped for the best and feared for the worst. Time and again, new commanders promised grand successes against Lee's forces only to be thrown back with massive casualties—Irwin McDowell in First Bull Run, George McClellan's Peninsular Campaign, John Pope at Second

Bull Run, Ambrose Burnside in Fredericksburg, Joe Hooker at Chancellorsville, and so on. If Grant were to falter, Northern morale might not recover. Almost assuredly, Lincoln would lose his nomination bid for a second term, with a candidate willing to negotiate a peace to replace him.

Updates on the Wilderness came into Washington piecemeal. Then, on May 7, nineteen-year-old *New York Tribune* reporter Henry Wing entered the Executive Mansion with a brief message from Grant: "He told me to tell you, Mr. President, that there would be no turning back." Reportedly, an elated Lincoln kissed Wing. The following day, there were indications that Lee had disengaged. Losses were high on both sides, but so was Unionist optimism, including Lincoln's. On May 9, it was clear that Grant had succeeded where so many others faltered. The field commander himself expressed cautious optimism, but witnesses back in the War Department Telegraph Office saw a different side of their president. Stanton spoke of a great victory, even a turning point. Papers resounded the good news. "Gen. Grant Driving Lee Back . . . Rebel Dash Foiled at Last," declared the *New York Tribune*. The *New York Times* echoed, "Glorious News, Defeat and Retreat of Lee's Army . . . Immense Rebel Losses . . . Capture of City Point and Reported Occupation of Petersburg."[13]

WEDNESDAY, NOVEMBER 9, 1864

Lincoln knew from his own **election record** that losing was always a possibility. In addition, although economic and military conditions were improving by late 1864, experience taught him that devastating news was only a telegraph transmission away. There was also the question of the soldiers' affection for Democratic nominee George McClellan, a relationship that bordered on mutual adoration when he was in command. On the eve of the election, Lincoln confessed to journalist Noah Brooks, "About this thing I am far from certain." To be sure, there were no certainties in politics. Lincoln had won in 1860, and it had sparked the exodus of seven states from the Union.[14]

On election night, sometime around 7:00 p.m., Lincoln and his secretary John Hay walked from the White House to the adjacent War Department in the cold rain. Waiting for them at the Telegraph Office were a visibly tense Edwin Stanton, Gideon Welles, and others from the

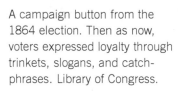

A campaign button from the 1864 election. Then as now, voters expressed loyalty through trinkets, slogans, and catch-phrases. Library of Congress.

War and Navy Departments. Reporters came in and out. Returns showed close contests, especially in the Midwest. Around midnight the entourage and telegraphers shared a dinner of oysters, and Lincoln periodically read from a book of satire, much to Stanton's displeasure.[15]

By 1:30 a.m., November 9, the outcome was confirmed. Lincoln would win the electoral vote by a massive landslide. Outside the War Department, a band serenaded the president as crowds of civilians and soldiers gathered to cheer. Lincoln declined to telegraph a personal declaration of victory, stating, "I don't believe it would look well for a message from me to go traveling around the country blowing my own horn," so he had Noah Brooks send one instead.[16]

Days later, details expanded on just how big the landslide was. Lincoln received 212 electoral votes to McClellan's 21 (to date, Lincoln's 1864 victory margin is the eighth-largest electoral landslide in US history). He took particular pleasure in learning about the support he received from the troops. In Baltimore, where in 1861 anti-government rioters clashed in a deadly exchange with Union troops traveling through the city, the atmosphere in 1864 could hardly have been more different. Of the Union soldiers from that city, there were 1,428 votes cast, and 1,160 of them went to Lincoln.[17]

Tuesday, January 31, 1865

In February 1861, the US House and Senate passed an amendment to the US Constitution. Had the states ratified the measure, it would have prohibited any federal obstruction of slavery within the states. Four years later, a very different Thirteenth Amendment entered the House for consideration. Introduced by moderate and radical Republicans in 1864, the wording was succinct and monumental: "Neither slavery nor involuntary servitude, except as a punishment for crime whereof the party shall be duly convicted, shall exist within the United States, or any place subject to their jurisdiction." Passing easily in the Republican-dominated Senate, heavy Democratic and conservative Republican opposition in the House left it shy of the required two-thirds majority. But in the 1864 elections, not only did Lincoln win a second term, but his party also gained seats in both the upper and the lower chambers. Armed with the spoils of pending contracts and government appointments, Lincoln and associates convinced lame-duck members that it was in their best personal interests to support the measure. The strategy worked. On January 31, 1865, the Thirteenth Amendment passed 113 to 56, just three votes more than the required two-thirds majority. Thunderous applause swelled throughout the packed chambers, especially among the radicals, and lasted unbroken for several minutes. The recently finished Capitol dome shook as nearby batteries fired a one-hundred-gun salute. Lincoln celebrated with an outing to the theater. The following day, Lincoln signed the proposal, releasing it to the states for ratification, and crowds gathered outside the Executive Mansion to serenade him.[18]

Alas, Lincoln would not live to see the Thirteenth Amendment enter the Constitution. Not until December 1865 did the required three-fourths of all states ratify the change. Even then, a crucial loophole plagued the nation for generations. Within the amendment, the words "except as a punishment for crime whereof the party shall be duly convicted" became an open invitation to widespread, racialized abuse. Armed with this passage, white law enforcement in states, counties, and cities arrested African Americans for any perceived infringement, forcing them to work without pay. Working in tandem, lawmakers passed a series of "Black Codes," criminalizing such activities as peaceable assembly, unemployment, drinking, owning a firearm, and refusing to sign work contracts. By the end of Reconstruction, Jim Crow laws codified segregation in states and communities, including areas that were not part of the former Confederacy.[19]

SUNDAY, APRIL 9, 1865

Just a few days earlier, Lincoln did something that would have seemed inconceivable a year before: with son Tad in tow, he entered the Confederate White House in Richmond and sat at Jefferson Davis's desk. The Confederate experiment had mere weeks left to live. He spent most of this day aboard the luxury steamer *River Queen*, traveling back to Washington up a placid Potomac. For company, he had the lively Tad, Mary, Joshua Speed's brother James, Senator Charles Sumner, and the Harlan family of Iowa, among others. Despite the political power on deck, Lincoln set aside business and simply enjoyed the brief sensation of feeling like a civilian again. The party discussed literature, among other cerebral pleasures. Lincoln read to them as the sun set, including passages of Shakespeare.

Their serene voyage ended at sundown as they docked to the sights of roaring bonfires dotting the city and raucous crowds shouting the news. Lee had surrendered that day in central Virginia. Already feeling better than he had for some time, Lincoln looked visibly at peace. One of the first things he did was head to the Seward home to check on his secretary of state. A carriage accident had left him severely injured, recuperating from a broken arm and fractured jaw. Whispering to his president, Seward said, "You are back from Richmond." Lincoln confirmed, "Yes, and I think we are near the end at last."[20]

Part III
Lincoln's Death and Legacy

CHAPTER SIXTEEN

Lincoln's Long Path to Final Rest

THE AMERICAN CIVIL WAR REPEATEDLY DISTURBED THE LIVING AND the dead. Union and Confederate bodies were commonly moved at least three times postmortem. Gettysburg is a prime example. Several of the famous postbattle images showed rows of corpses. These indicated not where the combatants had fallen but where burial crews had moved them for initial burial. In addition, some photographers, including Alexander Gardner's team around Devil's Den, took artistic license by dragging and posing the deceased in melodramatic positions. Also, families of the dead arrived weeks and months after hearing the worst. With spades in hand, they probed shallow graves in search of their loved ones. Over the years, Confederate bodies in the area were transferred to a multitude of other plots, primarily Hollywood Cemetery in Richmond, Virginia. Seen in context, Lincoln's long and winding road to a final resting place was the rule rather than the exception.[1]

DEATHBED, WILLIAM PETERSEN BOARDING HOUSE, WASHINGTON, D.C.
April 14–15, 1865
As with James Garfield in Washington, William McKinley in Buffalo, and John F. Kennedy in Dallas, Lincoln did not die instantly. He was carried from Ford's Theatre still breathing, but the .44-caliber bullet that had entered his brain had caused enough damage that death within hours was all but assured. Army doctors, who had seen this kind of wound before, knew the end was near. They calculated he would die on

the way to a medical facility or the Executive Mansion, and yet they felt compelled to remove him from the crime scene. Across the street and diagonally from the theater, a boarding house with its lights on seemed to be the nearest possible option. Heading upstairs to the bedrooms, his carriers stretched his ebbing body diagonally across a bed designed for the average person; the median height of adult males at the time was around five feet, seven inches. Altogether, ten doctors tended to him. His initial pulse hovered around 45 beats per minute, and respiration averaged a breath every three seconds or so. At 1:30 a.m., his pulse spiked to 95 bpm, and then it slowly grew weaker. By 6:30 a.m., his breathing became labored. At 7:22 a.m., his heart stopped.[2]

The phenomenon of the "deathbed" was commonplace in most societies. The phrase "to die with your boots on" would not enter the American vernacular until several decades later, stemming not from some ideal bravery but from the hardships of cowboy life, in which poor laborers would literally work themselves to death. Ironically, the idiom's origin probably stems from one of Lincoln's favorite books, **Shakespeare's Macbeth**, in which the main figure laments that he will likely succumb in a final, desperate battle like a beaten draft animal, rationalizing, "At least we'll die with harness on our back." In more civilized realms, during the nineteenth century especially, the process of dying was intended to be a communal affair, usually at home, where family and friends would be present in witnessing the final hours. In 1878, Thomas Edison proclaimed in the *North American Review* that his new cylinder phonograph was the ideal instrument to record a loved one's dying words. The ritual was meant as a calming effect in its consistency, in a world where death was not at all strange.[3]

Lincoln's demise had the opposite effect, transpiring, as it had, violently and in a very public space. First came the severe wounding not only of the president but also of young Lieutenant Henry Rathbone, his forearm slashed open by the assailant's dagger. In front of hundreds of witnesses, from the box sprang a person well known in the theater, a billow of blue smoke shrouding his egress. Collective confusion ensued, lasting several moments, broken only by screams from the President's Box. One person, recognizing the limping figure onstage, recalled that he had enough time to peruse the night's program to see whether John Wilkes Booth was part of the production. Minutes passed before the majority of the audience realized there was an emergency, and even then the overriding emotion appeared to be shock and pain rather than hysteria and panic.[4]

That Lincoln remained alive for more than eight hours after the shooting cannot be understated. Military personnel, his wife, his oldest son, and government officials were able to arrive and watch him struggle and die. Their experience mirrored that of countless combat veterans, who underwent similar scenes among their mortally wounded friends and comrades. This was no quiet departure. Blood oozed from the wound and onto the bed, visible testimony to the violence of the president's passing.[5]

Surgeon General Joseph Barnes took the deceased's leaden hands and folded them across the chest. Reverend Phineas Gurley of the New York Avenue Presbyterian Church offered a short prayer. It is unknown whether Secretary Edwin Stanton actually said, "Now he belongs to the ages." The last word may have been "angels." Of simple speech, Stanton was not prone to poetry, even in the most melancholy moments. However, it is known for certain that the otherwise stalwart war secretary did weep.[6]

GUEST ROOM, EXECUTIVE MANSION
April 15–18, 1865

At about 9:30 a.m., Lincoln's body was removed from the boarding house and taken by hearse, draped in an American flag, to the Executive Mansion. Carried to a guest room on the northeast corner on the second floor, he was first subjected to an autopsy, during which surgeons removed the brain as well as bone fragments and the bullet within. That same day, Lincoln became the first US president to be embalmed. Undertaker Henry Cattell, who had also embalmed young Willie, pumped a solution of zinc chloride into the femoral artery of the president's right thigh, which soon rendered the body's liquids and tissue into a solid mass. Lincoln was then dressed in the suit he wore for his recent second inauguration.[7]

The war itself became a catalyst for the art and science of embalming, with thousands of families hoping to have their dear ones returned in a search for closure. Technicians charged according to rank, usually

$5 for an enlisted man, $100 for a colonel, and $200 for a general, or about two months' income for a middle-class family. Lincoln's morticians charged $260.[8]

The East Room, Executive Mansion
April 18–19, 1865

This is where Willie's funeral transpired three years previous. The day before the funeral, over twenty-five thousand people, equivalent to a quarter of the population of Washington, D.C., filed past his open casket.[9] The following day, the service consisted of six hundred invited guests. Absent was William H. Seward, still in critical condition from the attempt on his life on the night of the assassination. Also missing was Mary. Devastated and traumatized, she remained upstairs during the proceedings. In attendance were General U. S. Grant, Admiral David Farragut, Lincoln's secretaries, George Templeton Strong of the US Sanitary Commission, members of Congress, the cabinet members, including Andrew Johnson, plus multitudes more crammed into the eighty-by-forty-foot room. Long-winded clergy turned the memorial into a two-hour marathon. For the mourners, many of whom cried openly, it was an emotionally wrenching and physically exhausting endeavor. Immediately after the final prayers, an honor guard carried the casket to a waiting horse-drawn hearse. Along the route were thousands of mourners, black and white.[10]

Federal Capitol Rotunda
April 19–21, 1865

Lincoln was the second person to lie in state at the Capitol. The first was congressional leader and Lincoln's longtime hero Henry Clay in 1852. By April 19, news of his death had reached most corners of the country, including the war-torn South, where Union telegraph and mail linkages connected the former Confederacy far better than its own government ever managed. In the North, mourning spread among all but the coldest toward him. Most Copperheads knew to keep divisive statements to themselves. In the Rotunda, long lines assembled to pay their respects, including some forty thousand people on April 21 alone.[11]

THE FUNERAL TRAIN
April 21–May 3, 1865

Fitting was the medium of Lincoln's return home. Since his first days in elected office he had championed the rail system. When he became a senior partner in his law practice, his most frequent client was the Illinois Central. From his entry into Washington as president-elect to his one and only trip to Gettysburg, Lincoln traveled on a system that did not exist when he was born, yet he helped raise the industry from infancy into a network of over thirty thousand miles of rail, much of which held his Union together in war and peace. Mary wanted a nonstop journey, but the populace needed more time. Aboard the nine-car train were hundreds of officials and several family members. There were also two caskets, the other being little William Lincoln's, disinterred from Georgetown's Oak Hill Cemetery, where it had been since his death in 1862. He would travel with his father one last time.

Lincoln's funeral train, bedecked in symbols of mourning. The engine was known as the *Nashville*, notably the first Confederate state capital taken by the Union Army. Library of Congress.

Baltimore was the first major stop on the seventeen-hundred-mile journey, followed by Harrisburg; then eastward to Philadelphia; a northerly loop through New York, Albany, Buffalo, and Cleveland; then Columbus, Indianapolis, Chicago; and on to Springfield. At each place, President Lincoln's casket was removed from the train and opened for public viewing—at Independence Hall in Philadelphia, in New York's City Hall, the public square in Cleveland. In between were scores of other halts—fuel and water for the boilers, passengers disembarking and others climbing on. For the long stretches in between, day and night, people came with timetables in hand, saying prayers, playing dirges, lofting banners, lighting candles and bonfires, decorating the route with flowers and evergreen branches. Many people simply knelt and wept. Drew Gilpin Faust offers the compelling hypothesis that the procession functioned as a surrogate funeral for countless families who lost their own fathers, sons, and brothers during the war.[12]

Once the ensemble reached Springfield, Lincoln would lie in state yet again, this time at the Old State Capital, within sight of his old law office and mere blocks from his home on Eighth and Jackson.

OAK RIDGE CEMETERY RECEIVING VAULT
May 1865–December 1865

Burial in Springfield's new cemetery on the edge of town was not a certainty. Lincoln stated many times that he wished to return after his presidency and resume his law practice, but he did not specify a final resting place. Historian Jeremy Prichard finds that the town's politically divided populace did forgo their differences when they heard of their slain neighbor, and thereafter they remained dedicated to the proposition that he should remain among them in perpetuity. Yet, regardless of their political affiliations, locals could not agree on where.[13]

Several prominent townspeople, including the chief justice of the state supreme court, lobbied for interment near the center of town, complete with a towering monument. Within days of Lincoln's death, patrons created the National Lincoln Monument Association, with the intention of the downtown shrine, in large part because they feared Springfield itself was on the verge of replacement. Not three months before the assassination, bills began to appear in the state legislature calling for yet another relocation of Illinois's capital. Though growing steadily, Lincoln's adopted hometown was not keeping pace with rapid urbanization elsewhere. Many viewed the seat of government's transfer as a matter of when rather than if.[14]

Left on the outside, yet again, was Mary Todd. In life, her husband's law partnerships, his party, the war, and now the Association dictated his monthly itinerary, with his consent. Now that Lincoln could not speak or act on his own behalf, Mary understandably considered herself the final authority. If it were up to her, he would be interred in Chicago. She

Often labeled "Lincoln's Tomb" in photos at the time, the still extant Receiving Vault at Oak Ridge held caskets until burial spaces were readied for interment. Library of Congress.

longed to live in the metropolis and not in the political hive of Springfield. But during his last days, Lincoln and Mary came upon a serene setting along the James, and he reportedly told his spouse, "When I am gone, lay my remains in some quiet place like this." Springfield's Oak Ridge was such a place, three miles distant from town, with rolling hills and mature oaks nestling its tombstones. Willie and Eddie would be buried by his side, as would the rest of the family when their time came.[15]

Days before the funeral, the Monument Association tried yet again to keep Lincoln in the city, claiming that construction of a downtown tomb was already underway with no such preparations at the cemetery. Incredulous, Mary summoned support from any sympathetic ear, including her son Robert. The Lincolns were going to be in Oak Ridge, Chicago, or even Washington, D.C. Terse words and covert schemes continued up to and beyond the eleventh hour, cursing any chances that Lincoln's widow and his hometown would ever develop a warm relationship. Ultimately the Association acquiesced, by an 8–7 vote.[16]

In the interim, Lincoln and William would be held in Oak Ridge's grand Receiving Vault, still extant on the base of the hill where the First Family would eventually reside. Normally reserved for those who died in wintertime, when the Midwest prairielands could freeze four feet deep and refuse the work of pick and shovel, the vault held the two caskets for the entire summer and autumn of 1865.[17]

Oak Ridge Cemetery, Lincoln Monument Association Temporary Vault
December 1865–September 1871

In 1868, the Association requested designs for the grand monument and received thirty-seven different concepts from thirty-one artists. Meanwhile, labor crews built a temporary, modest crypt farther up the hill. That December, morticians transferred little Eddie Lincoln's casket from another Springfield cemetery, where it had been since 1850, to be with his father's and brother's. Soon after, when the depths of winter came, and less famous families needed the temporary vault's services, the three Lincolns were taken to their new location, which would hold them for another six years while the towering Lincoln Memorial took shape at the hillcrest. Today, a simple stone memorial marks the location of this provisional tomb.[18]

OAK RIDGE CEMETERY, LINCOLN TOMB CATACOMBS, FAMILY SARCOPHAGI
September 1871–November 1876

Neither Abraham nor Eddie, or even Willie, was the first Lincoln to lie beneath the Lincoln Monument. That distinction went to young Thomas, better known as Tad. Nicknamed "Tadpole" by his dad for having a large head on a tiny body, Tad and his older brother William were inseparable—and insufferable. Among **Abe and Mary's commonalities**, they were excessively lenient parents, much to the annoyance of nearly every adult who had to endure their little hellions' incessant shenanigans. When Willie died from the same illness that nearly killed Tad in 1862, the young survivor and his mother grew increasingly dependent on each other, a connection intensified by the murder of Abraham.

After living in Chicago with Mary's oldest son Robert, Tad and his mom traveled to Europe in 1868, where the son became uncharacteristically studious and learned German. After staying abroad for almost three years, the pair return to Chicago, where Tad developed a persistent cough. Possibly a case of recurring tuberculosis, the ailment intensified to the point that every breath became painful. After rallying, he became feverish and feeble. On July 15, 1871, Thomas Lincoln died at age eighteen. Taken by train to Springfield, Tad's remains were placed in the recently completed catacombs of the Lincoln Monument, to occupy the westernmost of five white marble sarcophagi. Two months later, his father and two deceased brothers were placed in the crypts next to him. There they would have remained undisturbed ad infinitum, had it not been for a bizarre plot to kidnap Abraham's body.[19]

Among the occasional bodysnatching incidents in the nineteenth-century United States, most victims were impoverished, taken soon after burial and sold to medical schools. The threat to society's more powerful strata was so limited that neither federal nor Illinois law addressed grave robbery. Then, on election night in 1876, a Chicago counterfeiter hired several men to steal a president's corpse while the rest of the nation awaited returns on who was going to be the next live one. Unfortunately for the perpetrator, some of the men he selected were undercover agents of the US Treasury Department—specifically, Secret Servicemen. Unfortunately for the agents, they botched their sting just as badly as the real thieves bungled their robbery. Just as the two would-be snatchers realized they couldn't move Lincoln's several-hundred-pound lead casket from its crypt, a nearby agent inadvertently fired his weapon and scared off the henchmen. Adding insult to injury, the Secret Service began shooting at each other in the darkness. Luckily, their aim was as poor as their timing.[20]

LINCOLN TOMB CATACOMBS, BENEATH A DEBRIS PILE
November 1876–November 1878

Feeling that Lincoln's publicly accessible crypt posed too much risk for a more coordinated crime, his defenders secretly opted for a ruse so risky that it defies logic. On November 15, just a few days after the attempted kidnapping, a small group of aging men, including sixty-nine-year-old **John Todd Stuart**, removed Lincoln's heavy coffin, resealed his sarcophagus, and hauled the container thirty feet away. Attempts to dig a shallow grave revealed a rising water table. In a desperate move, to blend the scene with ongoing construction of the memorial above, trusted members from this self-appointed "Lincoln Guard of Honor" piled lumber on top of the casket. There, hidden in plain sight, the president would stay for nearly two years.[21]

LINCOLN TOMB CATACOMBS, SHALLOW GRAVE
November 1878—April 1887

Word eventually leaked concerning a possible ad hoc burial arrangement, and rumors began to circulate that tourists had been paying homage to an empty marble container. The "Guard of Honor" acted quickly, dragging the casket from its hiding place to a drier side of the basement. There they built a wooden crate to contain the casket and its lead container and buried the ensemble under six inches of dirt. So as not to create an obvious scene, they once again masked the area with bricks and scrap wood. When Mary died in 1882, Robert Lincoln quietly requested that the guards place her next to her husband in the ground, leaving two empty sarcophagi in the chamber nearby for visitors to revere.[22]

Lincoln Tomb Catacombs, Brick-Lined, Concrete Grave
April 1887–April 1900

Long after his death, twenty-two years to the day, Lincoln would be moved yet again, although this time for a very short distance. Facing their own ends of life, members of the "Guard of Honor" decided to reveal the existence of their group as well as confirm the long-held suspicions that the Lincoln crypt was empty. It was time to bury the president safely, with public knowledge that although he was not next to his sons, he was with his wife and the people of Springfield. With a journalist present, workers removed husband and wife from their humble "digs," and, as was done several times before, the soft lead box around Lincoln was cut open near his face to confirm his presence. Laborers then created a wide, brick-and-mortar chamber in the earth, reinterred their caskets, built a brick arch above them, and poured concrete above. Remarkably, the general public reaction was one of relief; their fallen Lincoln was now confirmed to be in his famous tomb beneath more than three feet of hardened cement. One writer referred to the entire operation as "a labor of love."[23]

Temporary Vault Next to the Lincoln Tomb
April 1900–September 1901

Alas, thick walls of brick beneath a solid slab of concrete topped by marble flooring could not keep Lincoln in place. Time revealed that the tomb, with its massive superstructure, was poorly designed. Subjected to crushing weight and water seepage, its base was on the verge of collapse after just thirty years of life. Before major renovations could be done, the family had to be relocated yet again, this time to a new temporary vault, made with thick concrete walls, to the northeast side of the hill behind the looming monument. First to be moved were Abe and Mary, requiring days of chiseling into the hardened concrete and brickwork. From there the caskets were placed in the new chamber, and above them lay the crypts of their sons. Sealing them all were stone blocks weighing four thousand pounds each.[24]

A steam crane lowers Lincoln's boxed casket after removing it from a temporary vault behind the towering Lincoln's Tomb in 1901. The monument and its base required extensive reconstruction, necessitating removal of the Lincoln family to this humble holding space. Officials were still so concerned that the president's body could be stolen from this site that they considered piling thirty feet of earth atop the vault while the memorial underwent renovations. Library of Congress.

LINCOLN MEMORIAL—OAK RIDGE CEMETERY, SPRINGFIELD, ILLINOIS
September 1901–present

When the time came to move the family into the reconstructed catacombs, proprietors intended to place Lincoln with his family yet again into an aboveground marble sarcophagus. Robert Lincoln refused to subject his father to the same threat of grave robbing that had transpired a quarter century earlier. Instead, he demanded that the martyred president be entombed deep into the tomb's base, in a heavy steel cage, and then encased under ten feet of concrete. Officials obliged, but not before opening his metal casket yet again to confirm that Lincoln was still inside. Altogether, Lincoln's coffin had been opened at least five times, and moved nearly twenty times, since his funeral train arrived in Springfield thirty-six years before.[25]

Lincoln's Tomb, 1901. It is said that Oak Ridge is the second-most visited cemetery in the United States behind only Arlington. Library of Congress.

CHAPTER SEVENTEEN

Assassination Conspiracy Theories

THE DESIRE TO SEE SOME GRAND CAUSE BEHIND ANY TRAUMATIC EVENT is understandable. Humans by nature prefer order over chaos, even in negative form. For some believers, an intricate plot with a cast of thousands can seem more plausible than a few rogue actors creating tragedy on their own. At approximately 10:30 p.m. on Good Friday 1865, a tragedy occurred nonetheless—a muffled crack, a cloaked man leaping from the Presidential Box, and a wailing Mary.

Fueled by countless unknowns, imaginations quickly swirled into a tempest of wild rumors. Several sources claimed both Seward and his son were dead. Others reported that War Secretary Edwin Stanton had been severely wounded and that U. S. Grant had been shot. Overwhelmed by the rising terror, Chief Justice Salmon P. Chase murmured that the entire capital seemed paralyzed by "a night of horrors." The Washington-based *National Intelligencer* soon declared to its readers that a slew of people were involved, announcing in its headline "Conspirators Are Among Us!"[1]

In its hasty assessment, the *Intelligencer* was technically right. The attacks on Lincoln and Seward were a conspiracy—a clandestine effort by a group of people intending to commit harm. Seward's assailant was Lewis Powell (a.k.a. Lewis Payne), a Confederate veteran and survivor of Gettysburg. Acting as a guide for Powell was college-educated David Herold of Maryland. Assigned to kill Vice President Andrew Johnson, but backing out at the last minute, was George Atzerodt, a German émigré living in Maryland.[2]

COURIER---EXTRA.

National Calamity!

Lincoln & Seward Assassinated!!

WASHINGTON, April 15, 1865.

President Lincoln was shot through the head last night, and died this morning.—The Assassin is supposed to be Wilkes Booth the Actor. About the same time a desperado called at Secretary Seward's, pretending to be a messenger from his physician Being refused admittance, he attacked Frederick Seward, son of the Secretary, knocking down the male attendant, he cut Mr. Seward's throat, the wound was not at first considered fatal. Letters found in Booth's trunk shows that this assassination was contemplated before the fourth of March but fell through from some cause or other. The wildest excitement prevails at Washington. Vice President's and residences of the different Secretaries are closely guarded.

LATER—Seward died this A. M. 9:45. E. M. STANTON, Sec'y of War.

This sad intelligence falls like a dark pall on the hearts of the people so joyous and hopeful, yesterday, so terribly overwhelmed to-day. What rebels in Richmond dare not do, their accomplices and sympathizes have accomplished in our own capitol.

NOTICE.

All who abhor assassination, deplore murder, and detest the "deep damnation" of the taking off of our Chief Magistrate and Secretary of State, and who sincerely grieve for the great and good men gone are called on to meet

ON THE PUBLIC SQUARE,

AT

3 O'clock, this afternoon, April 15, 1865.

Early rumors that Secretary of State William H. Seward had died from his wounds only exacerbated public confusion and anguish. Alfred Whital Stern Collection, Library of Congress.

These four, and a handful of others, initially hoped to kidnap the president. The postmortem discovery of this small circle led government prosecutors and the public at large to believe the murder plot involved far more people than it actually did. This widening lens of conjecture gave rise to multiple wild hypotheses. Over the decades, the list of accused only lengthened, eventually including international banking, officers of the US Army and Navy, industrialists, Jews, the director of the War Department Telegraph Office, opposition editors, and secret lovers of John Wilkes Booth. Below are the most prominent of these accusations, listed in order of when they were formulated. Though few shed much light on what happened, all reflect the intense fear, anguish, and anger that prevailed. Sadly, some of these suspicions manifested into revenge killings, adding to the war's horrific toll.[3]

THE CONFEDERATE GOVERNMENT

On April 15, the *New York Times* issued the headline "The Act of a Desperate Rebel." The seminal paper admitted, "Who the assassins were no one knows, though everybody supposes them to have been rebels." It was a plausible assumption. Although the Army of Northern Virginia had surrendered just six days before, the war was not yet over. Nearly 150,000 Confederate combatants were still in the field, from the eastern Carolinas to central Texas. Washington itself teemed with Southern refugees— forty thousand by some estimates. Surely more than a few members of the Confederate hierarchy would entertain a last-ditch effort to prevent a Union victory. Andrew Johnson believed it. Edwin Stanton believed it.[4]

On April 16, Stanton announced that evidence had emerged connecting John Wilkes Booth directly to the Confederate government. "It appears from a letter found in Booth's trunk," claimed Stanton, "that the murder was planned before the 4th of March, but fell through then because the accomplice backed out until 'Richmond could be heard from.'" Stanton stretched the truth. The letter did exist, but it spoke only of kidnapping Lincoln. Nothing was mentioned of assassination, nor did the reference to "Richmond" necessarily mean the Confederate administration.[5]

Regardless, by April 17, Booth's associates started falling into federal hands, and the circle of suspects soon grew beyond those directly involved.

Federal authorities captured Powell when he returned to the boarding house of Mary Surratt, mother of John Surratt and owner of the property where the conspirators met. She was soon taken into custody as well. On April 20, while Booth was still on the run, Stanton issued a reward of $50,000 for his capture (nearly $800,000 in 2021), along with $25,000 for David Herold (who was riding with Booth at the time) and John Surratt.[6]

On April 16, the *New York Times* published a report saying the US Government Provost Marshall's Office believed several suspects were trying to reach Canada (and John Surratt actually was). Large bounties were given for Clement Clay and Jacob Thompson (CSA diplomats stationed in Canada), among others. Clay surrendered on May 11, and Stanton ordered his arrest. When Federals apprehended Jefferson Davis, former Confederate assistant secretary of war and former US Supreme Court justice John Campbell, and the Confederacy's secretary of war James A. Seddon, Stanton had them imprisoned as well, partly because he suspected some connection to the murder plot. Multitudes thought the same, including William Tecumseh Sherman, though he was skeptical that anybody in uniform was involved, stating, "I doubt if the Confederate military authorities had any more complicity with it than I had."[7]

COPPERHEADS AND THE PEACE DEMOCRATS

In Washington, George Templeton Strong considered Lincoln "despised and rejected by a third of this community, and only tolerated by the other two-thirds." Strong's assessment could also describe how the nation viewed itself before, during, and after the war. In the summer of 1864, Northerners were so divided that Lincoln doubted he would win his party's nomination, let alone be reelected. This "fire in the rear" did not sit well with Unionists, especially the soldiers in the field. As one soldier in the Ninth Ohio Battery told his hometown paper, "Hang the enemies in the rear and show our enemies that we don't want them to live and enjoy peace when we have gained it by our hard toils."[8]

After Lincoln's mortal wounding, it did not take long for the Unionist and ardently Republican *Extra Star* of Washington to form its conclusion: "Developments have been made within the past twenty-four hours, showing conclusively the existence of a deeply laid plot of a gang of con-

Hard-line Unionists, especially those in the military, developed seething hatred for Northerners who opposed the war, often lumping them into the category of "Copperheads." The above lithograph, with accompanying sardonic song lyrics, refers to the opposition as "Home Traitors." Library of Congress.

spirators, including members of the [Copperhead] Order of the Knights of the Golden Circle, to murder President Lincoln and his cabinet."[9]

Lincoln's death also unleashed pent-up frustrations among his civilian supporters, many of whom turned on outspoken opponents of the administration. In New York, a man by the name of William Stewart was arrested for allegedly celebrating the news of the assassination. When a Baltimore congregation displayed pleasure in Lincoln's death, a Union general publicly warned that if "unable to control evil disposed members of your flock, I suggest . . . you should close the doors of your church for a season at least." The people of Estherville, Iowa, hanged one of their neighbors for stating Lincoln deserved to die. An angry mob confronted the editor of the Westminster, Maryland, *Democrat* for his anti-Lincoln rhetoric and killed him.[10]

For weeks, Northern incidents of property destruction, assault, and murder were not uncommon. Ironically, the majority of Copperheads and Peace Democrats were pro-Union, but the war's cost in blood and money repulsed the progressives among them, and the vast conservative wing balked at emancipating the enslaved. Such was the hatred of Democrats altogether that one would not be elected president until Grover Cleveland in 1884 and 1892, and no Southern-born Democrat would win the post until Woodrow Wilson in 1912. In all three contests, it took a severely divided Republican Party to make it happen.[11]

JEFFERSON DAVIS

In the last week of April, with Lincoln dead and the killer still at large, former president Franklin Pierce addressed a distraught crowd at his New Hampshire home. Sharing in their grief, he offered condolences, but he would not subscribe to the possibility of a grand conspiracy. Instead, he told the mournful gathering, "It is to be hoped that the great wickedness and atrocity was confined, morally and actually, to the heads and hearts of but two individuals." Focusing on the two known attackers—Booth and Powell—Pierce wanted to dispel rumors that his dear friend and former secretary of war, Jefferson Davis, was involved.[12]

The Confederate president was on the run in North Carolina when he first heard of the shooting. He had just reached the city of Charlotte when a crowd of locals gathered around him and begged for inspiration as the Confederacy lay dying. He could give them none, other than the pledge that he would fight on. Davis did, however, read a telegram to them that he had just received. "Here is a very extraordinary communication," he said, reporting that Lincoln had been mortally wounded in Washington. Davis's reaction hardly conveyed an air of sadness, probably because he had little reason to believe the news to be true. Papers printed innumerable rumors throughout the war, many of which proved patently false. He had read of his own death many times, as well as the fall of Richmond in 1862, the death of James Longstreet in 1863, and other apocryphal reports.[13]

When confirmation of Lincoln's death surfaced, Davis was still somewhat oblivious to the possibility that he was now among the prime suspects. On Sunday, April 23, he attended a church service, where he heard a pastor condemn the events at Ford's Theatre and, in doing so, stared in Davis's direction. "I think the preacher directed his remarks at me," Davis observed, "and he really seems to fancy I had something to do with the assassination."[14]

The preacher was not alone. By May 2, President Johnson made an executive proclamation: "Whereas it appears from evidence in the Bureau of Military Justice that the atrocious murder of the late President, Abraham Lincoln, and the attempted assassination of the Hon. William H. Seward, Secretary of State, were incited, concerted, and procured by and between Jefferson Davis, late of Richmond." Johnson proceeded to name others in the Confederate government, offering massive bounties for their capture, including an incredible $100,000 for Davis (a century of wages for an average skilled laborer). The new commander-in-chief had his suspect in hand when Davis was captured on May 10, and the investigation began.[15]

No concrete evidence emerged. Weeks turned into months. War Secretary Stanton delayed a trial time and again, hoping for some link to surface between a rogue Southern sympathizer and the leader of the seceded states. Johnson and the US Army judge advocate general pushed for an indictment, with no success. In May 1867, Jefferson Davis was released from federal prison without ever being charged for murder or any other crime against the United States, and yet many people remained convinced that he was a co-conspirator. In 1868, President Johnson wrote to a friend, "I shall go to my grave with the firm belief that Davis, Cobb [Howell Cobb, CSA general and Confederate founder], Toombs [Robert Toombs, CSA officer and first Confederate secretary of state], and a few others of the arch-conspirators and traitors should have been tried, convicted, and hanged for treason. . . . If it was the last act of my life I'd hang Jeff Davis as an example."[16]

Andrew Johnson

On the day of the shooting, a man left a note at Pennsylvania Avenue's Kirkwood House Hotel, residence of Vice President Andrew Johnson. The little card would become the troubling Exhibit No. 29 at the May–June assassination trial, for it read, "Don't wish to disturb you. Are you at home? J. Wilkes Booth." Who else would benefit more from the death of a chief executive than the next in line? How did Johnson go untouched while Seward's throat was slit and the president lay dead? South Carolinian Grace Brown Elmore wrote in her diary, "We have hardly heard the strange account of Lincoln's death authenticated, then the news follows fast, that Andy Johnson was the instigator of the plot."[17]

Sincerely fearing defeat in the election of 1864, Republican officials balanced their ticket by dumping Hannibal Hamlin of Maine for a loyal Southern Democrat. Johnson was certainly qualified, having formerly served as a mayor, state congressman, US representative, governor, and US senator, as well as the current military governor of Tennessee. Yet the chummy language from an assassin's note posed serious questions. Strange, too, that former Wisconsin governor Leonard Farwell invited Johnson to see *Our American Cousin*, and Andy declined (though Johnson avoided plays as a habit, rarely having time or interest). The mounting clues, plus his ascension to the presidency, stirred ire among Lincoln's many dedicated followers, including abolitionist Henry Ward Beecher, Benjamin Butler, members of Lincoln's cabinet, and Mary Todd Lincoln.[18]

Some of this suspicion eroded once it was discovered that Booth's cadre also intended to kill the vice president on that fateful night, with the assigned perpetrator choosing instead to run rather than perform the dark act. Johnson also made it clear that he desired a far harsher punishment of Confederate hierarchy than Lincoln intended, up to and including several hangings. Yet his innocence, and the extent of Union victory, would come into doubt in the following years. His veto of the 1866 Civil Rights Act, his vehement opposition to the Fourteenth Amendment granting African Americans citizenship, and his attempt to remove Edwin Stanton from his cabinet, plus a multitude of other repressive performances (not to mention his utterly irascible nature), only solidified hatred and suspicions for generations.[19]

THE CATHOLIC CHURCH

Rather than a melting pot, mid-nineteenth-century America was more like a simmering cauldron. In 1820, not one in forty residents was foreign born. By 1850, the ratio was one in six. Much of this influx came from a crippling famine in Ireland and failed revolutions in Bavaria, resulting in a rapidly increasing number of Catholics in a predominantly Protestant United States. Growing tensions became too much for many communities to bear, and an ensuing *Kulturkampf* produced the xenophobic American Party (a.k.a. the Know-Nothings). So strong was this nativist movement that in the 1856 presidential election, the American Party and its nominee, former president Millard Fillmore, carried over 20 percent of the popular vote and won the state of Maryland. Their growing power led Lincoln to write, "When the Know-Nothings get control, it [the Declaration of Independence] will read 'all men are created equal, except negroes, and foreigners, and catholics.'"[20]

Yet Lincoln's own fledgling Republicans would soon absorb a number of Know-Nothings in shared opposition to the spread of slavery or, in the case of many members, the spread of African American populations into predominantly white regions. When suspects in the Lincoln assassination included four Catholics—Mary Surratt (a convert), Dr. Samuel Mudd, Michael O'Laughlin, and John H. Surratt—some believed there was a papal connection. It was John Surratt's alleged involvement that piqued suspicions. After the assassination, several Catholic clergy helped him escape to Canada and then to the Vatican, where he subsequently served as a guard in the Papal Zouaves. When Pius IX and other church hierarchy called for his arrest and extradition, Surratt somehow managed to escape to Egypt, where he was later captured and brought to the United States for trial. Deemed no longer liable under a statute of limitations, he was released.[21]

The most emphatic accuser of the Catholic Church was a defrocked (for sexual misconduct) priest named Father Chiniquy. In 1886, Chiniquy released *Fifty Years in the Church of Rome*, in which he proclaimed that the assassination had Roman roots and that Booth was Catholic (though he was actually Episcopalian). "Booth was nothing but a tool of the Jesuits," wrote Chiniquy. "It was Rome who directed his arm, after corrupting his heart and damning his soul." The author also claimed to have been a dear friend of Lincoln's, adding that Lincoln had become a fundamentalist evangelical late in life and that the Rail Splitter believed the pro-slavery South to be a product of Catholic intrigue. In 1922, prohibitionist and anti-Catholic Burke McCarty

John Surratt in the uniform of the Papal Guard. Library of Congress.

echoed these accusations in *The Suppressed Truth about the Assassination of Abraham Lincoln*, in which, without evidence, he insisted that Lincoln was the third US president killed by the Order of Jesuits, the others being William Henry Harrison and Zachary Taylor by poison.[22]

EDWIN M. STANTON

When Booth slipped through the cracks and into infamy, no one expressed more anguish and sadness, nor moved with greater speed to catch the assassin, than Secretary Stanton. According to his detractors, however, the breakdown of security and Stanton's ready condemnation of others were all part on an intricate scheme.[23]

The most formal accusation came in 1937, when Austrian-born chemist and businessman Otto Eisenschiml produced a scathing review of Lincoln's top guardian. In a book called *Why Was Lincoln Murdered?*, Eisenschiml directly blamed Stanton for conspiring to kill the more moderate Lincoln. Theodore Roscoe repeated this assertion in his 1959 conjecture titled *The Web of Conspiracy*.[24]

How was it possible, Eisenschiml and Roscoe asked, that both Booth and accomplice John Surratt were able to escape the capital? Also odd was Stanton's apparent absence among the Booth clan's list of targets. The writers and their admirers likewise sowed suspicions over Stanton's insistence that he assign and direct search operations as well as be the lead government spokesperson during the crisis. Was this not a prime moment for a power grab, with Congress in recess and the two men above him out of his way? The shooting of Booth and the abrupt trial of his associates all seemed to be part of a cover-up.

In reality, Lincoln often felt annoyed by the safety measures that Stanton placed upon him. Contrary to Lincoln's wishes, Stanton frequently ordered a company of troops to escort the president during his travels around Washington, and the detail sometimes exceeded one hundred men. Though his protectors often enjoyed mingling with Lincoln during downtime, many concurred that such a large bodyguard constituted overkill. Most members of the Light Cavalry Guard of Ohio, watching over their charge at the **Soldiers' Home**, eventually grew tired of the mundane assignment and longed for deployment into the field. Aside from the affection he developed for "his boys," Lincoln felt more at ease when left unguarded. For example, on his nightly walks to the Old Executive Building and its telegraph office, he often went by himself. By 1865, warnings of impending harm had become so commonplace that they approached the mundane.[25]

When harm did come, Stanton ordered guards to protect his fellow cabinet members and the vice president. He also stopped all rail travel south and ordered the immediate questioning of witnesses at Ford's. In the days and weeks that followed, Stanton so doggedly pursued suspects and information that the sifting could have easily unearthed evidence about his own complicity, had any existed.[26]

THE US GOVERNMENT

Perhaps they were inspired by the litany of conspiracy theories surrounding the John F. Kennedy, Dr. Martin Luther King Jr., and Robert Kennedy assassinations or the very real cover-up attempt of the Watergate scandal. Whatever the case, in 1977 amateur sleuths David Balsiger and Charles Sellier produced a grandiose exposé titled *The Lincoln Conspiracy*, with a "documentary" to accompany it. In their investigation, Balsiger and Sellier claimed to have found the missing eighteen pages of John Wilkes Booth's diary, supposedly from descendants of Edwin Stanton (thereby linking the former secretary of war with the assassination). In addition, the pair claimed "scientific proof" of secret messages hidden in the diary proper that implicated over seventy members of the US government, from Andrew Johnson on down.[27]

When public awareness of Balsiger and Sellier's claims grew, Vice President Walter Mondale instructed the Federal Bureau of Investigation to conduct a formal exploration. Starting with the original Booth diary (possessed by the Ford's Theatre Museum under the Department of Interior) and other materials, the FBI found no evidence of any secret messages. But this ruling did little to suppress a national skepticism, spurred by the recent Watergate cover-up and the cynicism generated around the collapse in Vietnam. Nonetheless, *The Lincoln Conspiracy* lost considerable weight when its authors failed to show where in the original diary these secret messages could be found. When asked to present the alleged missing pages, Balsiger and Sellier claimed the sheets were unavailable due to contract disputes and legal issues with the professed owner.[28]

CHAPTER EIGHTEEN

Lincoln Tributes

A BUST OF ABRAHAM LINCOLN ADORNS THE INTERIOR OF ST. ANDREWS Church in Hingham, England, a silent reminder of his English lineage. One hundred miles to the southwest, Christ Church in London features an entire steeple raised in his honor, dedicated on a Fourth of July, ironically. A stone tablet within it reads, "In commemoration of the abolition of slavery effected by President Lincoln and as a token of international brotherhood." From Mount Rushmore to schoolroom walls, Lincoln's image is often used to convey a sense of steady strength, calm, and assured progress. Yet if we look into the origins of these stoic tributes, the majority were born from open hostility.[1]

A prime example is his first appearance on a dollar bill in 1862. The Civil War was beginning to escalate beyond any reasonable control, and a shocked public began to hoard their federal coin currency, which in turn threatened to implode the entire national economy. In a desperate attempt to thwart a catastrophic depression, Congress passed the unprecedented Legal Tender Act, ordering citizens to accept a strange, new, and possibly unconstitutional creation as payment for all debts private and public. They were paper notes with green backs, and among their iterations was a $10 slip with Lincoln's face on it. Article I of the US Constitution clearly stated that Congress alone had the authority to *coin* federal money, but it didn't stipulate whether the legislature had any right to *print* currency. The public commonly traded similar scraps quite frequently, but those notes were the product of local banks and businesses. The fact that the government would resort to such legally and literally flimsy productions served notice that the country was indeed in financial peril.

The silt of time often buries such tumultuous origin stories, and we are left with objects so common in our everyday lives that it is easy to lose sight of their historical origins. Significantly, more recent movements have spurred greater reflection on such mementos and memorials, enabling us to revisit history in all of its very human complexities. Though Lincoln himself was frequently self-effacing, he possessed considerably foresight concerning the power of imagery (for instance, allowing himself to be photographed more often than nearly all of his political contemporaries). Thus, it is altogether fitting and proper that we should take another look at his representations that adorn our landscape, to better understand his time and our own.

LINCOLN, ILLINOIS

A fellow lawyer once asked him whether Lincoln in Logan County was named in his honor. "Well, it was named after I was," he said. The Rail Splitter actually received the homage after some insider trading.[2]

In 1852, state legislator Colby Knapp informed three friends— including the Logan County sheriff—that a new rail line was about to pass through some open real estate in the rapidly populating area. The sheriff then rushed to Pennsylvania and offered the owner a modest sum. Once the transaction was completed, Knapp conveniently proposed that the county seat be moved to this new location. In a gesture of seeming goodwill, the sheriff granted a right-of-way to the rail company constructing the line. Handling much of the paperwork for this right-of-way was their mutual friend and counsel Abe Lincoln.

To his credit, Lincoln only profited via legal fees and the naming. The three land speculators made the killing, although they offered a money-back guarantee to those who bought plats in the newly surveyed town if it did not become the new county seat. Fortunately for the three men and their investors, Lincoln did become the official center of Logan County, a status it enjoys to this day.[3]

LINCOLN, NEBRASKA

Like a Soviet statue in Cold War Poland, or a Confederate memorial in a Jim Crow town square, monuments are often public declarations of power. Behold a state capital. Becoming a state just two years after the Civil War, Nebraska adopted a host of place names that bore the imprint of the conflict. Its counties alone sounded like the roll call of Union legends—Armstrong, Chase, Grant, Hooker, Howard, Logan, McPherson, Seward, Sheridan, Sherman, Stanton, Thomas. Yet the nomenclature was less a declaration of victory and more the reverberations of an ongoing fight.

Nebraska itself was born from the incendiary Kansas-Nebraska Act of 1854, which led to a civil war in microcosm, especially in Kansas, where free-soil "Jayhawkers" fought openly with "Ruffians" over the fate of slavery within the region. Nebraska's provisional seat of government was Omaha, a village turned metropolis, thanks to a Northern-dominated Congress making the remote location (rather than the far-larger New Orleans) the terminus of the emerging Union Pacific Railroad.

Yet even within Nebraska itself, animosity raged over where its capital should be once the territory applied for statehood. Republicans who were more Northern and urban in mind-set saw no reason to abandon Omaha, by far the largest and most productive city for hundreds of miles. In contrast, rural Democrats, some of them sympathetic to the dead Confederacy, called for a different location that better reflected the predominantly pastoral populace. What plagued the anti-Omaha faction was finding a plausible alternative. When they proposed a distant site along the Platte River, territorial governor Mark Izard protested, because there didn't seem to be a town anywhere near it—nor any people, for that matter.[4]

By 1867, rural Democrats outnumbered the more urban Republicans, and thus began to throw their weight against Omaha. It was not uncommon for legislators to openly brawl and flash guns within the state assembly. By 1869, the Democrats were the dominant force, but rather than show preference for any existing town, they chose a virtually unpopulated spot, which they blandly dubbed Capital City. In a desperate attempt to block the move, pro-Omaha state senator J. H. N. Patrick rose from his seat and demanded that the site be named after the recently martyred Lincoln. Much to his surprise and disappointment, some of the most conspicuous Confederate sympathizers smelled the ruse and accepted the motion. Weeks later, a small party in two covered wagons set out in a bitter winter to locate the new capital. Traveling sixty miles southwest of the dethroned Omaha, the team stopped along a nondescript spot along the meandering Platte, bordered by marshes and thick with cold mud. At that moment, Lincoln became the latest of many places named after political leaders, for very political reasons.[5]

LINCOLN'S BIRTHDAY

George Washington's birthday was once a major holiday in the national calendar. Festivals, fireworks, dances, and dining marked the anniversary, a tradition begun soon after Washington's death in 1799. During the Civil War, both the Confederacy and the Union continued to pay tribute. In a brash declaration of ownership, Federal garrisons in the South would mark the event with military parades, grand parties, and booming artillery. Established as a national holiday in 1885 and moved to the third Monday in February with the Uniform Monday Holiday Act in 1971, it continues in comparative quietude as Presidents' Day. Contrary to popular belief, Presidents' Day does not act as a shared commemoration of Lincoln's and Washington's birth. In fact, Lincoln's birthday has never been a federal holiday, partly because sectionalism prevented it from becoming one.

In 1892, the State of Illinois became the first to declare that Lincoln's birthday should also be an official holiday. That same year, in a direct countermove, Florida declared Jefferson Davis's birthday (June 3) a state holiday, and several more former Confederate states followed suit. Thus the era of Jim Crow sowed the lasting discord, one that spread northward. The turn of the century witnessed the apex of Confederate statuary and memorial construction, segregation of entities public and private, and the legalization of "separate but equal" under *Plessy v. Ferguson* in 1896. Official and unofficial celebrations of Lincoln's birth continued nonetheless, with Northern white and African American war veterans participating together, as they had done with Emancipation Day events

Competing with Lincoln hagiography as well as an increasingly diverse and modernizing society, the Ku Klux Klan conducted multiple daylight rallies in the 1920s, including this parade on Washington, D.C., in 1925. Library of Congress.

for decades. Yet even these demonstrations of unity became increasingly separated, to the point that February 12 celebrations were nearly all segregated by the 1909 centennial.[6]

On July 20, 1921, a nonplussed Benjamin Focht rose before his colleagues in the US House of Representatives to discuss the matter. "As I understand it, this is the only division of Government in the country that does not observe Lincoln's birthday anniversary." A vote three years later permitted the day to be honored in the District of Columbia but not nationwide. Simultaneously, a resurgent Ku Klux Klan openly rallied in communities north and south, including 25,000 members in the nation's capital in 1925.[7]

As of 2021, just six states classify Lincoln's birthday as a state holiday—Illinois, California, Connecticut, Missouri, New York, and Indiana, the last designating the day after Thanksgiving as its date for recognition. For Jefferson Davis, Alabama still officially recognizes his birth anniversary with state offices and courts closed in commemoration.[8]

THE LINCOLN MEMORIAL

The Washington Monument and the Lincoln Memorial have much in common. Both took fifty-five years to design and build, went far over budget, were ultimately much less grandiose than originally envisioned, and received widespread criticism. And, over time, both grew into their setting and became cherished symbols.

Just two years after Lincoln's death, Congress established the Lincoln Monument Association, and because the Civil War increased the national debt more than 4,000 percent, legislators hoped they could fund the project through private donations. Such wishes proved delusional, largely because the populace was hardly in a celebratory mood. A half million combat survivors still carried physical wounds from the conflict, ranging from hearing loss to quadruple amputations. Untold thousands also suffered from mental trauma. On the financial front, around 40 percent of military dead were the primary breadwinners in their family, and inflation rates emaciated what holdings families still possessed. Such limitations apparently did not register with the Association's sculptor of choice, Clarke Mills. He envisioned a seventy-foot-high statue of the sixteenth president, encircled by life-size Union infantry and cavalry milling about the base. A myriad of other proposals followed, mostly in the form of pyramids, obelisks, and statuary, with locations consisting primarily of hilltops north of town.[9]

Passion and plans floundered thereafter. Not until the passing of Lincoln's centennial birthday did work regain momentum, and once again, Congress was at the vanguard and bitterly divided. Two prominent factions emerged—one desiring a national shrine, the other looking to build a memorial highway.

Pushing for the monument, the powerful former House Speaker Joseph Cannon stated that it would be "profanity" to link Lincoln's name to a road project. A firm believer in the great man theory and generally dismissive of the lower classes, the North Carolina–born Cannon went on to say that "Washington, Lincoln, Lee, and Jefferson Davis . . . were the greatest men in American history." In support was senatorial powerhouse Elihu Root. Former secretary of the State and War Departments, Root led an aggressive expansionist policy into the Americas and the Pacific, seeing the United States as a "civilizing" force in the developing world.[10]

Several House members vehemently opposed the gentrified senators, arguing that a lavish memorial was not in keeping with the spirit of

A multiracial crew sets the Lincoln Memorial cornerstone in 1915. Ewing and Harris Collection, Library of Congress.

the prairie lawyer. Representative Isaac Sherwood of Ohio considered a proposed Greek temple "absurd" for such a commoner as Lincoln. The design itself was cause for mockery. William Borland of Missouri mocked it as a "little Greek temple down by the brewery" and predicted the American people would laugh at the project as well. In contrast, some legislators believed the mall area was in desperate need of beautification. Cannon and Henry Cooper from Wisconsin called the existing Pension Building "a cross between an affliction and a secretion" and the central Post Office "a cross between a canning factory and a refrigerator plant."[11]

Eventually the Greek monument won out, but there were still problems and contestations galore. The budget ran in excess of $2 million—a record for a public monument at the time. Placement was to be at the end of the evolving mall, an area that was quite literally a swamp. Any construction would require diversion of the wide and wandering Potomac and intense excavation into epochs of sediment. Even interior décor caused issues. Popular was the inclusion of the Gettysburg Address, but one hundred some versions were known to exist in publication, causing Senator Root to form a joint resolution to find the "correct" version.

Finally, in 1922, after several failed bills and 50 percent over budget, the Lincoln Memorial opened to its public. Millions would flock to its steps every year thereafter, and milestone events would grace its steps over the proceeding generations. Whether the self-effacing Lincoln would have approved of such a rendition is debatable, but he likely would have warmed to its frequent hosting of the common people and declarations of new dreams.[12]

Lincoln Highway

Despite losing the fight over a monumental pike from Washington to Gettysburg, the modern-minded accomplished something far greater a few years later, something quite in keeping with the rustic but economically progressive Lincoln. Much credit goes to Carl Fisher for championing the idea—as the president of a headlight company, he could see a bright path where others only saw darkness. Yet his ideal ran into stark realities on the ground when politicians and communities competed fiercely to have their areas be included on the route. When Fisher and an entourage of motorcar executives announced a fact-finding foray from Indianapolis to the West Coast, towns in between lured them with sumptuous banquets, free gasoline, and newly constructed byways. Colorado alone built thirty bridges and sixty miles of newly laid roads and hosted the grand announcement of the highway's ultimate route, only to discover that the state would be excluded entirely from the final design.[13]

Today's Interstate 80 roughly mimics the path of the groundbreaking Lincoln Highway of 1915. The highway itself also followed a number of historic pathways. Effectively beginning at the nation's first federal capital of New York City, it proceeded to the second in Philadelphia. Tracing along the more industrial North, the path then went to Chicago and Omaha before eventually linking with the Salt Lake Trail. From that Mormon terminus it proceeded to Reno and then to the former Spanish mission of San Francisco. Over 3,300 miles long, the road's enormous length, ongoing alterations, dearth of signage, and limits of cartography made its exact trajectory somewhat of a mystery, leaving a great deal of guesswork for adventurers looking to drive its entire distance. The route's manifestation, and the roaring growth of

A stretch of the Lincoln Highway in 1968, outside West Wendover, Nevada. Library of Congress.

the auto industry, turned a chain of meandering paths into an industrializing, urbanizing causeway. Before 1913, no more than a few dozen drivers and companions managed to traverse the continent. Within two years, the total numbered in the tens of thousands.[14]

Though Ford's affordable Model T was just entering mass production, the cost of travel remained prohibitive. Completion still took around thirty days, and, barring any major breakdowns, expenses could reach $5 per day per traveler (about $130 per day in 2021), leaving the experience almost exclusively to the extremely wealthy plus any mechanics they brought along. Still, Lincoln's long lane was not a trip for dandies. Accommodations consisted mostly of ad hoc lodgings or rustic camping, most of the "highway" was dirt, and driving usually consisted of ten-hour days at around 18 mph, weather permitting. Ironically, much of this elite situation was made possible by local road taxes and the laboring class, as there was yet no such thing as a federal highway.[15]

Much like the wagons trails before it, the highway came and went within a few decades, all but abandoned by the grinding Great Depression and New Deal programs that looked for other routes to unify the country. While fragments still exist, including a short ascent of a quiet hill in this author's hometown of Cedar Rapids, Iowa, the Lincoln Highway has a direct descendant in the behemoth Interstate System. Popular belief cites the German Autobahn as Dwight Eisenhower's inspiration to build a similar network in the United States. In reality, the head of Allied forces in Europe during the Second World War first saw the promise and need of such an undertaking when he traveled along the Lincoln Highway in 1919 as a youthful lieutenant colonel. His was a journey to test the military's ability to transport troops and material overland, an exam that existing equipment largely failed, but the experience tracked in his mind thereafter. In 1956, President Eisenhower signed into law the Federal Aid Highway Act, which to date has laid nearly forty-seven thousand miles of interstate roads across the country, or about twice the circumference of Earth.[16]

THE LINCOLN PENNY

Months before the coin became available to the public, Brooklyn's *Daily Herald* announced, "Abraham Lincoln is the first individual in the history of the republic on whom has been bestowed the honor of minted portraiture in the coinage of the realm." People living and dead had already appeared upon US stamps and paper scrip; yet since its inception the US government avoided placing political leaders on federal currency for fear of re-creating Europe's divination of monarchs. In 1909, a culmination of minor events created a major shift in attitude.[17]

Looking to honor a fellow progressive Republican on the centennial of his birth, President Teddy Roosevelt proposed casting Lincoln's face on a US coin. Capitalizing on the moment, and banking on the Rough Rider's admiration for his bronze portraiture of Lincoln, artist Victor David Brenner insisted that he, rather than someone at the US Mint, should craft the image. Once again, vehement opposition arose. Many lamented the break in tradition, as, ideally, the government was supposed to be about the people rather than presidents. Some decried the great Lincoln appearing on the lowly penny, while others believed the humble cent to be a fine homage to his humble roots. Not a few white Southerners condemned the idea of Lincoln's likeness being on anything, let alone on potentially millions of coins swimming in and around their communities. Others inside the US Mint were nonplussed to see an outsider considered for the job.[18]

Lost in the shuffle of larger issues—US expansion, workers' rights, rapid immigration, electrification of cities, inventions galore—legislative particulars over coinage styles garnered little attention—that is, until the Lincoln penny became publicly available in August 1909. Much like its predecessor greenback, the new one-cent piece rapidly became highly popular. Demand was such that the Philadelphia mint alone was ordered to produce up to eight million units each month.[19]

Controversy continued, however, when (for reasons still debated) the artist's initials, VDB, appeared on the finished work. When rumors soon surfaced that the issue would be withdrawn and a new version without the lettering would take its place, desire for the original skyrocketed. Reportedly the cleverest of collectors were street-corner paperboys, who hoarded their stash of VBD coins and later sold the rarified mints for thirty to three hundred times their face value.[20]

Yet the next iterations became nearly as popular. By autumn, store owners ran advertisements promising shoppers shiny new Lincoln pennies as change for every purchase. Multitudes of proprietors turned the phenomenon into cash-back promotions, including a Burlington, Kansas, Rexall drugstore that offered shiny new cents as instant rebates on school supplies. Many entrepreneurs went a long step further, including a clothing store in Fresno, California, that sold gold-plated Lincoln pennies as brooches, cuff links, and hat pins.[21]

Initially featuring shocks of wheat to symbolize the nation's agricultural bounty, the penny's tail side did not host an image of the Lincoln Memorial until 1959. Currently, the "Union Shield" design serves as the standard. First applied in 2010 but taken from similar themes on past US coins, the shield's thirteen stripes and emblazoned *E Pluribus Unum* are in homage to Lincoln's preservation of the Federal Union. To date, the US Mint has struck more than three hundred billion Lincoln pennies, or about forty per each human being currently living.

Chapter Nineteen

Lincoln Myths and Misconceptions

From Mount Rushmore to the American mind, Lincoln is larger than life. Post-assassination biographies canonized him as a saint. Lost Cause vitriol painted him as a tyrant. In the twentieth century, monuments, memorials, movies, and currency kept him in power and public view. Politicians still quote him ad nauseam. For the foreseeable future, he will remain cloaked in hearsay, nostalgia, and alterations after the fact.

Why is he still a mystery to us? Lincoln himself bears much of the responsibility. He had very few **close friends**; never wrote a journal, diary, or memoir; and preferred the wide latitude of the middle ground. Judge David Davis spent months working with the young attorney on the Eighth Circuit, became one of his closest political advisers during Lincoln's presidential bid, was appointed by him to the US Supreme Court, and, after Lincoln's death, served as the executor of his estate. Yet, when asked to describe the real Lincoln, Davis said, "He was the most reticent, secretive man I ever saw, or expect to see."[1]

The general public also plays a role. An avid reader, he was very much in the minority in his time, as he would be today—busy people prefer easy answers to hard questions. We can also level charges against his murderer. Though we have no way of knowing how much longer Lincoln would have lived, nearly the entirety of his second presidential term, and any remaining years, disappeared into the ether by the deed of a lone gunman. There is also the psychological effect to consider—we may still be struggling with the gravity of Lincoln's abrupt, traumatic death. While truth is often in the eye of the beholder, fable can become entrenched in the public mind. Following is just some of a litany tangled in his legacy.

HE EMANCIPATED THE ENSLAVED

Today, Lincoln's most acclaimed act is the Emancipation Proclamation. In 1862, it was widely unpopular, manipulative, and opportunistic, but it was a work of Machiavellian genius. In his famous public letter to abolitionist Horace Greeley in August 1862, Lincoln confirmed yet again his loathing for human slavery; however, he acknowledged that emancipation was a tactical option in his quest for military victory. "If I could save the Union without freeing any slave I would do it; and if I could save it by freeing all the slaves I would do it; and if I could save it by freeing some and leaving others alone I would also do that. What I do about slavery, and the colored race, I do because I believe it helps save the Union."[2]

Technically, Lincoln's Proclamation was a move to free some, eventually. As many observers noted, upon its enactment on January 1, 1863, the Proclamation emancipated no one. The Federal military would need to take new territory for the decree to create any direct liberations. In areas already under de facto US control (including the border states of Delaware, Maryland, Kentucky, and Missouri; the entirety of Tennessee; large sections of Arkansas, Louisiana, Virginia; and elsewhere), slavery would remain. In addition, the preliminary Emancipation Proclamation gave each Confederate state the option of keeping their enslaved if they opted to return to the Union by January 1. Lincoln also continued to advocate recolonization to Central and South America and/or Africa. For the remainder still in bondage after the war, Lincoln contemplated promoting a bill that would free slaves in the United States by the year 1900.[3]

On the ground, most of the liberation taking place came not from national decrees but through exceptionally dangerous, courageous personal decisions. Before, during, and after the Proclamation went into effect, it was the enslaved who freed themselves. Wherever Union lines were near, African Americans increasingly left their masters. At the war's outset, escapes were rare, near the same low rate of around one hundred or so per month. By 1862, the rate increased to hundreds per week. At the end of 1863, escapes to freedom approached one hundred per day, most of whom had no idea that the Proclamation existed.[4]

Yet Lincoln's keystone edict was a masterpiece. With the power of the pen, Lincoln placed the Union on the moral high ground, struck fear and anguish within all ranks of the Confederacy, and unleashed a massive and motivated power, the assembly of nearly 180,000 free and enslaved African Americans into the federal armed forces. No battle, no general, no other act of government had bolstered the Union war effort so much and so fast.

HIS ONE TRUE LOVE WAS ANN RUTLEDGE

The legacy of a disturbed and despotic Mary Lincoln stems largely from **Billy Herndon**, who disdained his senior partner's lively wife. She in return disliked Billy, whom she believed was an inebriate and poor law partner to her husband. Overtly, both were extremely possessive of Mr. Lincoln. Consequently, Mary made it clear that Herndon would not be invited inside the Lincolns' home in Springfield or Washington, and Herndon found his revenge on the speaking circuit.

When Herndon stumbled upon a story of New Salem resident Ann Rutledge and her death at age twenty-two, along with circumstantial evidence and the possibility that a heartbroken mourner might have been twenty-six-year-old Lincoln, he interviewed multiple former New Salem residents for more information. Nothing conclusive emerged, other than Ann's sudden death being a terribly sad event for Abe, for he knew the family well. He resided with the Rutledges for some time, and Ann's father had become his in many respects.

Despite lacking hard evidence, Herndon still felt confident enough to declare in an 1866 lecture in Springfield that the couple were engaged. Herndon further alleged that Ann's demise devastated Lincoln, turned him suicidal, and emotionally scarred him for life. Lincoln's bodyguard Ward Hill Lamon parroted the story soon after, adding a tone of legitimacy (though Lamon never knew Ann, having first met Lincoln in the 1850s). The yarn lengthened in 1890 with Ann's reinterment in Petersburg, Illinois. Her lengthy epitaph included the words "I am Ann

Rutledge who sleep beneath these weeds, Beloved of Abraham Lincoln, Wedded to him, not through union, but through separation."[5]

HE OWNED SLAVES

At the time of Lincoln's election to the presidency, more than 390,000 US residents owned human chattel, or approximately 1.25 percent of the national population. Lincoln was not one of them, nor was his wife. The argument is often made that Mary's family owned people, and, by extension, so did Mr. and Mrs. Lincoln. It is true that actual ownership usually applied to the head of the family. Thus the seemingly miniscule percentage of Americans owning other Americans noted above was by extension much larger. The actual ratio of white families in the South who owned one or more people was closer to 30 percent. Mary's family on average owned five.[6]

It is also true that slaveholding families clung to their possessions. County archives in cash crop regions are rife with antebellum cases where children fought over their inheritance, including who would get which people. It was common for enslaved people to weep openly when an owner died, usually not from sentimental attachments, but from the stark awareness that any assets the deceased owned would be distributed among multiple heirs and creditors. White death meant black separation. Such was the case in the passing of Mary's dad Robert Todd in 1849, father of thirteen adult children from two marriages. Married to Lincoln at the time and living in the free-soil state of Illinois, she took possession of no one in her father's will.[7]

HE WAS DEEPLY RELIGIOUS

The fight over Lincoln's soul began as soon as he died, and the tug-of-war has not yet ceased. Evangelicals selectively plucked references of the supernatural in his writing and speeches. Immediately after Lincoln's assassination, throngs of Northerners elevated him from a relative skeptic to a religious martyr, especially those preaching from the pulpits. This image of the devout Abraham was further evangelized in 1866 by Josiah Holland, a Massachusetts journalist and a strident fundamentalist. His early biography *Life of Abraham Lincoln* proved immensely popular and equally fanciful. According to Holland, "Father Abraham" was an intensely religious president. The message was an easy sell, considering Abraham's demise on Good Friday.[8]

In contrast, his stepmother recalled, "Abe read **the Bible** some, though not as much as said," which was true when he was young. Mary Todd observed, as did others, that Lincoln never considered Jesus a celestial being. Billy Herndon was more adamant, stating that for most of his life, Lincoln was a deist, if not at times an atheist.[9]

His sentiments changed later, though not to the extent that he underwent an "awakening." His son Robert and others noticed Lincoln reading the Bible with greater frequency later in life, and his public statements—particularly his Second Inaugural—became increasingly laden with references to Providence and fate, as if humankind ultimately could not override a mysterious divine will. Simultaneously, as president, he certainly exercised the power of the office as if humans could form their own national future. That he did not connect to any specific denomination and was never baptized, nor was he a Sabbatarian, neither confirms nor denies a religious streak in him. Overall, Lincoln's

Anthony Berger's portrait of Lincoln and Thomas was often captioned "Lincoln reading the Bible to Tad." Actually it was a picture book. In 1984 the US Postal Service issued a stamp with the image, sporting the more accurate caption, "A Nation of Readers."[10]

relationship with deities was not unlike how he viewed other intensely profound concepts, such as liberty, constitutionalism, and freedom. His thoughts were complex, his study ongoing, and his perspective evolving. As for those who stated definitively what Lincoln did or did not believe in, they usually were addressing their own convictions more than his.[11]

HE SUFFERED FROM MARFAN SYNDROME

The idea first gained traction in the 1960s, when the medical and historical fields contemplated whether the malady, defined by French doctor Antoine-Bernard Marfan, was the very condition that gave Lincoln his unique facial features and extraordinarily long limbs. The hypothesis also held a somewhat macabre attraction, in that sufferers of Marfan syndrome tend to die prematurely. Had John Wilkes Booth not killed Lincoln, so went the thinking, Lincoln's own heart would have done the deed soon after.[12]

Marfan is a genetic disorder that often results in exceptional height, elongated digits, loose joints, heart murmurs, tremors in the hands and feet, nearsightedness, physical weakness, a sunken chest, and, significantly, heart valve deformations that can dangerously affect blood flow. Death can come at an early age and suddenly, usually from a bursting aorta. A sufferer might possess only some of the symptoms and in varying severity. Lincoln's exceptional physical strength, ability to work long hours, lack of major eyesight problems, normal joints, and living to age fifty-six suggest that his unique features came from a different genetic causation. Hypotheses that his birth mother suffered and died from Marfan are even more suspect, considering she perished from drinking contaminated cow's milk (see **Animals in Lincoln's World**).[13]

In 1991, a team of medical experts discussed testing Lincoln's DNA to verify whether he possessed the affected gene. Despite the medical subject being rather out of reach, entombed as he was (and still is) under several feet of reinforced concrete, samples of his tissue were available. Several people assisted in transferring the wounded president from **Ford's Theatre** to the **Petersen House**, and their clothes consequently became stained with his blood. Some of these clothes were saved. Also extant are the pillow and pillowcase from his **deathbed**, which had become partially drenched by the time of Lincoln's death. Yet concerns arose. Involved in the study, geneticist Dr. Philip Reilly acknowledged there were inherent complications—for example, for what purpose was the study, and was it ethical to test without consent? Ultimately, technical challenges formed the decisive roadblock, as modern iterations of Marfan appear in manifold forms. The genetic form has mutated over the generations to such an extent that any examination of Lincoln's DNA, at present, would be inconclusive.[14]

THE GETTYSBURG ADDRESS WAS WRITTEN
ON THE BACK OF AN ENVELOPE

Normally a dedication of a mass burial site would be a somber affair, but when Lincoln and associates arrived in Gettysburg from Washington, they witnessed massive, festive crowds milling about the depot and filling the main square. Interspersed among them were journalists, souvenir peddlers, and food vendors. The time was 6:00 p.m., the night before he was to deliver "a few appropriate remarks" at the Gettysburg National Cemetery. After dinner with more than a score of guests, Lincoln peered from his second-floor bedroom at David Wills's home, and among the patriotic flags, bunting, wreaths, and evergreen branches, he saw the Fifth New York Artillery band with throngs in tow looking to serenade him.[15]

By November 1863, Unionists had rewritten the costly draw of Gettysburg into a decisive Federal triumph. This development, paired with the far more substantive capture of Vicksburg and improving chances on the Chattanooga front, provided good reason to think the Confederacy's life expectancy could now be measured in months. In contrast, Lincoln could not afford to be optimistic. From his own experiences as commander-in-chief up to that point, and keenly aware of life's unforeseeable turns, Lincoln knew to treat the future as utterly unknowable. He knew the prudence of careful steps. He left very little to chance, including public speaking.

Then why the legacy of an immortal address crafted at the eleventh hour? The *New York Evening Post* had something to do with it, when in 1865 its columns insisted Lincoln penned his speech just moments before the dedication. Harriet Stowe repeated the tale in 1868. David

Wills, president of the Gettysburg Cemetery Commission, claimed Lincoln started writing the speech the night before. In 1906, Mary Raymond Shipman Andrews's fawning *A Perfect Tribute* claimed the president penciled the address on brown wrapping paper during the train ride into town. When her unsubstantiated book became a classroom text in 1910, the myth embedded itself into the American psyche thereafter.[16]

In reality, Lincoln wrote the first page in Washington. True to form, he spent time mentally assembling his thoughts before committing pen to paper. Writing in longhand, he began at least three days before departure. Two days before he left, someone asked about his composition. He responded that it was "short, short, short. . . . Written but not finished."[17]

The second page is in lead and on different paper, suggesting, as many observers contended, that Lincoln finished the work either the night before or the morning of the commencement. No verifiable account has him writing anything during his six-hour train journey. Packed cars, several transfers, and a string of meetings prevented him from physically working on the speech, a fact confirmed by his attending secretaries. Likely, the masterpiece came together late on November 18 at the Wills home. It is true, however, that partisan newspapers dismissed the address as forgettable and that Lincoln was subdued afterward, but the reasons for these tepid responses were quite different. For Democratic journalists, it was standard operating procedure for them to placate their readership and downplay anything done by the opposing party. For Lincoln, he was struggling through a mild case of smallpox.[18]

THE SOLDIERS' NATIONAL MONUMENT MARKS WHERE LINCOLN DELIVERED THE GETTYSBURG ADDRESS

Inductive reasoning can lead a person to believe that Lincoln uttered his immortal words from where the Soldiers' National Monument now stands. From that towering epicenter, rows of flush Union headstones emanate outward in semicircles, like ripples in a pond. Stand near this memorial, and almost certainly you will soon hear passersby remark with varying levels of confidence that the imposing structure marks where Lincoln stood. Occasionally someone might disagree, pointing to the cemetery's southern end and its Speaker's Rostrum (completed in 1879) or the nearby Gettysburg Address Memorial (completed in 1912) as the actual location. Though several presidents have indeed used the rostrum for their own speeches, including Grover Cleveland and the Roosevelts, Lincoln spoke from none of these locations.

For decades, the National Park Service incorrectly assumed the Soldiers' Monument marked the spot, even creating a metal sign at the Address Memorial stating so. In their defense, NPS officials were working with limited information. At the event itself, no journalist or any eyewitness specified the stage's exact location. Recollections were vague and often contradictory, with some claiming the stage faced toward the soldiers' burial plots, while most have it facing away or to the side.[19]

A circa 1903 stereo card photo titled "Monument Where Lincoln's Famous Address Was Made," perpetuating the myth that the Soldiers' Monument was where he stood on November 19, 1863. In the background is the New York State Monument closer to the famous Gatehouse. Lincoln actually stood around one hundred meters to the right of the Soldiers' Monument, near the high point of the adjacent Evergreen Cemetery. Library of Congress.

Later photographic analyses revealed the speaker's platform actually stood to the southeast of the Soldiers' Monument in the adjacent Evergreen Cemetery, on or very near the apex of Cemetery Hill. Former park historian Kathleen Georg Harrison estimates the location to be what is now the Brown family vault (erected in the 1950s). In 1863, that particular area was void of graves, trees, shrubs, and the tall iron fence that currently separates the burial sites. Judging by the faint image of the famous Gatehouse far to the left of the stage, Lincoln was facing away from the National Cemetery, a logical position for the event, for it provided the dramatic backdrop of a thousand Union graves, and beyond them an evocative vista of the battlefield itself.[20]

HE WAS ALWAYS KNOWN AS HONEST ABE

This is a rather harmless misconception, although it is evidence of how legends can differ from what Leopold von Ranke called "wie es eigentlich gewesen"—how it actually was. After Lincoln's death, his adult son Robert vehemently argued that "Honest Abe" was a sobriquet fabricated by election newspapers in 1860, saying that it was a "temporary and not very widely extended vulgarity." Robert was not far off. Though some neighbors and acquaintances as far back as New Salem frequently described Lincoln as scrupulous, they didn't use the nickname in doing so.[21]

New Salem neighbor Henry McHenry remembered Lincoln working at Denton Offutt's general store. "He was a good—obliging clerk, and an honest one." **Mentor Graham** told Lincoln's old law partner **Billy Herndon**, "You ask what gave him the title of honest Abe. That is answered in these few words, he was strictly *honest truthful and industrious* and in addition to this he was one of the most *companionable* persons you will ever see in this world."[22]

The tag didn't emerge until the Great Debates of 1858—specifically October 18, after Lincoln and Stephen Douglas clashed in Peoria. The rather pro-Whig *Peoria Transcript* reported that their man verbally walloped the Little Giant: "We predict that Douglas, giant though he has the reputation of being, will never again consent to meet honest Abe Lincoln in joint discussion." Eventually the adjective "Old" attached itself, as it had with other prominent public figures: "Old Man Eloquent" (John

Quincy Adams); "Old Hickory" (Andrew Jackson); "Old Kinderhook" (Martin Van Buren); "Old Fuss and Feathers" (Winfield Scott); "Old Rough and Ready" (Zachary Taylor); "Old Tippecanoe" (William Henry Harrison). Certainly, "Old" was not terribly original when it came to nicknames. One of the first known applications appeared in the November 11, 1858, issue of the *Chicago Daily Democrat*, noting how the Great Debates were becoming nationally known: "It is not only in his own state that Honest Old Abe is respected." Far more frequently, journalists focused on Lincoln's physical altitude rather that his age, such as "Long Abe," "The Giant Killer," and "Tall Sucker."[23]

Chapter Twenty

Sites of Lincoln Historic Preservation

MANY A HERITAGE TOURIST WILL ATTEST THAT TO KNOW THE HIS-tory intimately, one must go to the place where it transpired. Inch by inch and brick by brick, key places in Lincoln's life have been rediscovered and rebuilt. In their renaissance, each followed a pattern familiar to historic preservation.

For any given event, great or small, the first thing that happens is life moves on. When incidents are relatively commonplace, such as the birth of a child, the purchase of a house, or the delivery of a short speech, there is little indication that such an incident will resonate much beyond its immediate circle. Concerning episodes of stark trauma impacting thousands, like a horrific military engagement or a horrific murder at a theater, survivors must labor through the immediate consequences. Coping often includes an overwhelming desire to forget. Whether tender or tragic, it is the moment itself, rather than the land and structures upon which it transpires, that commands the attention of witnesses.

In some cases, the passage of time brings a critical second phase, when a handful of committed people develop a connection to that time and place—usually people who were not directly present during the event itself. They will labor to save a particular building or plot they personally hold dear but that the public has moved beyond. Their step toward action usually begins when the site becomes endangered through neglect or replacement. If and when rescue occurs, the result frequently proves paradoxical. With obliteration avoided, these passionate protectors usually imprint their own focus and fascinations upon their labor of love, culminating in memorials and museums long on sentimentalism and short on historical accuracy.

Phase three tends to be the most emotional and contentious. When academics and government entities move to bring their professional resources to the effort, site matriarchs and patriarchs have difficulty letting go. Understandably, private groups that saved decaying places can wonder where these major players were when the work began. Conversely, qualified specialists often struggle with well-meaning citizenry who might be doing more harm than good. These transitions from amateur to professional preservation can take decades, sometimes generations. When they do, generally speaking, public access widens, preservation techniques improve, and interpretation becomes more inclusive. Of course, all sites will and should evolve, as our understanding of history and our relationship with it evolves. Following are some of the key protected sites of Lincoln's past and their evolution into our present.

ABRAHAM LINCOLN BIRTHPLACE NATIONAL HISTORIC PARK, LARUE COUNTY, KENTUCKY

Fittingly, the site of his birth became the first Lincoln site in the National Park system, though its journey would be a long one. Biographer Louis A. Warren calculates that the property changed hands eighteen times between Thomas Lincoln's residence and the federal government attaining possession of some 110 acres, or about one-third of the original farm, in 1916.[1]

If there is an overriding theme to the National Historic Park today, it is symbolism. Remote, hilly, with stands of massive trees and thick undergrowth, the landscape reveals how hard it was to fight nature in Kentucky and spawn cropland. Before European and African arrival, Natives set fires to create grasslands to attract more wild game, with limited success.[2]

The task proved just as challenging for wealthy and poor whites who tried to make the area more productive, including those who wanted to obtain and commemorate the place of Lincoln's birth. One such individual included Alfred Dennett, a religious businessman with questionable motives. Purchasing the land in 1894 plus adjacent property, he dismantled a nearby cabin and reassembled it near the sinking spring after which the farm was named. Failing to attract many visitors, he dismantled the logs, along with another collection said to be the birth cabin of Jefferson Davis, and took them to Nashville for that city's centennial celebration, where politicians gave speech after speech exalting civilizations based on slavery, including ancient Egypt, Hellenistic Greece, and the American Confederacy. From there, the rough-hewn timbers eventually made their way to the 1901 Pan-American Exposition in Buffalo, where President William McKinley suffered the same fate as Lincoln.[3]

By that time Dennett had become insolvent, and the intermingled logs languished in storage on Long Island. Eyeing the one hundredth anniversary of Lincoln's birth, Robert Collier of *Collier's Weekly* and supporters aspired to restore what they believed to be the original cabin to the farm, and to create a memorial befitting the centennial. Richard Lloyd Jones, the magazine's managing editor, envisioned a place that offered a counternarrative to the conflict and death themes that pervaded among battlefield parks, a site that "will express our national unity rather than preserve our lamentable differences."[4]

In short order, the Lincoln Farm Association (LFA) formed in New York to raise funds. Fees for membership ranged from a minimum 25 cents to a maximum $25, to symbolize a collection of, by, and for the common people. Yet, in the end, the association opted to rebuild a cabin that was almost certainly inauthentic, surrounded by a grandiose Memorial Building with a sprawling granite stairway of fifty-six steps representing the years of Lincoln's life. Notably, plans for an even more ostentatious Washington Mall–style vista leading up to the Memorial Building proved too costly to undertake.[5]

In 1916, by an act of Congress, the government accepted the grounds and construction, transferring responsibility from the War Department to the National Park Service in 1933. Leading up to the Civil War centennial, the NPS began to question the appropriateness of such an opulent presentation of a birth site that was anything but glamorous in its time. To tone down the centrality of the boastful Beaux-Arts Memorial Building, the NPS constructed a Visitor Center nearer to the park entrance to "intercept" the public and present to

Completed in 1911, the Memorial Building housing the Symbolic Cabin was designed by John Russell Pope, a young and promising architect who years later would draft several buildings in the national capital, including the National Archives and the Thomas Jefferson Memorial. Carol Highsmith, Library of Congress.

them depictions of Lincoln's early life that better represented his humble beginnings. For the birthplace itself, officials adeptly renamed it the "Symbolic Cabin." Walking trails and picnic areas were added to create a more natural and relaxed visitor experience, countering the exaggerative hagiography of the Lincoln Farm Association's original layout. In 1998, the NPS incorporated the Knob Creek farmstead site into the Birthplace Park area, allowing tourists to view the rural settings that would have been familiar to young Abe.[6]

LINCOLN BOYHOOD NATIONAL MEMORIAL, SPENCER COUNTY, INDIANA

In Indiana as in Kentucky, determining the exact layout of the Lincoln homestead proved elusive, largely because the family left such a light archaeological footprint. Adding to the challenge, local interest in the Spencer County farm site began soon after Lincoln's death, which unfortunately led to scavenging of logs that may have been part of the original structures. As a result, the site began as the Nancy Hanks Lincoln Memorial, because the one verifiable remnant in situ was her burial place. As it turned out, placing focus on his mom became the locale's central theme. From then on, preservationists in Indiana strove to promote their state as Lincoln's *alma mater*, Latin for "nurturing mother." As a figurative and literal cornerstone, advocates placed a grave marker on her plot in 1879. A larger, more ornate memorial was installed in 1902, made from rock left over from the recently completed **Lincoln's Tomb** at Oak Ridge Cemetery in Springfield.[7]

During the First World War, locals believed they had found hearthstones of the Lincoln home. Whether their discovery was accurate was debatable, but the search signaled renewed interest, and by 1926 an organization called the Indiana Lincoln Union assumed management of the growing enterprise. Despite the onset of the Great Depression, by the 1930s, the ILU managed to construct two large memorial halls joined by an arcing passageway. Modestly, and arguably more suitable for the setting, the union also established a Trail of Twelve Stones, a pathway representing Lincoln's milestones, including rocks from his birthplace, New Salem, Gettysburg, and the White House. The forest in which all of this resides is largely of human construct, planted during the New Deal by the Civilian Conservation Corps and during other areas for three primary reasons—to establish an ambience for quiet contemplation, to create a park that is environmentally sustainable, and to represent the untamed woodlands that the Lincolns saw when they first arrived here in 1816.[8]

In 1962, the National Park Service accepted conservatorship and transformed the memorial halls into the Visitor Center. To better depict the atmosphere present during Lincoln's youth, the nearby highway was moved farther south to reduce noise pollution, and the NPS partnered with the Smithsonian Institute and Department of Agriculture to create a living history farm. To this day, the Lincoln Boyhood National Memorial sustains its secluded character, and its home of Spencer County remains ostensibly rural, with a total population of just 22,000.[9]

Lincoln's New Salem State Historic Site, Menard County, Illinois

In 1906, locals gave publicist extraordinaire William Randolph Hearst a tour of the abandoned village of New Salem. The eccentric magnate was so struck by the experience that he purchased over sixty acres of the site

The State of Illinois has reconstructed most of the structures that existed in Lincoln's time, taking pains to make them operational rather than simply decorative. Carol Highsmith, Library of Congress.

and gave it to a regional trust. In 1917, a younger generation of Lincoln enthusiasts from nearby Petersburg, Illinois, invited every living person who had once lived in New Salem to return to their old haunts for a Fourth of July celebration. There the former residents shared their stories, reminisced about their most famous neighbor, and located the footprints of the long-gone structures and roads. By 1918, the State of Illinois accepted the vanguard of site restoration and interpretation by accepting the property deed, constructing a small museum, and reconstructing homes and stores based on excavations and recorded memories.[10]

Federal assistance arrived via the New Deal, manifesting in a Civilian Conservation Corps project that employed hundreds of young men. Officially known as CCC Camp 1683, it aptly operated for seven years—as long as Lincoln's stay in the village. Part of the CCC's legacy includes pathways and buildings that are still in use.[11]

As historic preservation evolved into a social scientific profession, so did New Salem. Rebuilding involved as many period methods and materials as feasible, including producing bricks from nearby clay pits and fashioning log houses out of surrounding stands of trees. In the interest of structural longevity, builders employed more modern techniques when necessary—foundations built below the frost line, logs treated with zinc chloride to prevent rot, concrete in place of lime mortar and mud for chinking. For furnishings, regional families donated hundreds of relics, each vetted by a committee for appropriate age and design, with some verified as having been on-site during Lincoln's seven-year stay. Today the site continues as a state park with a visitor center, theater, and living history, with a caveat. The future of New Salem's interpretation will depend on how far public sentiment and professional practice will allow the town to return to its former, less civilized self. Its history of blood sports including fist fighting and gander pulls, lives filled with recurring diseases and abject poverty, the persistence of gangs and prevalence of alcohol, not to mention the raw necessities of animal slaughter and culling, are beyond the general public's willingness to witness firsthand. Yet the dangers of presenting that time and place in sentimental and sanitized vistas is to hide the world from which Lincoln emerged, to mask his driving motive for leaving that town and that hard life far behind.[12]

LINCOLN HOME NATIONAL HISTORIC SITE

Essentially every historic preservation project is a comeback story, and Lincoln's Springfield footprint is a prime example. After the assassination, the family home on Eighth and Jackson was on track to becoming like any other American middle-class home, valued primarily for its familial memories and real estate market worth. In 1865, its occupant was Lucian Tilton, executive president of the Great Western Railroad. He continued to rent the home from Robert Lincoln until moving to Chicago in 1869. Robert sold some of the Lincoln furnishings to the rail magnate, which were consumed in the Great Chicago Fire of 1871. A physician resided next until 1883, when Union veteran and Lincoln devotee Osborn Oldroyd moved in, bringing with him some two thousand Lincoln photos and artifacts he had collected since the war. Oldroyd proceeded to pack much of the first floor with his eclectic compendium for display to a paying public.[13]

In 1887, Robert deeded the home to the State of Illinois, and trustees of the property kept Oldroyd on as a curator and caretaker. Over time, Robert loathed the transformation of his old family home into a heavily trafficked knickknack shack. It wasn't until 1893 that a new governor interceded and essentially evicted Oldroyd, who took his stacks of paraphernalia and set up shop at the **Peterson House** across from **Ford's Theatre**.[14]

Thereafter, relatives on Mary's side served as custodians up to the 1950s. The home thereafter became a tourist magnet, drawing in thousands of car-driving visitors riding the highways and newly created Interstate System to the Land of Lincoln. The neighborhood increasingly transformed into a strip of souvenir shops catering to family vacationers and disposable consumerism. In 1971, the NPS began to shepherd the home back to its roots, restoring its exterior and interior as closely as possible to its character and contents of the late 1850s. In 1987, a year-long restoration project ensued, including installation of the latest available techniques in climate control. In addition, the NPS acquired over four square blocks of the surrounding area, saving and restoring (and, in some cases, reconstructing) homes and buildings present in Lincoln's time. Interpretation also expanded considerably, to include the Lincoln story in far greater context, including the economic, social, ethnic, and technological features that were fundamental parts of his everyday existence.[15]

Today, downtown Springfield is the first destination for anyone looking to better understand Lincoln. Led, self-guided, and virtual walking tours, the Illinois Old Capitol Building, the Benjamin Edwards Place Historic Home (Mary Todd's nephew's house), interpreting family life in the 1850s, and other features allow several days of heritage tourism opportunities. The flagship is the Lincoln Presidential Library and Museum. Opened in 2004, it is a state-of-the-art interactive center for study and experiential history.

GETTYSBURG

Lincoln visited Gettysburg only once and his address never mentioned the battle by name—yet a two-day journey and two minutes have fused the two names ever after. Fortunately for the heritage tourist, the site and its eponymous battle possessed traits that enabled considerable preservation over time. Though the overall cost in deaths and casualties was the highest in the war, the warring parties stayed less than seventy hours, sparing most structures in the city, a fate not enjoyed by places such as Atlanta, Richmond, and Vicksburg. Nor was it a location subjected to postwar urban sprawl, unlike Manassas, Nashville, and Washington. As the largest and deadliest Civil War engagement, not to mention Lincoln's immortal speech bearing its name, Gettysburg held unique status among the war's ten thousand battlefields. Lastly, its legacy as the Confederate "high-water mark" and a pivotal Union victory deemed it worthy of exaltation for sentimentalists on both sides. Consequently, the Gettysburg Battlefield Memorial Association, organized mere weeks after the engagement, bought up acres and gathered eyewitness accounts. In 1895, Gettysburg became a national park under the protection of the War Department, transferring in 1933 to the Department of the Interior.[16]

To trace the president's footsteps, begin at the Gettysburg Train Depot (renovated in 2006) on the north side of town. Here he arrived from a six-hour train journey from Washington the day before he was to deliver remarks at a new national cemetery. To truly set the mood, consider arriving at 6:00 p.m. as he did, and know that seeing throngs of tourists would not be out of context. Thousands of people were in the area when Lincoln and his entourage arrived, and a festive air prevailed—a perplexing ambience indeed considering that the president saw, among other things, stacks of caskets around the depot awaiting use for the dead yet to be interred in the growing gravesite.[17]

From there, head south to the town square and the extant David Wills home (added to the National Park in 2009). The ceremony and the cemetery were largely Wills's creations, and the thirty-two-year-old lawyer personally greeted Lincoln at the station. Lincoln stayed at the Wills home that night, dining with more than twenty guests, and completing the last lines of his speech, while bands and crowds serenaded him from outside.[18]

The following morning, before the procession to the cemetery, Lincoln and **William H. Seward** took a carriage ride down the existing Chambersburg Pike, the same road many Confederates used to reach the fight on July 1. The president and secretary of state then proceeded northwest to the Lutheran Theological Seminary (since 2013, the Seminary

Ridge Museum and Education Center) and into the countryside. Their destination—McPherson Ridge, where Major General John Reynolds was shot and killed on the battle's first day (Stop 1 on the National Park Service Driving Tour). One account states that Lincoln dismounted the carriage and walked among the trees in somber reflection. Lincoln knew Reynolds personally and spoke with him at the White House shortly before the general's fate at Gettysburg.[19]

The president and Seward then returned to the Wills home to dress and prepare, emerging around 10:00 a.m. to thousands of people in the plaza. By this late November day, most of the trees had lost their leaves, but a warm sun shone through the crisp autumn air. The weather was far brighter than Lincoln's mood. The long column then proceeded down Carlisle Street, with Lincoln on horseback. While some people took the shorter route through the iconic gatehouse, the official procession entered on the far side through what is now the main pedestrian entrance. To see where he spoke, look through the iron gate between the National Cemetery and its predecessor Evergreen Cemetery. Neither the fence nor most of the civilian burials were present during the commemoration. Look to the apex of the hill and a family vault labeled "Brown." Close to that spot is where the stage and Lincoln stood, his back to you, as he recited his two-page homage to the dead and living around you.[20]

The ceremony, having lasted nearly three hours, ended with Lincoln returning to the Wills home and a late lunch. From there, he and others proceeded to the Gettysburg Presbyterian Church (rebuilt on its original site, with its old rafters and the very pew in which Lincoln sat). After the services, a weary Lincoln almost immediately returned to the train station for the long trek back to Washington. Unbeknownst to him, much of his exhaustion came from an oncoming bout of mild smallpox.[21]

PRESIDENT LINCOLN'S COTTAGE AT THE SOLDIERS' HOME

Every year, the National Trust for Historic Preservation lists the eleven most endangered sites related to US history. These clarion calls frequently inspire critical massing of support required for rescue. Success stories include James Madison's Montpelier, Joe Frazier's Gym in Philadelphia, Cincinnati's Union Terminal, and Ellis Island. In 2000, the **Soldiers'**

Home three miles north of the White House made the list. Support from the federal government enabled the National Trust to begin saving the main cottage and immediate landscape. After eight years of meticulous work, including the removal of more than a dozen layers of paint from the aging interior walls, the Trust opened the site to the public. Within the modern urban sprawl of the Washington area, a hectic environment that weighed on Lincoln as it does his fellow humans who live and work there today, this quiet hilltop enclave with its majestic vistas of the Potomac Valley resonates with peace.[22]

One historic feature that needed very little restoration was the adjacent National Cemetery. Established during the Civil War, this and other National Cemeteries grew precipitously from thousands of Union fatalities, most of whom died not from combat but from pandemics and infections that flourished in times of national stress. Lincoln walked these very grounds during his stay, contemplating the war's meanings and costs. These dead lay yards away from the cottage in which Lincoln partially drafted his Emancipation Proclamation, a critical expansion of the war from restoration of the political Union to a larger, greater human cause.

FORD'S THEATRE NATIONAL HISTORIC SITE

Of the building's outer shell, only the back wall is not original, although the rest have undergone multiple restorations. Inside, nearly everything is a facsimile. Despite calls to destroy the building altogether in the wake of the assassination, the federal government purchased the theater after the war and converted it into an office building, and then the Army Medical Museum up to 1877. Following a horrific collapse of interior floors in 1893, which killed twenty-two government employees, the structure remained abandoned. It would have disappeared altogether were it not for the New Deal and its push to create jobs from the rubble of the Great Depression. Functioning as a museum yet again, this time to Lincoln himself, the building possessed historic gravity only because of its location. The structure itself held virtually no resemblance to its previous life as one of Lincoln's favorite Washington performance halls.[23]

As the Civil War centennial neared, and all things Lincoln gained public attention, there emerged movements to restore the theater based

A 1980 interior view of the fully restored Ford's Theatre. A living venue today, the site was home to many public joys as well as tragedies. A chilling example of the latter, on June 9, 1893, a large portion of the front of the structure collapsed, killing twenty-two civil servants and injuring sixty-five more.[24]

on period photos, sketches, testimonials, construction reports, and excavations. The idea was not without considerable opposition, as many people questioned the ethical implications of commemorating a national crime scene, a backlash that recurred when preservationists called for saving the Texas Book Depository in Dallas and the Lorraine Motel in Memphis. Yet public and private support won out, enabling the Department of the Interior's meticulous restoration of Ford's Theatre starting in the 1950s. On January 30, 1968, the building reopened, appearing very much as it did on the night of the assassination. As an homage, the Presidential Box is never used, but the rest of the structure remains a living museum and an active performance venue.[25]

THE PETERSEN HOUSE

It initially seemed that the three-story brick building in which Lincoln breathed his last would be as temporary as his life. There was little initial indication that the site would or should endure. As one contemporary said, "The house is built of material too frail to induce the hope that it will long stand as a memento of the great man who died in it, being built rather on the tenement style." Adding to this pessimism, souvenir seekers immediately preyed upon the boarding establishment, grabbing up and cutting out anything of perceived interest. After the owner's death in 1871, the blockhouse changed hands and uses several times, all while random sightseers begged for an inside look.[26]

Exasperated owners sold the Petersen House to the US government, and it became a one-man show of sorts. The aforementioned Osborn Oldroyd arrived in 1893 and proceeded to cover the walls with random Lincoln pictures and paraphernalia, ironically masking the story of the historic death room and building itself.

Before the aging Oldroyd passed away, the government purchased his collection and stored it in the basement of the Ford's Theatre Museum, with the intention of vetting and cataloging the material at a later time. In 1933, with the guidance of 1865 photos and drawings, the National Park Service began restoring the building, particularly the room in which Lincoln died, to as close as possible to the way it appeared on April 15. Next to the Peterson House today is the Center for Education and Leadership, a building acquired in 2012 by the Ford's Theatre Society.

CHAPTER TWENTY-ONE

Seven Must-Reads on Lincoln

IT IS SAID THAT ONLY JESUS AND SHAKESPEARE HAVE HAD MORE BOOKS written about them. Volumes on Lincoln number some sixteen thousand and rising. Consequently, this list could rightly number in the hundreds, and there would still be excellent works excluded. By delving into the following, at least a reader could sympathize with the book hound in Lincoln. Nearly every book he read widened his world, which in turn compelled him to keep exploring.

Remarkably, over 160 years of meticulous searching has not yet exhausted primary materials related directly and indirectly to the sixteenth president. A solid base formed with the 128-volume *Official Records of the Union and Confederate Armies* (1894–1922) and Roy Basler's eight-volume *Collected Works of Abraham Lincoln* (1953). The digital age slammed our access and accumulation into overdrive, including invaluable databases such as the Illinois Historic Preservation Agency's Law Practice of Abraham Lincoln and the 40,000-plus documents within the Abraham Lincoln Papers at the Library of Congress. Cross-discipline fertilization has fostered further growth, including archaeology, economics, environmental history, and medicine. As the following tomes attest, the number of topics related to the man, and the ways of traversing those topics, are truly enormous. Following is a starter list for those beginning their journey into the universe that is Lincoln, as well as an incentive to add one or two more to the bookshelf of the avid Lincoln explorer.

ABRAHAM LINCOLN: A LIFE
Michael Burlingame
Johns Hopkins University Press, 2008

Arguably the standard single-volume text remains the highly readable, Pulitzer Prize–winning *Lincoln* by David H. Donald (1995). A stalwart among overarching political profiles is Benjamin Thomas's seminal *Abraham Lincoln* (1952), with a deeper search of the man's political psyche in Ronald C. White's *A. Lincoln* (2009). Yet for an honestly raw, exhaustive depiction, Michael Burlingame's two-volume opus *Abraham Lincoln: A Life* is now the highest milestone among biographies. The eleven-year project involved not only the latest in digital collections but also an enormous amount of old-school research, traveling to state and local archives, scrolling through miles of microfilm, sifting through countless files, diaries, family collections, and period local newspapers, mining every conceivable vein. The result is the most complete picture of Lincoln's relationship with his personal world and how the world viewed him. For example, Burlingame presents the most substantive argument to date that the Lincoln marriage was an abusive one, in which Mary's accumulation of personal traumas and physiological maladies turned her into a broken spirit, whose primary target was her exceptionally accommodating husband. In turn, Burlingame finds, Lincoln turned to others in search of stability, especially while president.

One of the biography's greatest strengths, among many, is Burlingame's willingness to fully humanize his subject. As stated many times in the text you are currently reading, Lincoln was an elusive figure by his own design—paradoxical, purposefully vague, often emotionally detached except with animals and children, and excruciatingly complex. Yet, to date, Burlingame has come closest to finding the inner man.

In case this nearly two-thousand-page exploration is not immersive enough, Johns Hopkins University Press has also released an extended version containing all the prose and documentation trimmed from the original version.

LINCOLN AND THE ECONOMICS OF THE AMERICAN DREAM
Gabor S. Boritt
Memphis State University Press, 1978

By his own admission, Gabor Boritt has a strange advantage over most Lincoln scholars—he was born outside the United States. Raised in Budapest, the Jewish Boritt survived Nazi occupation in World War II. As a teenager, he fought against the 1956 Soviet suppression of Hungary. Escaping to the United States with his sister and in utter poverty, he taught himself English and trudged through his studies to earn his doctorate in history at Boston University. Consequently, Boritt possessed an intense familiarity with oppression and liberation.

His early life outside the United States also allowed him to approach Lincoln largely free of preconceptions. Boritt consequently found the American perception of Lincoln to be "as much the creation of mythology as history." When he began to form his own perspective, he discovered something hiding in plain sight. "In his public life," Boritt observed, "Lincoln probably talked more about economics, to use the term in a broad sense, than any other issue, slavery included."

Since his first bid for office and thereafter, Lincoln wrote, spoke, and legislated extensively on internal improvements, capital flow, public and private credit, trade, and protectionism. He chastised the Democratic practice of minimal governance and avoidance of debt, as it starved the economy of precious investment, that "the revenue is to be collected, and kept in iron boxes until the government wants it for disbursement; thus robbing the people of the use of it . . . and while the money is performing no nobler office than that of rusting in iron boxes." Boritt articulated how Lincoln wanted the nation to build up, not out, through internal improvements. And foremost, the historian maintained that Lincoln argued against slavery not on racial terms but as an issue of the rights of labor—that to rob a worker of wages, as Lincoln's father ostensibly did to him as a young man, destroyed the chance for millions of people to work for themselves, to maximize their own motivation and talents, and to inject their own earnings back into the market.

A common critique of Boritt's conclusions is that he overemphasizes a "rag-to-riches" theme, seeing Lincoln as an idealized self-invention like himself. But in delving deeper into the micro- and macroeconomic language that is indeed pervasive in Lincoln's thought processes and political actions, one cannot unsee it. Lincoln does transform from a moral idealist to a market pragmatist.

Lincoln's Citadel: The Civil War in Washington, D.C.
Kenneth J. Winkle
W.W. Norton, 2013

Masterful is Kenneth Winkle's central theme: the man and the place evolved in parallel. When Lincoln first arrived as a US congressman, the capital city and he were clearly works in progress. Both were relatively young, reaching for refinement, yet still modest and rough. As Winkle also notes, both failed to flourish under the overbearing weight of ultra-conservative politics, including the ancient institution of human slavery. At the same time, *Lincoln's Citadel* details the hairline cracks in the old system—the ongoing debates over whether slavery should continue in the District of Columbia, the growing proportion of Northern representation in governance, and the sectional hostilities erupting over the conquest of Mexico, while the city itself wallowed in mud and discord like a frontier mining town.

Turning to the Civil War, the author deftly describes (often through ground-level accounts) Washington's explosive transformation from a small city to an overcrowded metropolis. In this regard, one of the book's most valuable contributions is its use of D.C. as a harbinger of America's immediate future, in which rapid industrialization and immigration hyper-urbanizes the East Coast, packing ever more animals and humans into finite spaces, with the resulting bursts of disease, poverty, ethnic segregation, and accentuated disparities in wealth.

As for the war itself, Winkle presents the capital as the nation in microcosm, internally divided, multiracial, a spectrum of classes, forcefully militarized, indirectly and directly traumatized by combat, and entrenched for the duration. Placed in the center of this tumult, the reader gains greater empathy for Lincoln, a person weighed down not only by gargantuan political and military uncertainties but also by ever-present physical and emotional pressure, assaults upon the senses, the hospitals, factories, graveyards growing larger seemingly by the hour.

During the Civil War's centennial, publications focused on battle-fields, the word "battlefield" itself being a misnomer. Combat occurred in people's towns, in and around their homes, overriding their lives and mutating their landscapes. *Lincoln's Citadel* is a prime example of how sesquicentennial histories emerged as a far more complex and encom-passing representation of what Lincoln and the nation endured.

LINCOLN IN THE ATLANTIC WORLD
Louise L. Stevenson
Cambridge University Press, 2015
One of the greatest benefits of the discipline of history is that it pro-vides perspective. In the past half century, historians have increasingly viewed the Atlantic Ocean not as a barrier but as a superhighway. As evidence: you are currently reading a European language, the majority of people who arrived in the Americas between 1500 and 1800 came quite involuntarily from Africa, and part of what fuels your body (and, in some cases, your car) today comes from plants first domesticated in the Americas. Before the Civil War, the United States began to divide between those who looked to Europe's 1848 revolutions and their liberal ideals and those who looked instead to the Caribbean and the Gulf of Mexico to prosper from cash crops and human slavery.

Louise L. Stevenson cleverly selects specific objects and experi-ences in Lincoln's life that illuminate not only his own direct connec-tions to the four Atlantic continents but also the larger national and international questions of his time. Among these chosen lenses are political work with Illinois's German immigrants, a book he had read concerning Barbary pirates capturing and enslaving American sailors, the Emancipation Proclamation as an act of foreign policy (preventing British and French recognition of the Confederacy), and a compelling examination of *Our American Cousin*, a play written by a British citizen about the irreconcilable worldviews of a haughty member of the landed gentry and a rough-hewn Northerner looking for his fair share of the family wealth. Through this approach, Stevenson offers a compelling history approachable to scholars and the general public alike, on a subject that increasingly sees Lincoln's life, the Civil War, and US history altogether as global phenomena.

THE FIERY TRIAL: ABRAHAM LINCOLN AND AMERICAN SLAVERY
Eric Foner
W.W. Norton, 2010
Winner of the Bancroft Prize, the Lincoln Prize, and a Pulitzer, Eric Foner's *Fiery Trial* will certainly resonate with fans of Lincoln, as well as with anyone looking for a politician willing to learn from their mistakes. One of the preeminent historians on the interconnections and continuities between the Civil War and Reconstruction, Foner contends that Lincoln was capable of navigating the Union through the war while simultaneously fracturing its long addiction to legalized slavery not because of any intrinsic genius or destiny. Instead, Lincoln achieved these ends because he was capable of change.

The point is certainly compelling, made more so by Foner charting Lincoln's path from youth through the presidency. Time and again, Lincoln was open to new ideas. A voracious reader, he partook of many genres, from mathematics and law to poetry and logic (see chapter 5, **Books That Most Impacted Lincoln**). By Lincoln's own admission, he was slow to judge or react, rarely succumbed to base emotions (including severe bouts of depression), brooded over problems for long periods, and preferred the middle ground for its inherent room to maneuver. This adaptability, Foner shows, enabled Lincoln to better read and react to the most emotional, divisive issue of the age.

Simultaneously, Foner does not paint his subject as enlightened. Lincoln was very much a product of his time and place—hating slavery but unwilling to attack it wholly and directly until the very end of the Civil War; able to see African Americans as humans, though not as fully equal to his own race; and marrying into a slaveholding family with eyes wide shut. Foner's audience may recognize the intent here. We can come to understand Lincoln better, along with much of his fellow Americans of all ethnicities who hated slavery but didn't know how to eradicate it. Lincoln and his nation were living contradictions, were born so and lived so. It may have required a war to destroy enough of what existed in order to form a more perfect Union.

In the end, Foner wonders, as many of us do, what kind of progress Lincoln could have made during Reconstruction had he lived. While optimistic that the outcome would have been better than what actually transpired, Foner recognizes that it is ultimately unknowable, in no small part because Lincoln himself would likely have changed his own strategies as events unfolded.

Battle Cry of Freedom: The Civil War Era
James M. McPherson
Oxford University Press, 1988

Simultaneously detailed and succinct, James McPherson's Pulitzer Prize winner stands the test of time as one of the most encompassing single-volume works on the war, and it includes Lincoln within its economic, military, political, and social coverage throughout.

Beginning with a snapshot of the nation as a whole in the mid-nineteenth century and moving into a compelling reexamination of the war with Mexico and its effects on a country in transition, McPherson commits considerable space to the foundations of sectional discord. Only the most impatient reader will miss his intent. The Princeton professor interprets the war as inseparable from a myriad of national transformations, especially industrialization and its effect on human labor, and westward expansion's disruption of regional balances.

McPherson's greatest strength is his ability to blend a multitude of facts into flowing prose, crafting more illuminating evidence within a page than some historians accomplish in a chapter. Few corners of the struggle are left untouched, from the plight of the slave to the paper trails of the desk clerk, from the struggles on the home front to the logistics of warfare. Each subject is presented with considerable documentation and sobriety, establishing a level of credibility to this work rarely matched by other histories of popular appeal. He may at times overemphasize the leverage of battles in the course of the war, but he also places those acute engagements within the larger framework of the military campaigns, as well as the economic and political atmospheres, from which they spring.

TEAM OF RIVALS: THE POLITICAL GENIUS OF ABRAHAM LINCOLN
Doris Kearns Goodwin
Simon and Schuster, 2005

Fundamentally, history is the story of human relationships. Goodwin deftly describes the intertwined lives of Lincoln and his key cabinet members, as well as the critical roles of their spouses, in navigating the country through its most lethal struggle to date. Regarding the First Lady in particular, Goodwin presents the image of a political partnership, providing a sympathetic view in the same compelling way as Mary's biographers Jean Baker and Betty Boles Ellison.

Key to the book's popularity, aside from its flowing and informative prose, was its timing. At the time of publication, the United States had become entangled in Afghanistan and Iraq. As the commander-in-chief steadily swept aside his ablest advisers for less scrupulous figures, *Team of Rivals* presented a time when competitive, political animals were able to summon the better angels of their nature. Was Lincoln a political genius? The shortcomings of emancipation and excessive military casualties suggest otherwise. Concerning internal differences, George Washington's cabinet was certainly more divided. Yet Goodwin produced an insightful, engaging view of true icons when the nation needed them most.

Epilogue

It is altogether fitting and proper that we still struggle to understand Lincoln. He was friendly to nearly anyone and yet a mystery to virtually everyone around him. He repeatedly spoke out against slavery but hesitated to abolish it. He lived in the most rural and most urban corners of the country, but he never completely felt at home in either environment. Uncouth in appearance and believing himself ugly, he repeatedly used photography to broadcast his likeness far and wide. Gentle and kind, he presided over the deadliest US war to date. He was a collection of paradoxes, very much like his birth nation.

The United States has not yet come to terms with its own intrinsic, enduring contradictions. Perhaps that is why so many of us keep exploring Lincoln, as a vicarious path to better understand ourselves. We still contend with the same issues Lincoln did—racism, wealth disparities, gender relations, diseases, wars, urbanization, immigration, mental health, the promises and limits of democracy.

One of my favorite takes on the sixteenth president comes from Charles Starling at Lincoln's New Salem State Historic Site. Several years ago, we conversed about the village's most celebrated resident, wondering whether there would ever be an end to the number of books and articles written about him. Starling eventually offered a compelling thought—that conceivably we could never fully exhaust all possible ways to write about him because, said Starling, in the American mind, "Lincoln is infinite."

Conversely, if it were possible to describe the man with a single word, it may be "surveyor," an occupation intimately familiar to him. By his own admission, Lincoln preferred to move forward, navigating "point to point," venturing to guess no further than he could see. It was certainly true that he favored the future. His first law partner John Todd Stuart stated that Lincoln "didn't know anything about history—had no faith in it nor biography." Another contemporary, Joseph Gillespie, confessed, "Mr. Lincoln never I think studied history except in connection with politics. . . . He regarded it as of trifling value as teaching by example." It is indeed ironic that he cared so little for history, especially his own. Famous is his reply to a prying and frustrated campaign biographer during the 1860 campaign for the presidency, John Locke Scripps: "Why, Scripps, it is a great piece of folly to attempt to make anything out of my early life. It can all be condensed into a single sentence and that sentence you will find in Gray's Elegy—'The short and simple annals of the poor.'"

Never fond of his childhood, or his background in general, he loathed to reminisce. He preferred instead to remember a story about something else, usually a humorous one, and even then, the purpose was never to be nostalgic. His tales invariably applied to the moment at hand, the prevailing landscape, and how best to read it.

Arguably, of his primary destinations, he definitely reached one by 1860—the middle class. It is fitting that he spoke of returning to Springfield while president. Life on Eighth and Jackson suited him. A neighborhood that was neither rural nor urban, free from the extremes of either environment, his was the model American dream—kids, a dog, a nice house with a fence (Lincoln had a picket fence installed in 1854).

About anything else, he refused to predict, opting instead to continue moving forward. His most famous speech embodies that conviction. The United States, he told his audience, will always be unfinished work, a great task remaining before us, and one that requires dedication, devotion, resolve. I wish to think that in any national opportunity, problem, question, or crisis, we heed his advice and conduct the hard labor ourselves, rather than hail a lone leader or hallow yet more ground. Lincoln's Gettysburg ideal was not a destination but a form of navigation. And, like the search for the real Lincoln, it *should* be ongoing.

Time Line of Lincoln's Life

1809

February 12:   Nancy Hanks Lincoln gives birth to second child
and first son, Abraham. Delivered in the family
cabin on Sinking Spring Farm, Nolin Creek, near
Hodgenville, Kentucky.

1811

Lincoln family moves ten miles to Knob Creek farm.

1812

Hanks gives birth to second son, Thomas, who dies in
infancy.

1815

Abraham sporadically attends school.

1816

Family moves late in the year to frontier Indiana.

1818

October 5:   Mother Nancy Hanks Lincoln dies of milk sickness.

1819

December 2:   Thomas Lincoln marries widow Sarah Bush Johnston,
who has three children.

1824

Abraham's affection for reading becomes apparent.

1828

January 20:   Abraham's sister Sarah dies in childbirth.
April: Abraham (nineteen) and Allen Gentry pilot a flatboat
              of produce to New Orleans.

1830

March: Lincoln family moves two hundred miles west to
              Illinois along Sangamon River near Decatur.
              Reportedly Abraham gives first public speech,
              promoting improvement of Sangamon River for
              commercial shipping.

1831

Abraham moves to New Salem, Illinois, without his
family.

1832

March: Becomes a candidate for Illinois General assembly.
April: Black Hawk War breaks out. Abraham serves but does
              not see combat.
August: Loses the election for the assembly.
              Lincoln and William Berry purchase village store in
              New Salem.

1833

His store fails, leaving Lincoln badly in debt.
Appointed New Salem postmaster. A few months
later, he becomes deputy county surveyor.

1834

August 4:   Lincoln, twenty-four, elected to the Illinois General
              Assembly and begins to study law.

December: Meets Stephen A. Douglas, twenty-one, for the first
              time.

1835
August 25:   Ann Rutledge, Lincoln's friend, dies at twenty-two.

1836
August 1:   Reelected to the Illinois General Assembly.
September 9: Lincoln receives his law license. Courts Mary Owens,
              twenty-eight.

1837
              Lincoln aids in getting the Illinois state capital moved
              from Vandalia to Springfield.
April 15:   Lincoln settles in Springfield. Partners with lawyer
              John T. Stuart.

1838
August 6:   Reelected to the Illinois General Assembly. Becomes
              Whig floor leader.

1839
December 3:   Admitted as attorney into the United States Circuit
              Court. Meets Mary Todd, twenty-one, at a dance.

1840
June: Lincoln argues his first case before the Illinois Supreme
              Court.
August 3:   Elected to third term in Illinois General Assembly.
Fall: Engaged to Mary Todd.

1841
January 1:   Breaks engagement with Mary Todd. Falls into a deep
              depression.
March 1:   Establishes law partnership with Stephen T. Logan.

1842

Summer: Reinitiates courtship with Mary Todd.
September 22:   Nearly duels with state auditor James Shields over
                letters that mocked Shields.
November 4:   Lincoln weds Mary Todd in Springfield.

1843

August 1:   Mary gives birth to their first child, Robert Todd
                Lincoln.

1844

May: The Lincolns move into home at Eighth and Jackson.
                Begins to campaign for Henry Clay in the presidential
                election.
December: Dissolves law partnership with Logan and then sets up
                his own practice with William Herndon.

1846

March 10:   Mary gives birth to second child, Edward Baker
                Lincoln.
May 1:   Lincoln nominated as Whig candidate for US Congress.
August 3:   Elected to first and only term in US House of
                Representatives.

1847

December 6:   Lincoln and Thirtieth Congress take their seats.
December 22:   Lincoln questions President James K. Polk's actions
                against Mexico.

1848

January 22:   Gives a speech on floor of the House against President
                Polk's war with Mexico.

1849

March 31:   Lincoln returns home to Springfield, planning to
                concentrate on his legal career.
May 22:   Lincoln receives patent on flotation buoys for flatboats.

1850

February 1:   Second son Edward (nearly four years old) dies of
               illness.

December 21:   Third son, William, born in Springfield.

1851

January 17:   Father Thomas Lincoln dies. Abraham does not attend
               the funeral.

1853

April 4:   Fourth son, Thomas, is born.

1854

               Kansas-Nebraska Act passed in Congress, infuriating
               Lincoln and inspiring him to reenter politics.

1855

               Fails in first attempt to become US senator.

1856

               Receives over one hundred Republican Convention
               votes to be party nominee for vice president.

1858

May: Wins his famous "Almanac Case."

June 16:   Republicans nominate him for senator against
               Democrat incumbent Stephen A. Douglas. Great
               Debates follow.

1860

May 18:   Nominated in Chicago as Republican candidate for
               president.

November 6:   Elected sixteenth president of the United States.

December 20:   South Carolina becomes the first state to secede from
               the Union.

1861

January–   Before President-Elect Lincoln is inaugurated,
  March: Mississippi, Florida, Alabama, Georgia, Louisiana,
              and Texas declare separation from the Union
              and form a central government in Montgomery,
              Alabama.
February 11: Lincoln departs Springfield for Washington.
March 4:   Inauguration.
April 12:   South Carolina shells Fort Sumter in Charleston
              Harbor.
April 15:   President Lincoln issues a proclamation calling for
              seventy-five thousand militia and a special convening
              of Congress.
April 17:   Virginia leaves the Union.
April 19:   The president issues blockade of Southern ports in
              rebellion.
April 27:   Lincoln suspends writ of habeas corpus.
June 3:   Senator Stephen A. Douglas dies suddenly, probably of
              rheumatism.
July 21:   Union defeat at First Manassas.
July 27:   Major General George B. McClellan appointed
              military commander of the Department of the
              Potomac.
August 6:   Lincoln signs first Confiscation Act.
September 11: Lincoln revokes General John C. Frémont's
              emancipation decree in Missouri.
November 1:   Announces Major General McClellan as commander
              of Union Army.

1862

February 6:   Fort Henry falls to the Union Army and Navy.
February 16: Fort Donelson falls to the Union Army and Navy.
February 20: William Lincoln, age eleven, dies of illness at the
              White House.
March 11:   McClellan relieved as general-in-chief of Union armies.

April 6–7:   Battle of Shiloh, Tennessee.

April 16:   Slavery abolished in the District of Columbia.

May 20:   Passage of the Homestead Act.

June 19:   Slavery prohibited in future territories.

August 29–30:   Union defeated at Second Manassas. Lincoln dismisses General John Pope.

September 17:   Battle of Antietam, Maryland.

September 22:   Lincoln issues preliminary Emancipation Proclamation.

November 5:   Lincoln places Ambrose Burnside at the head of the Army of the Potomac.

December 13:   Army of the Potomac defeated severely at Fredericksburg, Virginia.

December 31:   West Virginia admitted into the Union.

1863

January 1:   Emancipation Proclamation goes into effect.

January 25:   Joseph Hooker appointed commander of Army of the Potomac.

January 29:   U. S. Grant appointed to lead Union armies in Western Theater.

May 1–4:   Union loses Battle of Chancellorsville, Virginia.

June 28:   George G. Meade appointed head of Army of the Potomac.

July 3:   Union victory at Gettysburg, Pennsylvania.

July 4:   Union capture of Vicksburg, Mississippi.

August 10:   Lincoln meets with Frederick Douglass.

September 19–20:   Union defeat at Chickamauga, Georgia.

November 19:   Gettysburg Address.

December 8:   Proclamation of Amnesty and Reconstruction.

1864

March 12:   Lincoln appoints Grant general-in-chief.

June 8:   Lincoln nominated by coalition "National Union Party."

September 2:   Atlanta falls to Union Army.

November 8:   Reelection over Democrat George B. McClellan, Electoral count 212–21.

December 20:   Sherman completes "March to the Sea" at Savannah, Georgia.

1865

March 4:   Second inauguration.

April 9:   Army of Northern Virginia surrenders at Appomattox, Virginia.

April 10:   Last known photo of Lincoln taken by Alexander Gardner.

April 11:   Last public speech.

April 14:   Shot at Ford's Theatre.

April 15:   Death from brain trauma, 7:22 a.m., Washington, D.C.

Notes

Chapter 1. Lincoln's Homes

1. Mark Neely Jr. and Harold Holzer, *The Lincoln Family Album* (New York: Doubleday, 1990), 13.

2. Kenneth J. Winkle, *The Young Eagle: The Rise of Abraham Lincoln* (Dallas, TX: Taylor Trade, 2001), 3.

3. "Birthplace Farm Title," *Lincoln Lore* (July 10, 1939).

4. Ralph Gray, *Following in Lincoln's Footsteps* (New York: Carroll and Graf, 2001), 215–17; Merrill D. Peterson, *Lincoln in American Memory* (New York: Oxford University Press, 1994), 178–81.

5. David Herbert Donald, *Lincoln* (New York: Touchstone, 1995), 22–23; Michael Burlingame, *Abraham Lincoln: A Life*, 2 vols. (Baltimore: Johns Hopkins University Press, 2008), 1:17–18.

6. "That Half-Faced Camp," *Lincoln Lore* (December 11, 1939). Winkle, *The Young Eagle*, 12.

7. Winkle, *The Young Eagle*, 18.

8. Winkle, *The Young Eagle*, 19.

9. Earl Schenck Miers, ed., *Lincoln Day by Day: A Chronology, 1809–1865* (Dayton, OH: Morningside, 1991), 1:12–15.

10. Burlingame, *Abraham Lincoln*, 1:60.

11. Winkle, *The Young Eagle*, 168.

12. Miers, *Lincoln Day by Day*, 1:151–93.

13. Stacey Pratt McDermott, *Mary Lincoln: Southern Girl, Northern Woman* (New York: Routledge, 2015), 56.

14. *Illinois State Journal* (Springfield, IL), January 2, 1850, p. 1.

15. Richard Lawrence Miller, *Lincoln and His World: Vol. 3, The Rise to National Prominence, 1843–1853* (Jefferson, NC: McFarland, 2011), 3–4. Robert L. Henn, *Lincoln and Darwin: Two Men Who Shaped the World* (Pittsburgh, PA: Dorrance Publishing, 2010), 48. Betty Boles Ellison, *The True Mary Todd Lincoln: A Biography* (Jefferson, NC: McFarland, 2014), 56–57.

16. Miers, *Lincoln Day by Day*, 1:219; Katherine B. Menz, *The Lincoln Home: Lincoln Home National Historic Site, Springfield, Illinois* (Harpers Ferry, WV: National Park Service, 1983), 5.

17. Bonnie E. Paull and Richard E. Hart, *Lincoln's Springfield Neighborhood* (Charleston, SC: History Press, 2015), 30.

18. Robert A. Nowlen, *The American Presidents from Polk to Hayes* (Denver, CO: Outskirts Press, 2016), 310.

19. Paul Angle, *"Here I Have Lived": A History of Lincoln's Springfield* (Springfield, IL: Abraham Lincoln Association, 1955), 148.

20. Ida M. Tarbell, *Life of Abraham Lincoln*, 4 vols. (New York: Lincoln Memorial Association, 1900), 1:209.

21. Ruth Painter Randall, *Mary Lincoln: Biography of a Marriage* (Boston: Little, Brown and Co., 1953), 139–41.

22. Angle, *"Here I Have Lived,"* 176.

23. "All the sorrows of my life" from Justin Turner and Linda Turner, *Mary Todd Lincoln: Her Life and Letters* (New York: A.A. Knopf, 1972), 273. "I am beginning to feel so perfectly at home" from Neely and Holzer, *The Lincoln Family Album*, 6.

24. "That damned old house" from Matthew Pinsker, *Lincoln's Sanctuary: Abraham Lincoln and the Soldiers' Home* (New York: Oxford University Press, 2003), 77.

25. Pinsker, *Lincoln's Sanctuary*, 7.

26. Ralph Gary, *Following in Lincoln's Footsteps* (New York: Carroll and Graf, 2001), 124.

CHAPTER 2. LINCOLN'S GREATEST MENTORS

1. Sumner quoted in M. L. Houser, *Lincoln's Education and Other Essays* (New York: Bookman Associates, 1958), 94. Historian Kenneth Winkle presents a compelling biography of the young Lincoln, with an underlying theme of "the myth of the self-made Lincoln," where Lincoln exaggerated his modest lineage and impoverished childhood for political effect.

2. Douglas Wilson, Terry Wilson, and Rodney Davis, eds., *Herndon's Informants* (Urbana: University of Illinois Press, 1998), 108.

3. William Barton, *The Women Lincoln Loved* (Indianapolis: Bobbs-Merrill, 1927), 66.

4. Barton, *The Women Lincoln Loved*, 65–66.

5. Lincoln biographer William Barton contends that the teenage Nancy Hanks "attended school and had gained the rudiments of a common education." Barton, *The Women Lincoln Loved*, 66.

6. Roy Basler, ed., *The Collected Works of Abraham Lincoln* (New Brunswick, NJ: Rutgers University Press, 1953), 1:456. Scripps's campaign biography quoted from Mark Neely Jr., *The Abraham Lincoln Encyclopedia* (New York: McGraw-Hill, 1982), 14. William H. Herndon and Jesse W. Weik, *Herndon's Lincoln: A True Story of a Great Life* (Reprinted New York: Cosimo, 2009), 11. For an insightful look into the merits of the mawkish Holland biography, see Allen C. Guelzo, "Holland's Informants: The Construction of Josiah Holland's 'Life of Abraham Lincoln,'" *Journal of the Abraham Lincoln Association* 23, no. 1 (Winter 2002): 1–53.

7. Harold Briggs and Ernestine Briggs, *Nancy Hanks Lincoln* (New York: Bookman Associates, 1952), 77. Louis A. Warren, *Lincoln's Youth* (Indianapolis: Indiana Historical Society, 2002), 193.

8. Mrs. Sarah Johnston Lincoln quoted in Arthur Bestor, David Mearns, and Jonathan Daniels, *Three Presidents and Their Books* (Urbana: University of Illinois Press, 1955), 51–52.

9. Wilson et al., *Herndon's Informants*, 122.

10. Mrs. Sarah Johnston Lincoln quoted in Bestor et al., *Three Presidents*, 51–52. Neely, *The Abraham Lincoln Encyclopedia*, 333. David H. Donald, *Lincoln* (New York: Touchstone, 1995), 24. Wilson et al., *Herndon's Informants*, 145, 149.

11. Barton, *The Women Lincoln Loved*, 102–3.

12. "Abraham gave me never one hard word . . ." from Barton, *The Women Lincoln Loved*, 108. "He was the best boy I ever saw," and "His mind and mine . . ." from Wilson et al., *Herndon's Informants*, 107, 108.

13. Houser, *Lincoln's Education and Other Essays*, 21–22.

14. Description of Rutledge from Benjamin Thomas, *Lincoln's New Salem* (New York: Knopf, 1954), 4, 29. Houser, *Lincoln's Education and Other Essays*, 23. Benjamin Thomas, *Lincoln's Humor and Other Essays* (Urbana: University of Illinois Press, 2002), 73–75.

15. Ronald C. White Jr., *A. Lincoln: A Biography* (New York: Random House, 2009), 48–49.

16. Neely, *The Abraham Lincoln Encyclopedia*, 126.

17. Neely, *The Abraham Lincoln Encyclopedia*, 126. Houser, *Lincoln's Education and Other Essays*, 92, 108–9. Rutledge quoted in John J. Duff, *A. Lincoln: Prairie Lawyer* (New York: Bramhall House, 1960), 11.

18. Thomas, *Lincoln's New Salem*, 71, and Duff, *A. Lincoln: Prairie Lawyer*, 11.

19. Duff, *A. Lincoln: Prairie Lawyer*, 11–12. Albert Woldman, *Lawyer Lincoln* (Boston: Houghton Mifflin, 1936), 20.

20. Benjamin Thomas, *Abraham Lincoln: A Biography* (New York: Modern Library, 1968), 41.

21. Woldman, *Lawyer Lincoln*, 24.

22. Houser, *Lincoln's Education and Other Essays*, 21–22. Thomas, *Lincoln's New Salem*, 44, 70. Duff, *A. Lincoln: Prairie Lawyer*, 11. Donald, *Lincoln*, 47.

23. Duff, *A. Lincoln: Prairie Lawyer*, 12. Ferenc Morton Szasz, *Abraham Lincoln and Robert Burns: Connected Lives and Legends* (Carbondale: Southern Illinois University Press, 2008), 61–63. Earl Schenck Miers, *Lincoln Day by Day, Vol. I* (Dayton, OH: Morningside, 1991), 38. Mary Turner, "Will the Real Jack Kelso Please Stand Up?" *For the People: Newsletter of the Abraham Lincoln Association*, 1, no. 4 (Winter 1999): 1–2. US Federal Census of 1850, District 52, Macon, Missouri, Roll M432, p. 169A [Ancestry.com]. Richard Lawrence Miller, *Lincoln and His World: The Early Years* (Mechanicsburg, PA: Stackpole Books, 2006), 240.

24. Herndon and Weik, *Herndon's Lincoln*, 93.

25. *History of Sangamon County, Illinois* (Chicago: Inter-State, 1881), 216.

26. *History of Sangamon County, Illinois*, 217. Bonnie E. Paul and Richard E. Hart, *Lincoln's Springfield Neighborhood* (Charleston, SC: History Press, 2015), 27.

27. Basler, *Collected Works of Abraham Lincoln*, 1:15. "Whether elected or not" from Herndon and Weik, *Herndon's Lincoln*, 134.

28. Herndon and Weik, *Herndon's Lincoln*, 179.

29. Neely, *The Abraham Lincoln Encyclopedia*, 116–17.

30. Thomas, *Abraham Lincoln: A Biography*, 46–47.

31. Brian Dirck, *Lincoln the Lawyer* (Urbana: University of Illinois Press, 2007), 21. Duff, *A. Lincoln: Prairie Lawyer*, 8. Herndon and Weik, *Herndon's Lincoln*, 270.

32. Duff, *A. Lincoln: Prairie Lawyer*, 9-10. Thomas, *Abraham Lincoln: A Biography*, 42–43.
33. Paul Angle, *"Here I Have Lived": A History of Lincoln's Springfield* (Springfield, IL: Abraham Lincoln Association, 1955), 110. Lincoln quoted in Daniel Stowell, "Almost a Father to Me," *Lincoln Legal Briefs* (October–December 2007), 1.
34. Logan quoted in Miers, *Lincoln Day by Day*, 1:29.
35. Dirck, *Lincoln the Lawyer*, 26. Kermit L. Hall, ed., *The Oxford Companion to American Law* (New York: Oxford University Press, 2002), 525. Duff, *A. Lincoln: Prairie Lawyer*, 94.
36. Duff, *A. Lincoln: Prairie Lawyer*, 95. Angle, *"Here I Have Lived,"* 238. Neely, *The Abraham Lincoln Encyclopedia*, 194.

CHAPTER 3. MARY AND ABE COMMONALITIES

1. Jean H. Baker, *Mary Todd Lincoln: A Biography* (New York: W.W. Norton, 1987), 19–20.
2. Baker, *Mary Todd Lincoln*, 20–21.
3. Catherine Clinton, *Mrs. Lincoln: A Life* (New York: Harper, 2009), 15.
4. Clinton, *Mrs. Lincoln*, 17. David H. Donald, *Lincoln* (New York: Touchstone, 1995), 85.
5. Baker, *Mary Todd Lincoln*, 117, 209–10, 290–92. Mark Neely Jr. and Harold Holzer, *The Lincoln Family Album* (New York: Doubleday, 1990), 20.
6. Baker, *Mary Todd Lincoln*, "imagine that others were as seldom gladdened," 91; "my dearest partner of greatness," 148.
7. Baker, *Mary Todd Lincoln*, 16.
8. Baker, *Mary Todd Lincoln*, 54–57.
9. Mary did write to her stepmother-in-law once, but it was two years after Lincoln's death. Neely and Holzer, *The Lincoln Family Album*, 14. The story of Lincoln comparing God to the Todds from Stephen Berry, *House of Abraham: Lincoln and the Todds, a Family Divided by War* (New York: Houghton Mifflin, 2007), xi; Clinton, *Mrs. Lincoln*, 5.
10. Neely and Holzer, *The Lincoln Family Album*, 15.
11. Neely and Holzer, *The Lincoln Family Album*, 7–8; Benjamin Thomas, *Abraham Lincoln* (New York: Modern Library, 1968), 484.
12. Baker, *Mary Todd Lincoln*, 32–35; "The Lone Whig from Illinois," *Lincoln Lore* (May 20, 1940).
13. *Sangamo Journal*, March 15, 1832; Earl Schenck Miers, ed., *Lincoln Day by Day* (Dayton, OH: Morningside, 1991), 1:32.
14. Justin Turner and Linda Turner, *Mary Todd Lincoln: Her Life and Letters* (New York: A.A. Knopf, 1972), 21.
15. Robert V. Remini, *Henry Clay: Statesman for the Union* (New York: W.W. Norton, 1991), xiii.
16. Berry, *House of Abraham*, 21–22.
17. Edgar De Witt Jones, *The Influence of Henry Clay on Abraham Lincoln* (Lexington, KY: Henry Clay Memorial Foundation, 1952), 21.

18. See Remini, *Henry Clay*, on Clay's slavery policy, 178–80; "It has been my invariable rule," xxix.

19. Mary Todd's niece quoted in Paul Angle, *The Lincoln Reader* (New Brunswick, NJ: Rutgers University Press, 1947), 123. For "ruddy pine knot," see Baker, *Mary Todd Lincoln*, 83.

20. Baker, *Mary Todd Lincoln*, 118, 195.

21. Benjamin Barondess, *Three Lincoln Masterpieces* (Charleston, WV: Education Foundation of West Virginia, 1954), 9.

22. For descriptions of Lincoln's physical appearance when he spoke, see Baker, *Mary Todd Lincoln*, 83–84; Donald, *Lincoln*, 274.

23. Thomas, *Abraham Lincoln*, 100.

24. Baker, *Mary Todd Lincoln*, 120.

25. Donald, *Lincoln*, 309.

26. Roy Basler, ed., *The Collected Works of Abraham Lincoln* (New Brunswick, NJ: Rutgers University Press, 1953), 8:395.

CHAPTER 4. LINCOLN'S CLOSEST FRIENDS

1. Roy P. Basler, ed., *The Collected Works of Abraham Lincoln* (New Brunswick, NJ: Rutgers University Press, 1953), 5:117, 125, 133. Robert Lincoln quoted in Mark Neely Jr. and Harold Holzer, *The Lincoln Family Album* (New York: Doubleday, 1990), 33. David H. Donald, *We Are Lincoln Men* (New York: Simon and Schuster, 2003), 213–17. Joshua F. Speed, *Reminiscences of Abraham Lincoln* (Louisville, KY: Bradley and Gilbert, 1896), 23.

2. Douglas L. Wilson, *Lincoln's Sword* (New York: Vintage Books, 2006), 28.

3. Brian Dirck, *Lincoln the Lawyer* (Urbana: University of Illinois Press, 2007), 48–50. Thomas J. Craughwell, *Stealing Lincoln's Body* (Cambridge, MA: Belknap Press, 2007), 139.

4. Jean H. Baker, *Mary Todd Lincoln: A Biography* (New York: W.W. Norton, 1987), 196.

5. "I can never be satisfied" from Paul Angle, *The Lincoln Reader* (New Brunswick, NJ: Rutgers University Press, 1947), 122. "I am quite as lonesome here" from Basler, *Collected Works of Abraham Lincoln*, 1:78.

6. John Hay's view of Mrs. Lincoln shown in a letter from Hay to John Nicolay, in Tyler Dennett, ed., *Lincoln and the Civil War: In the Diaries and Letters of John Hay* (New York: Dodd and Mead, 1939), 41.

7. Basler, *Collected Works of Abraham Lincoln*, 1:465.

8. Neely and Holzer, *The Lincoln Family Album*, 4.

9. David H. Bates, *Lincoln in the Telegraph Office* (New York: The Century Company, 1907), 208.

10. Basler, *Collected Works of Abraham Lincoln*, 1:320.

11. Joshua Speed quoted in Kenneth J. Winkle, *The Young Eagle: The Rise of Abraham Lincoln* (Dallas, TX: Taylor Trade, 2001), 168.

12. Bonnie E. Paull and Richard E. Hart, *Lincoln's Springfield Neighborhood* (Charleston, SC: History Press, 2015), 41; Earl Schenck Miers, ed., *Lincoln Day by Day* (Dayton, OH: Morningside, 1991), 1:295.

13. Basler, *Collected Works of Abraham Lincoln*, 2:323.

14. Basler, *Collected Works of Abraham Lincoln*, 2:320.

15. Douglas L. Wilson, Terry Wilson, and Rodney O. Davis, eds., *Herndon's Informants: Letters, Interviews, and Statements about Abraham Lincoln* (Urbana: University of Illinois Press, 1998), 499; Speed, *Reminiscences*, 26.

16. Douglas L. Wilson, *Honor's Voice: The Transformation of Abraham Lincoln* (New York: A.A. Knopf, 1998), 19–51.

17. Wilson et al., *Herndon's Informants*, 165.

18. Daniel W. Stowell, ed., *The Papers of Abraham Lincoln: Legal Documents and Cases* (Charlottesville, VA: University of Virginia Press, 2008), 2:1–2.

19. William Herndon and Jesse Weik, *Herndon's Life of Lincoln* (New York: Da Capo Press, 1983), xv.

20. Paul Finkelman and Martin Hershock, eds., *The Political Lincoln: An Encyclopedia* (Washington, DC: CQ Press, 2009), 324–26. Herndon quoted speaking to his coauthor Jesse Weik, *Herndon-Weik Collection*, Library of Congress, February 24, 1887. Mary Lincoln quoted in John J. Duff, *A. Lincoln: Prairie Lawyer* (New York: Bramhall House, 1960), 99.

21. Ted Widmer, *Lincoln on the Verge: Thirteen Days to Washington* (New York: Simon and Schuster, 2020), 108.

22. Douglas L. Wilson, "Herndon's Dilemma: Abraham Lincoln and the Privacy Issue," *Lincoln Lore* 1877 (Summer 2004): 3.

23. Mark Neely Jr., *The Abraham Lincoln Encyclopedia* (New York: McGraw-Hill, 1982), 15–16.

24. Harry C. Blair and Rebecca Tarshis, *The Life of Colonel Edward D. Baker: Lincoln's Constant Ally* (Portland: Oregon Historical Society, 1960), 116.

25. Basler, *Collected Works of Abraham Lincoln*, 8:293–94.

26. Neely, *The Abraham Lincoln Encyclopedia*, 299.

27. Robert S. Eckley, "Lincoln's Intimate Friend: Leonard Swett," *Journal of the Illinois State Historical Society* 92, no. 3 (Autumn 1999): 274–88.

CHAPTER 5. BOOKS THAT MOST IMPACTED LINCOLN

1. Sarah Bush Johnston Lincoln quoted in Douglas L. Wilson, *Lincoln's Sword* (New York: Vintage Books, 2006), 21. Historian David Mearns skillfully dismantles the myth that either Nancy Hanks Lincoln or Dennis Hanks taught Lincoln the basics of literacy (a myth initiated by Dennis Hanks himself). Instead, Mearns and others contend that learning to read for Lincoln was a sporadic and slow process, taking years to culminate into functionality. Arthur Bestor, David Mearns, and Jonathan Daniels, *Three Presidents and Their Books* (Urbana: University of Illinois Press, 1955). For a list of items President Lincoln checked out (but may have not read) from the Library of Congress, see *Lincoln Lore* no. 129 (September 28, 1931).

2. Farmer quoted in Brian Dirck, *Lincoln the Lawyer* (Urbana: University of Illinois Press, 2007), 15. "The things I want to know . . ." in Albert A. Woldman, *Lawyer Lincoln* (Boston: Houghton Mifflin, 1936), 11.

3. David H. Donald, *Lincoln* (New York: Touchstone, 1995), 51; Emanuel Hertz, ed., *Lincoln Talks: An Oral Biography* (New York: Bramhall House, 1986), 17–18; Carl H.

NOTES

Scheele, *A Short History of the Mail Service* (Washington, DC: Smithsonian Institute Press, 1970), 70.

4. Herndon's recollection of Lincoln's quote "When I read aloud . . ." from Bestor et al., *Three Presidents and Their Books*, 86.

5. Ralph Gary, *Following in Lincoln's Footsteps* (New York: Carroll and Graf, 2001), 372–73. "The great invention of the world" from Wilson, *Lincoln's Sword*, 41.

6. "A capacity and taste for reading" from Archer Shaw, ed., *The Lincoln Encyclopedia* (New York: Macmillan, 1950), 266. "My best friend" from Woldman, *Lawyer Lincoln*, 11.

7. The story of Lincoln discovering Blackstone's *Commentaries* at the bottom of a barrel is taken from Hertz, *Lincoln Talks*, 16. The version where he purchased the editions at an auction is from John J. Duff, *A. Lincoln: Prairie Lawyer* (New York: Bramhall House, 1960), 16; and Benjamin Thomas, *Abraham Lincoln: A Biography* (New York: Modern Library, 1968), 43.

8. Jefferson quoted in Kermit L. Hall, ed., *The Oxford Companion to American Law* (New York: Oxford University Press, 2002), 68.

9. Earl Schenck Miers, ed., *Lincoln Day by Day* (Dayton, OH: Morningside, 1991), 2:292.

10. Lincoln's reflections on Shakespeare from Bestor et al., *Three Presidents and Their Books*, 79–80.

11. David H. Bates, *Lincoln in the Telegraph Office* (New York: The Century Company, 1907), 223.

12. Bates, *Lincoln in the Telegraph Office*, 223; Miers, *Lincoln Day by Day*, 2:211, 243.

13. M. L. Houser, *Lincoln's Education and Other Essays* (New York: Bookman Associates, 1958), 124; Miers, *Lincoln Day by Day*, 2:203, 327; Bestor et al., *Three Presidents and Their Books*, 80.

14. Harold Holzer, ed., *Lincoln as I Knew Him* (Chapel Hill, NC: Algonquin Books, 2009), 14.

15. Houser, *Lincoln's Education and Other Essays*, 153. Robert Todd Lincoln quoted in Mark E. Neely Jr., *The Abraham Lincoln Encyclopedia* (New York: McGraw-Hill, 1982), 34. Though his public speeches contained an increase of spiritual language after 1862, it was not automatic. For example, Salmon P. Chase recommended the "God" passage in the Emancipation Proclamation, and Lincoln obliged. Houser, *Lincoln's Education and Other Essays*, 133, 166. For further reading, see Allen C. Guelzo, "Abraham Lincoln and the Doctrine of Necessity," *Journal of the Abraham Lincoln Association* (Winter 1997): 57–82; Ward Hill Lamon, *Recollections of Abraham Lincoln, 1847–1865* (Lincoln: University of Nebraska Press, 1994).

16. Roy Basler, ed., *The Collected Works of Abraham Lincoln* (New Brunswick, NJ: Rutgers University Press, 1953), 4:62.

17. Basler, *Collected Works of Abraham Lincoln*, 4:62. Bestor et al., *Three Presidents and Their Books*, 73.

18. Basler, *Collected Works of Abraham Lincoln*, 3:186.

19. Hertz, *Lincoln Talks*, 8.

20. "The wickedness of being cruel to animals" is a quote from Lincoln's Indiana schoolmate Nathaniel Grigsby in Louis Warren, *Lincoln's Youth* (Indianapolis: Indiana Historical Society Press, 2002), 169; Houser, *Lincoln's Education and Other Essays*, 115.

21. Basler, *Collected Works of Abraham Lincoln*, 1:308, 308n315.

22. Marcus Cunliffe, introduction to Mason Locke Weems, *The Life of George Washington* (Cambridge, MA: Harvard University Press, 1962), xxiv.

23. Shaw, *The Lincoln Encyclopedia*, 384. Basler, *Collected Works of Abraham Lincoln*, 4:234–35.

24. Weems, *The Life of George Washington*, 124.

25. Noah Brooks, *Abraham Lincoln: His Youth and Early Manhood, with a Brief Account of His Later Life* (New York: G.P. Putnam's Sons, 1901), 21; Houser, *Lincoln's Education and Other Essays*, 137.

26. Stanley Kunitz and Howard Haycraft, eds., *British Authors before 1800: A Biographical Dictionary* (New York: H.W. Wilson, 1952), 71–74. See also Carol McGuirk, ed., *Critical Essays on Robert Burns* (New York: Simon and Schuster, 1998).

27. Basler, *Collected Works of Abraham Lincoln*, 8:237.

CHAPTER 6. ANIMALS IN LINCOLN'S WORLD

1. Bill on Estrays, introduced December 6, 1834, Roy Basler, ed., *The Collected Works of Abraham Lincoln* (New Brunswick, NJ: Rutgers University Press, 1953), 2:27–28.

2. Henry Cabot Lodge, *George Washington, Vol. 2* (Berkeley: University of California Press, 1927), 168. Paul C. Nagel, *John Quincy Adams: A Public Life, a Private Life* (Cambridge, MA: Harvard University Press, 1999), 307. Joshua F. Speed, *Reminiscences of Abraham Lincoln* (Louisville, KY: Bradley and Gilbert, 1896), 25.

3. Sandra Choron and Harry Choron, *Planet Dog: A Doglopedia* (Boston: Houghton Mifflin, 2005), 18–21. Roy Rowan and Brooke Janis, *First Dogs: American Presidents and Their Best Friends* (Chapel Hill, NC: Algonquin, 2009), 123–35.

4. Emanuel Hertz, *The Hidden Lincoln: From the Letters and Papers of William H. Herndon* (New York: Blue Ribbon, 1940), 227–28.

5. Bonnie E. Paull and Richard E. Hart, *Lincoln's Springfield Neighborhood* (Charleston, SC: History Press, 2015), 135–36. Matthew Algeo, *Abe and Fido: Lincoln's Love of Animals and the Touching Story of His Favorite Canine Companion* (Chicago: Chicago Review Press, 2015), 54.

6. Charles M. Segal, *Conversations with Lincoln* (New Brunswick, NJ: Transaction Publishers, 1961), 272.

7. Basler, *Collected Works of Abraham Lincoln*, "as a bull-dog guards his master's door," 6:163; "better to give your path to a dog," 6:538; "hold on with a bull-dog grip," 7:499.

8. John C. Waugh, *Reelecting Lincoln* (New York: Crown Publishers, 1997), 48.

9. Rufus R. Wilson, *Lincoln among His Friends* (Caldwell, ID: Caxton Printers, 1942), 97.

10. David S. Reynolds, *Abe: Abraham Lincoln in His Times* (New York: Penguin Press, 2020), 920.

11. Lincoln trying to save the White House horses from a fire in Benjamin Thomas, *Abraham Lincoln* (New York: Modern Library, 1968), 304. Estimates of equine casualty rates in the Civil War from Gene C. Armistead, *Horses and Mules in the Civil War* (Jefferson, NC: McFarland, 2013), 7–8.

12. "Horse high, bull strong, and pig tight" axiom from Louis A. Warren, *Lincoln's Youth* (Indianapolis: Indiana Historical Society, 2002), 144. Mass production of cattle detailed in

William Cronon, *Nature's Metropolis: Chicago and the Great West* (New York: W.W. Norton, 2009), 221–22. Hogs roaming in Springfield from Paul Angle, *"Here I Have Lived": A History of Lincoln's Springfield* (Springfield, IL: Abraham Lincoln Association, 1955), 91. Hog population in Illinois from Basler, *Collected Works of Abraham Lincoln*, 1:401.

13. Basler, *Collected Works of Abraham Lincoln*, 4:63–65.

14. Basler, *Collected Works of Abraham Lincoln*, 2:245–46.

15. David H. Donald, *Lincoln* (New York: Touchstone, 1995), 26.

16. Amy Stewart, *Wicked Plants: The Weed that Killed Lincoln's Mother and Other Botanical Atrocities* (Chapel Hill, NC: Algonquin Books, 2009), 14.

17. Francis B. Carpenter, *Six Months at the White House with Abraham Lincoln* (New York: Herd and Houghton, 1866), 260–61.

18. David H. Donald, *Lincoln at Home: Two Glimpses of Abraham Lincoln's Family Life* (New York: Simon and Schuster, 2000), 27–28.

19. Leslie J. Perry, "Lincoln's Home Life in Washington," *Harper's New Monthly Magazine* 96 (December 1896–May 1897): 357.

20. Perry, "Lincoln's Home Life in Washington," 357. Basler, *Collected Works of Abraham Lincoln*, 7:371–72.

21. Charles G. Leland, *Abraham Lincoln and the Abolition of Slavery in the United States* (New York: G.P. Putnam, 1881), 21. Michael Burlingame, *Abraham Lincoln: A Life* (Baltimore, MD: Johns Hopkins University Press, 2008), 62.

22. Speed, *Reminiscences*, 25–26.

23. Speed, *Reminiscences*, 31–32.

CHAPTER 7. LINCOLN'S FAVORITE WASHINGTON SANCTUARIES

1. Kenneth J. Winkle, *Lincoln's Citadel: The Civil War in Washington, D.C.* (New York: W.W. Norton, 2013), 14–16.

2. Winkle, *Lincoln's Citadel*, 462n.

3. Matthew Pinsker, *Lincoln's Sanctuary: Abraham Lincoln and the Soldiers' Home* (New York: Oxford University Press, 2003), 7.

4. Pinsker, *Lincoln's Sanctuary*, 2.

5. Pinsker, *Lincoln's Sanctuary*, 5.

6. Pinsker, *Lincoln's Sanctuary*, 109.

7. David H. Bates, *Lincoln in the Telegraph Office* (New York: The Century Company, 1907), 277.

8. Tom Wheeler, *Mr. Lincoln's T-Mails* (New York: Collins, 2006), 9.

9. Douglas L. Wilson, *Lincoln's Sword* (New York: Vintage Books, 2006), 114–16.

10. Bates, *Lincoln in the Telegraph Office*, 9, 46; Earl Schenck Miers, ed., *Lincoln Day by Day* (Dayton, OH: Morningside, 1991), 3:294; "working as fast as you can" from Miers, 3:68.

11. Bates, *Lincoln in the Telegraph Office*, 302–3, 367–68.

12. Alexander Hunter and J. H. Polkinhorn, *History of the New National Theater* (Washington, DC: Polkinhorn, 1885), 44–46.

13. Richard Selcer, *Civil War America: 1850–1875* (New York: Facts on File, 2006), 349–50; Miers, *Lincoln Day by Day*, 3:171.

14. Ernest B. Furgurson, *Freedom Rising: Washington in the Civil War* (New York: Vintage Books, 2005), 375–76; Miers, *Lincoln Day by Day*, 3:175, 242–45, 251, 320.

15. Craig L. Symonds, *Lincoln and His Admirals* (New York: Oxford University Press, 2008), x.
16. Miers, *Lincoln Day by Day*, 3:99.
17. Ralph Gary, *Following in Lincoln's Footsteps* (New York: Carroll and Graf, 2001), 380.
18. George J. Olszewski, *Restoration of Ford's Theatre* (Washington, DC: US Department of the Interior, 1963), 7, 11.
19. Patricia Faust, *Historical Times Illustrated Encyclopedia of the Civil War* (New York: HarperCollins, 1991), 268.
20. Olszewski, *Restoration of Ford's Theatre*, xii, 105.
21. Browning quoted in Miers, *Lincoln Day by Day*, 3:82.
22. *Washington Chronicle*, April 1, 1863.

CHAPTER 8. LINCOLN'S EARLY JOBS AND PROFESSIONS

1. Archer Shaw, ed., *The Lincoln Encyclopedia* (New York: Macmillan, 1950), 179.
2. Roy Basler, ed., *The Collected Works of Abraham Lincoln* (New Brunswick, NJ: Rutgers University Press, 1953), 5:238.
3. "I was raised to farm work" from autobiography notes sent to Jesse Fell in 1859, quoted in Basler, *Collected Works of Abraham Lincoln*, 3:511.
4. On Lincoln's views on aspects of wage labor and the rights of the enslaved, see Gabor S. Boritt, *Lincoln and the Economics of the American Dream* (Memphis, TN: Memphis State University Press, 1978).
5. Earl Schenck Miers, ed., *Lincoln Day by Day* (Dayton, OH: Morningside, 1991), 1:10; Kenneth J. Winkle, *The Young Eagle: The Rise of Abraham Lincoln* (Dallas, TX: Taylor Trade, 2001), 19–20. Lincoln's 1834 campaign foray into a field of thirty harvesters from David H. Donald, *Lincoln* (New York: Touchstone, 1995), 52.
6. Description of Decatur convention wigwam from James T. Hickey, "Olgesby's Fence Rail Dealings and the 1860 Decatur Convention," *Journal of the Illinois State Historical Society (1908–1984)* 54, no. 1 (Spring 1961): 8–9.
7. Benjamin Thomas, *Abraham Lincoln: A Biography* (New York: Modern Library, 1968), 206–7.
8. Shaw, *The Lincoln Encyclopedia*, 18.
9. Louis A. Warren, *Lincoln's Youth* (Indianapolis: Indiana Historical Society, 2002), 144.
10. Warren, *Lincoln's Youth*, 144–45.
11. Josiah Holland, *The Life of Abraham Lincoln* (Springfield, MA: G. Bill, 1866), 34.
12. John J. Duff, *A. Lincoln: Prairie Lawyer* (New York: Bramhall House, 1960), 4. Albert A. Woldman, *Lawyer Lincoln* (Boston: Houghton Mifflin, 1936), 8–9.
13. There is a contention that Lincoln first took a flatboat to New Orleans in 1826. This is an unsubstantiated claim made by William Forsythe of Grandview, Indiana, who said that a seventeen-year-old Lincoln and Jefferson Ray made the trip. Lincoln himself refutes this statement in his campaign "autobiography" of 1860 penned by John Scripps. See also Warren, *Lincoln's Youth*, 259n.
14. Basler, *Collected Works of Abraham Lincoln*, 4:62; Ralph Gary, *Following in Lincoln's Footsteps* (New York: Carroll and Graf, 2001), 231.

15. Traditions persist that Lincoln, when seeing slaves being sold in New Orleans, responded with anger. The quote "If I ever get a chance to hit this thing, I'll hit it hard" comes from one Bess V. Ehrmann, who heard it from her relative Absalom Gentry, who stated that he heard it from his father Allen Gentry, who offered the recollection many years after his trip with Lincoln. There are similar statements from John Hanks regarding his trip with Lincoln to New Orleans in 1831. But Hanks could never have witnessed Lincoln make the statement, as he only went downriver with the flatboat party as far as St. Louis. Warren, *Lincoln's Youth*, 184–86, 261n48; Basler, *Collected Works of Abraham Lincoln*, 4:64.

16. Basler, *Collected Works of Abraham Lincoln*, 1:320.

17. Michael Allen, *Western Rivermen, 1763–1861* (Baton Rouge: Louisiana State University Press, 1994), 171; Warren, *Lincoln's Youth*, 175–76.

18. Basler, *Collected Works of Abraham Lincoln*, 4:64.

19. Thomas Reep, *Lincoln at New Salem* (Petersburg, IL: Old Salem Lincoln League, 1927), 98. Benjamin Thomas, *Lincoln's New Salem* (New York: Knopf, 1954), 62–63. Ronald C. White Jr., *A. Lincoln: A Biography* (New York: Random House, 2009), 46.

20. Miers, *Lincoln Day by Day*, 1:17.

21. Bogue quoted in *Sangamo Journal*, January 26, 1832.

22. Miers, *Lincoln Day by Day*, 1:16–17.

23. Donald, *Lincoln*, 43; William Herndon and Jesse Weik, *Herndon's Life of Lincoln* (New York: Da Capo Press, 1983), xv; John Nicolay, *A Short Life of Abraham Lincoln* (New York: Century, 1902), 28; White, *A. Lincoln*, 48.

24. Nicolay, *Short Life of Abraham Lincoln*, 38.

25. Basler, *Collected Works of Abraham Lincoln*, 4:62; Miers, *Lincoln Day by Day*, 1:17.

26. Kerry A. Trask, *Black Hawk* (New York: Henry Holt, 2006), 251.

27. Miers, *Lincoln Day by Day*, 1:21.

28. Miers, *Lincoln Day by Day*, 1:21. Taylor's quote at 1:24.

29. Spencer C. Tucker, ed., *Encyclopedia of American Military History* (New York: Facts on File, 2003), 1:101–2.

30. Donald, *Lincoln*, 47–49; Miers, *Lincoln Day by Day*, 1:32; Reep, *Lincoln at New Salem*, 103–4.

31. Donald, *Lincoln*, 47–48.

32. It is not definitely known whether Berry had a drinking problem, but he evidently possessed a marginal work ethic. See Donald, *Lincoln*, 49; Reep, *Lincoln at New Salem*, 103–4.

33. Miers, *Lincoln Day by Day*, 1:55–56; Nicolay, *Short Life of Abraham Lincoln*, 28.

34. Carl H. Scheele, *A Short History of the Mail Service* (Washington, DC: Smithsonian Institute Press, 1970), 63–74.

35. Richard R. John, *Spreading the News: The American Postal System from Franklin to Morse* (Cambridge, MA: Harvard University Press, 1995), 112–13; Scheele, *Short History of the Mail Service*, 66, 70.

36. "To make his politics an objection" from Miers, *Lincoln Day by Day*, 1:34. The story of the women of New Salem lobbying for Lincoln's appointment comes from Reep, *Lincoln at New Salem*, 57–58. Donald, *Lincoln*, 51; Emanuel Hertz, ed., *Lincoln Talks:*

An Oral Biography (New York: Bramhall House, 1986), 17–18; Scheele, *A Short History of the Mail Service*, 70; Thomas, *Abraham Lincoln*, 42.

37. "Studied Flint, and Gibson a little" from Thomas, *Abraham Lincoln*, 40, 52. For further detail on Lincoln's brief surveying career, see also Adin Baber, *A. Lincoln with Compass and Chain* (Rochester, IL: Professional Land Surveyors Association, 2002).

38. Andro Linklater, *Measuring America* (New York: Penguin Group, 2002), 5.

39. Basler, *Collected Works of Abraham Lincoln*, 1:20–21; Miers, *Lincoln Day by Day*, 1:36; Nicolay, *Short Life of Abraham Lincoln*, 40.

40. "Procured bread" from Mark E. Neely Jr., *The Abraham Lincoln Encyclopedia* (New York: McGraw-Hill, 1982), 44.

CHAPTER 9. LINCOLN'S ELECTION RECORD

1. Susan Cianci Salvatore, ed., *Civil Rights in America: Racial Voting Rights* (Washington, DC: US Department of the Interior, 2009), 4. Rosalind L. Branning, *Pennsylvania Constitutional Development* (Pittsburgh, PA: University of Pittsburgh Press, 1960), 26–27.

2. Roy Basler, ed., *Collected Works of Abraham Lincoln* (New Brunswick, NJ: Rutgers University Press, 1953), 1:5, 8. Account of Edmund Taylor and his suggestion of legal tender from Jean-Pierre Aubin, *Time Is Money: How Long and How Much Money Is Needed to Regulate a Viable Economy* (New York: Springer, 2014), 7.

3. Basler, *Collected Works of Abraham Lincoln*, 1:298–99.

4. Basler, *Collected Works of Abraham Lincoln*, 1:298–99. Benjamin P. Thomas, *Abraham Lincoln: A Biography* (New York: Modern Library, 1968), 40–42.

5. Basler, *Collected Works of Abraham Lincoln*, 1:298–99.

6. *Illinois State Register* (Springfield, IL), September 7, 1838, p. 2. Theodore C. Pease, ed., *Collections of the Illinois State Historical Library, Vol. 18, Statistical Series, Vol. I, Illinois Election Returns, 1818–1848* (Springfield: Illinois State Historical Library, 1923), 321. Fights between Stuart and Douglas in Thomas, *Abraham Lincoln*, 72–73.

7. Pease, *Collections of the Illinois State Historical Library*, 344. Kenneth J. Winkle, "The Second Party System in Lincoln's Springfield," *Civil War History* 44, no. 4 (December 1998): 267–84.

8. Mitchell Snay, "Abraham Lincoln, Owen Lovejoy, and the Emergence of the Republican Party in Illinois," *Journal of the Abraham Lincoln Association* 22, no. 1 (Winter 2001): 82–99. Lincoln quoted in Earl Schenck Miers, ed., *Lincoln Day by Day* (Dayton, OH: Morningside, 1991), 1:277.

9. Lincoln to Jesse Fell, December 20, 1859, in Basler, *Collected Works of Abraham Lincoln*, 3:512.

10. Basler, *Collected Works of Abraham Lincoln*, 2:293. Vote tabulations from *Journal of the Senate of the Nineteenth General Assembly of the State of Illinois* (Springfield, IL: Lanphier and Walker, 1855), 242–55. Thomas, *Abraham Lincoln*, 149.

11. Basler, *Collected Works of Abraham Lincoln*, 2:248.

12. Basler, *Collected Works of Abraham Lincoln*, 2:303–4.

13. *Ottawa Free Trader* (Ottawa, IL), December 30, 1854, p. 2.

14. William E. Gienapp, *Origins of the Republican Party, 1852–1856* (New York: Oxford University Press, 1987), 343–46. John Tweedy, *A History of the Republican National*

Conventions from 1856 to 1908 (Danbury, CT: J. Tweedy, 1910), 26–29. H. Edward Richardson, *Cassius Marcellus Clay: Firebrand of Freedom* (Lexington: University Press of Kentucky, 1976), 30–35. David H. Donald, *Charles Sumner and the Coming of the Civil War* (Naperville, IL: Sourcebooks, 2009), 245–52, 294.

15. Basler, *Collected Works of Abraham Lincoln*, 2:322.

16. *Rock Island Argus* (Rock Island, IL), November 5, 1858, p. 1.

17. Basler, *Collected Works of Abraham Lincoln*, 3:339–40. *Illinois State Journal* (Springfield, IL), November 3, 1858.

18. Alabama Ordinance of Secession from Edward Channing, *A History of the United States, Vol. 6* (New York: Macmillan, 1925), 261. Lincoln's election results in Springfield and Sangamon County from Jeremy Prichard, "'Home Is the Martyr': The Burial of Abraham Lincoln and the Fate of Illinois' Capital," *Journal of the Abraham Lincoln Association* 38, no. 1 (Winter 2017): 14–15.

19. *Richmond Daily Whig*, "Reflect Well and Vote Wisely," November 5, 1860, p. 2, c. 2; Texas media rumors from James McPherson, *Battle Cry of Freedom* (New York: Oxford University Press, 1988), 228. Lincoln officially received zero votes in Alabama, Arkansas, Florida, Georgia, Louisiana, Mississippi, North Carolina, Tennessee, and Texas, as well as no electoral votes from the legislature of South Carolina. *Richmond Daily Whig*, November 12, 1860, p. 2. Georgia newspaper quoted in McPherson, *Battle Cry of Freedom*, 230.

20. For a breakdown of results in the 1860 election, see Michael J. Dubin, *United States Presidential Elections: The Official Results by County and State* (Jefferson, NC: McFarland, 2002), 159, 168.

21. James Oakes, *The Radical and the Republican: Frederick Douglass, Abraham Lincoln, and the Triumph of Antislavery Politics* (New York: W.W. Norton, 2007), 225–29. Chase letter to Lincoln, February 23, 1864, Basler, *Collected Works of Abraham Lincoln*, 7:200–201.

22. Weed quoted in Basler, *Collected Works of Abraham Lincoln*, 7:514.

23. Basler, *Collected Works of Abraham Lincoln*, 8:25, 45. For a detailed rendition of the 1864 contest, see John C. Waugh, *Reelecting Lincoln: The Battle for the 1864 Presidency* (New York: Crown Publishers, 1997). For a reflection of Western Theater soldiers and their evolution on emancipationist thought, see Robert E. Hunt, *The Good Men Who Won the War: Army of the Cumberland Veterans and Emancipation Memory* (Tuscaloosa: University of Alabama Press, 2010).

24. Springfield and Sangamon votes detailed in Prichard, "'Home Is the Martyr,'" 14–42.

CHAPTER 10. IN THE STATE HOUSE: LINCOLN'S MOST SIGNIFICANT ACTIONS AS AN ILLINOIS LEGISLATOR

1. William Herndon, *The Hidden Lincoln* (New York: Viking, 1938), 425. Gibson Harris, "My Recollections of Abraham Lincoln," *Farm and Fireside*, December 1, 1904.

2. William E. Baringer, *Lincoln's Vandalia* (New Brunswick, NJ: Rutgers University Press, 1949), 53–54; Gabor Boritt, *Lincoln and the Economics of the American Dream* (Memphis, TN: Memphis State University Press, 1978), 5.

3. National debt estimates from *Budget of the United States Government: Historical Tables, Fiscal Year 2007* (Washington, DC: US Government Printing Office, 2006) and US Commerce Department, *Statistical Abstract of the United States* (Washington, DC: US Government Printing Office, 2005).

4. Jessica M. Lepler, *The Many Panics of 1837: People, Politics, and the Creation of a Transatlantic Financial Crisis* (New York: Cambridge University Press, 2013), 19–21, 106–7; Alasdair Roberts, *America's First Great Depression: Economic Crisis and Political Disorder after the Panic of 1837* (Ithaca, NY: Cornell University Press, 2012), 99–102; Ron J. Keller, *Lincoln in the Illinois Legislature* (Carbondale: Southern Illinois University Press, 2019), 103–4.

5. Boritt, *Lincoln and the Economics of the American Dream*, 5–6.

6. Boritt, *Lincoln and the Economics of the American Dream*, 5–6; Arthur C. Boggess, *The Settlement of Illinois, 1778–1830* (Chicago: Chicago Historical Society, 1908), 158; Elizabeth D. Putnam, *The Life and Services of Joseph Duncan, Governor of Illinois, 1834–1838* (Springfield: Illinois State Historical Society, 1921), 135–38.

7. Historian Paul Angle gives the legislator Lincoln enormous credit for moving the state capital to Springfield, stating that Lincoln, "more than any other individual," was responsible for the transfer. Paul Angle, *"Here I Have Lived": A History of Lincoln's Springfield* (Springfield, IL: Abraham Lincoln Association, 1955), 55–59.

8. Baringer, *Lincoln's Vandalia*, 22–23, 32.

9. Baringer, *Lincoln's Vandalia*, 108–10.

10. *Transactions of the Illinois State Historical Society for the Year 1904* (Springfield, IL: Phillips Brothers, 1904), 270–71; M. Scott Heerman, "In a State of Slavery: Black Servitude in Illinois, 1800–1830," *Early American Studies* 14, no. 1 (Winter 2016): 121–22.

11. Baringer, *Lincoln's Vandalia*, 100. For a detailed coverage of Lovejoy's abolitionist work and the general farce of his murder trial, see Paul Simon, *Freedom's Champion: Elijah Lovejoy* (Carbondale: Southern Illinois University Press, 1994).

12. Richard Lawrence Miller, *Lincoln and His World: Prairie Politician, 1834–1842* (Mechanicsburg, PA: Stackpole, 2008), chapter 1.

13. Lincoln's 1832 message to the people of Sangamon County from Roy Basler, ed., *The Collected Works of Abraham Lincoln* (New Brunswick, NJ: Rutgers University Press, 1953), 1:8. Lincoln's minor legislative role in supporting public education from Paul Simon, *Lincoln's Preparation for Greatness: The Illinois Legislative Years* (Urbana: University of Illinois Press, 1971), 278; Basler, *Collected Works of Abraham Lincoln*, 1:214; and Keller, *Lincoln in the Illinois Legislature*, 120.

14. Lawrence B. Stringer, *History of Logan County, Illinois* (Chicago: Pioneer Publishing, 1911), 214.

15. Lincoln quoted in Simon, *Lincoln's Preparation for Greatness*, 207.

16. Robert M. Owens, *Mr. Jefferson's Hammer: William Henry Harrison and the Origins of American Indian Policy* (Norman: University of Oklahoma Press, 2007), 4–5. Simon, *Lincoln's Preparation for Greatness*, 205–7.

17. Simon, *Lincoln's Preparation for Greatness*, 205–7; Keller, *Lincoln in the Illinois Legislature*, 108–12.

CHAPTER 11. LAWYER LINCOLN: NOTABLE CASES WON AND LOST

1. Albert A. Woldman, *Lawyer Lincoln* (Boston: Houghton Mifflin, 1936), 11–12.
2. Brian Dirck, *Lincoln the Lawyer* (Urbana: University of Illinois Press, 2007), 21.
3. Martha L. Benner and Cullom Davis, eds., *The Law Practice of Abraham Lincoln: Complete Documentary Edition*, 2nd edition (Springfield: Illinois Historic Preservation Agency, 2009), http://www.lawpracticeofabrahamlincoln.org (hereafter cited as *LPAL*), *People v. Truett*; *Peoria Register*, October 20, 1838.
4. Daniel W. Stowell, ed., *The Papers of Abraham Lincoln: Legal Documents and Cases* (Charlottesville: University of Virginia Press, 2008), 1:239–50; *LPAL, Grable v. Margrave.*
5. There were three cases in which Lincoln evidently helped defend individuals accused of protecting runaway slaves. See *LPAL, People v. Kern, People v. Pond*, and *People v. Scott*; Dirck, *Lincoln the Lawyer*, 148–49; Stowell, *Papers of Abraham Lincoln*, 2:11.
6. Stowell, *Papers of Abraham Lincoln*, 2:2–3.
7. Stowell, *Papers of Abraham Lincoln*, 2:2.
8. Although Lincoln did not defend an enslaved person in court, he did defend abolitionists accused of helping fugitives, specifically three cases; see *LPAL, People v. Kern, People v. Pond*, and *People v. Scott*; John J. Duff, *A. Lincoln: Prairie Lawyer* (New York: Bramhall House, 1960), 143–44; Paul Angle, "Aftermath of the Matson Slave Case," *Abraham Lincoln Quarterly* (June 1944), 147–48.
9. Duff, *A. Lincoln: Prairie Lawyer*, 155.
10. Jean H. Baker, *Mary Todd Lincoln: A Biography* (New York: W.W. Norton, 1987), 225.
11. Stowell, *Papers of Abraham Lincoln*, 2:358.
12. Stowell, *Papers of Abraham Lincoln*, 2:359.
13. Roy Basler, ed., *The Collected Works of Abraham Lincoln* (New Brunswick, NJ: Rutgers University Press, 1953), 2:194–95.
14. Ruth Painter Randall, *Mary Lincoln: Biography of a Marriage* (Boston: Little, Brown, and Co., 1953), 142–43; Stowell, *Papers of Abraham Lincoln*, 2:358.
15. Basler, *Collected Works of Abraham Lincoln*, 2:201.
16. Dirck, *Lincoln the Lawyer*, 97–98.
17. Stowell, *Papers of Abraham Lincoln*, 2:374–75.
18. *LPAL, Illinois Central RR v. Country of McLean, Illinois.*
19. Kermit L. Hall, ed., *The Oxford Companion to American Law* (New York: Oxford University Press, 2002), 526.
20. Duff, *A. Lincoln: Prairie Lawyer*, 314–17.
21. Stowell, *Papers of Abraham Lincoln*, 2:411.
22. Charles Warren, *A History of the American Bar* (New York: Howard Fertig, 1966), 457.
23. David H. Donald, *Lincoln* (New York: Touchstone, 1995), 185–86; Harry E. Pratt, *The Personal Finances of Abraham Lincoln* (Springfield, IL: Abraham Lincoln Association, 1943), 54–56.
24. Basler, *Collected Works of Abraham Lincoln*, 2:315.
25. Stanton quoted in Dirck, *Lincoln the Lawyer*, 88.
26. "I have nothing against the city" from William M. Dickson, "Abraham Lincoln at Cincinnati," *Harper's New Monthly Magazine* (June 1884), 62.
27. Stowell, *Papers of Abraham Lincoln*, 3:311–13.

28. Stowell, *Papers of Abraham Lincoln*, 3:381–82.

29. Dirck, *Lincoln the Lawyer*, 95–96.

30. Stowell, *Papers of Abraham Lincoln*, 2:1–2.

31. Daniel W. Stowell, "Murder at a Methodist Camp Meeting," *Journal of the Illinois State Historical Society* (Fall/Winter 2008), 27. For an analysis of the vague evidence surrounding the "Almanac Case," see Daniel W. Stowell, "The Promises and Pitfalls of Reminiscences as Historical Documents: A Case in Point," *Documentary Editing* (Winter 2005): 99–117.

32. Stowell, *Papers of Abraham Lincoln*, 4:18.

CHAPTER 12. MOST COMMON TYPES OF LINCOLN'S LEGAL CASES

1. Among admirers and early biographers who argued that Lincoln purposely or subconsciously threw cases he did not support, the principals include Albert Beveridge, William Herndon, and Albert Woldman. See Albert Beveridge, *Abraham Lincoln, Vol. 1* (Boston: Houghton Mifflin, 1928); Douglas L. Wilson, Terry Wilson, and Rodney O. Davis, eds., *Herndon's Informants: Letters, Interviews, and Statements about Abraham Lincoln* (Urbana: University of Illinois Press, 1998); and Albert A. Woldman, *Lawyer Lincoln* (Boston: Houghton Mifflin, 1936).

2. Roy Basler, ed., *The Collected Works of Abraham Lincoln* (New Brunswick, NJ: Rutgers University Press, 1953), 2:81; Brian Dirck, *Lincoln the Lawyer* (Urbana: University of Illinois Press, 2007), 106–7. *The Oxford Companion to American Law* calculates that the attorney Lincoln was involved, in whole or in part, with 5,669 cases; Kermit L. Hall, ed., *Oxford Companion to American Law* (New York: Oxford University Press, 2002), 525.

3. Hall, *Oxford Companion to American Law*, 526.

4. From Martha L. Benner and Cullom Davis, eds., *The Law Practice of Abraham Lincoln: Complete Documentary Edition*, 2nd edition (Springfield: Illinois Historic Preservation Agency, 2009) (hereafter cited as *LPAL*), *Sugg v. Morris*.

5. *LPAL*, *Lincoln v. Brown*.

6. Woldman, *Lawyer Lincoln*, 18.

7. Dirck, *Lincoln the Lawyer*, 60–62, 67. Charles Warren, *A History of the American Bar* (New York: Howard Fertig, 1966), 446–47.

8. *LPAL*, *Rothschild v. Langenbahn*; R. L. Allen, *Domestic Animals: History and Description* (New York: C.M. Saxton, 1848), 185–90; *LPAL*, table 8: Lincoln's Role in Cases.

9. *LPAL*, *Herndon v. Ledlie et al.*, *Ide v. Ledlie*, *Ledlie v. Burgess*, *Bunn v. Winn and Ledlie*.

10. Daniel W. Stowell, ed., *The Papers of Abraham Lincoln: Legal Documents and Cases, Vol. I* (Charlottesville: University of Virginia Press, 2008), 42–43.

11. Dirck, *Lincoln the Lawyer*, 133–34; *LPAL*, *Bancom v. Bancom*, *Beerup v. Beerup*, *Clarkson v. Clarkson*.

CHAPTER 13. ON THE HILL: LINCOLN'S MOST SIGNIFICANT ACTIONS AS A US REPRESENTATIVE

1. Benjamin Thomas, *Abraham Lincoln: A Biography* (New York: Modern Library, 1968), 117.

2. Roy P. Basler, ed., *Collected Works of Abraham Lincoln* (New Brunswick, NJ: Rutgers University Press, 1953), 1:421.

3. Geoffrey R. Stone, *Perilous Times: Free Speech in Wartime* (New York: W.W. Norton, 2004), 123.

4. Basler, *Collected Works of Abraham Lincoln*, 1:440–41.

5. Earl Schenck Miers, ed., *Lincoln Day by Day: A Chronology, 1809–1865* (Dayton, OH: Morningside, 1991), 2:297, 302. Basler, *Collected Works of Abraham Lincoln*, 2:323.

6. Chris DeRose, *Congressman Lincoln* (New York: Simon and Schuster, 2013), 77.

7. Louise L. Stevenson, *Lincoln in the Atlantic World* (New York: Cambridge University Press, 2015), 68; Basler, *Collected Works of Abraham Lincoln*, 2:20–22; Miers, *Lincoln Day by Day*, 2:297, 298, 300, 308.

8. Miers, *Lincoln Day by Day*, 2:308.

9. Basler, *Collected Works of Abraham Lincoln*, 1:471.

10. For works presenting the American Civil War within a global context, see Don H. Doyle, ed., *American Civil Wars: The United States, Latin America, Europe, and the Crisis of the 1860s* (Chapel Hill: University of North Carolina Press, 2017); Timothy Mason Roberts, *Distant Revolutions: 1848 and the Challenge to American Exceptionalism* (Charlottesville: University of Virginia Press, 2009); Mischa Honeck, *We Are the Revolutionists: German-Speaking Immigrants and American Abolitionists after 1848* (Athens: University of Georgia Press, 2011); and Wim Klooster, *Revolutions in the Atlantic World: A Comparative History* (New York: New York University Press, 2009).

11. Basler, *Collected Works of Abraham Lincoln*, 2:62.

12. Roberts, *Distant Revolutions*, 1–2.

13. Roberts, *Distant Revolutions*, 149.

14. *Illinois Journal* (Springfield, IL), January 12, 1852, p. 1.

15. Basler, *Collected Works of Abraham Lincoln*, 1:463. On Lincoln's opposition to national expansion, see Gabor S. Boritt, *Lincoln and the Economics of the American Dream* (Memphis, TN: Memphis State University Press, 1978), 146–50.

16. Miers, *Lincoln Day by Day*, 1:319–21.

17. Joseph G. Rayback, *Free Soil: The Election of 1848* (Lexington: University Press of Kentucky, 1970), 288–302.

18. Miers, *Lincoln Day by Day*, 1:469–71.

19. Jon D. Schaff, *Abraham Lincoln's Statesmanship and the Limits of Liberal Democracy* (Carbondale: Southern Illinois University Press, 2019), 171.

20. Milo M. Quaife, ed., *Publications of the State Historical Society of Wisconsin, Vol. 1* (Madison: State Historical Society of Wisconsin, 1916), 48.

21. Basler, *Collected Works of Abraham Lincoln*, 1:450, 474–75. James Traub, *John Quincy Adams: Militant Spirit* (New York: Basic Books, 2016), 529–30. Harlow Giles Unger, *John Quincy Adams* (Philadelphia, PA: Da Capo Press, 2012), 311.

22. Traub, *John Quincy Adams*, 531.

CHAPTER 14. WORST DAYS IN THE PRESIDENCY

1. Quoted in Ruth P. Randall, *Colonel Elmer Ellsworth* (Boston: Little, Brown and Co., 1960), 7.

2. Roy Basler, ed., *The Collected Works of Abraham Lincoln* (New Brunswick, NJ: Rutgers University Press, 1953), 4:273. E. Phelps Gay, "Lincoln's Letter to Colonel Elmer Ellsworth's Parents: A Study in Literary Excellence," *Lincoln Lore* (Summer 2007), 1889: 12–13.

3. Randall, *Colonel Elmer Ellsworth*, 258. Telegraph operator David Bates claims that Lincoln was in the War Department Telegraph Office when he received the news of Ellsworth's death. David H. Bates, *Lincoln in the Telegraph Office* (New York: The Century Co. 1907), 8.

4. Mark Neely Jr., *The Abraham Lincoln Encyclopedia* (New York: McGraw-Hill, 1982), 15–16.

5. Ralph Gary, *Following in Lincoln's Footsteps* (New York: Carroll and Graf, 2001), 351.

6. Typhoid deaths calculated in Bell I. Wiley, *The Life of Johnny Reb: The Common Soldier of the Confederacy* (Baton Rouge: Louisiana State University Press, 1978), 253; and Frank R. Freemon, *Gangrene and Glory* (Madison, NJ: Fairleigh Dickinson University Press, 1998), 206. Battle statistics derived from Mark M. Boatner III, *The Civil War Dictionary* (New York: Vintage Books, 1988); Thomas L. Livermore, *Numbers and Losses in the Civil War in America: 1861–1865* (Bloomington: Indiana University Press, 1957); and Frederick Phisterer, *Statistical Record of the Armies of the United States* (New York: Charles Scribner and Sons, 1893).

7. Lincoln quoted in Benjamin Thomas, *Abraham Lincoln: A Biography* (New York: Modern Library, 1968), 303. Mary Todd quoted in Matthew Pinsker, *Lincoln's Sanctuary: Abraham Lincoln and the Soldiers' Home* (New York: Oxford University Press, 2003), 22.

8. Pinsker, *Lincoln's Sanctuary*, 32. Description of William Lincoln's flower arrangements from *National Republican* (Washington, DC), February 25, 1862, p. 2.

9. National Portrait Gallery, *First Ladies of the United States* (Washington, DC: Smithsonian Institute, 2020), 86.

10. Stephen W. Sears, ed., *The Civil War Papers of George B. McClellan* (New York: Ticknor and Fields, 1989), 187.

11. James McPherson, *Battle Cry of Freedom* (New York: Oxford University Press, 1988), 571–74. Lincoln quoted in Geoffrey C. Ward, *The Civil War: An Illustrated History* (New York: Alfred A. Knopf, 1990), 174.

12. Lincoln quoted in James McPherson, *Tried by War: Abraham Lincoln as Commander in Chief* (New York: Penguin Press, 2008), 146.

13. Thomas, *Abraham Lincoln*, 351–55.

14. Michael Burlingame, *Abraham Lincoln: A Life* (Baltimore: Johns Hopkins University Press, 2008), 2:496.

15. Lee quoted in Stephen W. Sears, *Chancellorsville* (Boston: Houghton Mifflin, 1996), 444.

16. Sumner quoted in Gideon Welles, *Diary of Gideon Welles* (Boston: Houghton Mifflin, 1909), 1:293. Brooks quoted from McPherson, *Tried by War*, 177. George Gordon Meade III, ed., *The Life and Letters of George Gordon Meade* (New York: Charles Scribner's Sons, 1913), 1:372–73. "My God! My God!" from Michael Burlingame, ed.,

Lincoln Observed: Civil War Dispatches of Noah Brooks (Baltimore: John Hopkins University Press, 1998), 50.

17. Bates, *Lincoln in the Telegraph Office*, 155–58.

18. Lincoln quoted in Bates, *Lincoln in the Telegraph Office*, 157.

19. Gabor S. Boritt, ed., *Lincoln and His Generals* (New York: Oxford University Press, 1994), 89. John Hay Diary, July 14, 1863, Hay Papers. Lincoln quoted in Benjamin Thomas, *Abraham Lincoln: A Biography* (New York: Modern Library, 1968), 389.

20. Lincoln's unsent letter to Meade from Thomas, *Abraham Lincoln: A Biography*, 389. Chase quoted in McPherson, *Tried by War*, 184.

21. "Rosecrans has been whipped" from Pinsker, *Lincoln's Sanctuary*, 120.

22. For William Rosecrans's official report on the battle, see *War of the Rebellion: A Compilation of the Official Records of the Union and Confederate Armies* (Washington, DC: Government Printing Office, 1880–1901) (hereafter listed as O.R.), ser. I, vol. 30, pt. 1, 59–64. For an illuminating exchange of accusations and counter-accusations involving the gap created in the Union lines at Chickamauga, see O.R., ser. I, vol. 20, pt. 1, 101–5.

23. Battle report to Mary from David H. Donald, *Lincoln at Home* (New York: Simon and Schuster, 2000), 93. "I really wish to see you" from Pinsker, *Lincoln's Sanctuary*, 121.

24. Earl Schenck Miers, ed., *Lincoln Day by Day: A Chronology, 1809–1865* (Dayton, OH: Morningside, 1991), 3:329.

25. Miers, *Lincoln Day by Day*, 3:329.

26. Louis Weichmann, *A True History of the Assassination of Abraham Lincoln and the Conspiracy of 1865* (New York: A.A. Knopf, 1975), 148; Edward Steers Jr., *Blood on the Moon: The Assassination of Abraham Lincoln* (Lexington: University Press of Kentucky, 2005), 104–5.

27. E. Lawrence Abel, *A Finger in Lincoln's Brain: What Modern Science Reveals about Lincoln, His Assassination, and Its Aftermath* (Santa Barbara, CA: Praeger, 2015), 93–105.

CHAPTER 15. BEST DAYS IN THE PRESIDENCY

1. Earl Schenck Miers, ed., *Lincoln Day by Day: A Chronology, 1809–1865* (Dayton, OH: Morningside, 1991), 3:94–95.

2. Bruce Catton, *Terrible Swift Sword* (New York: Doubleday & Co., 1963), 156.

3. Thomas L. Connelly, *Army of the Heartland* (Baton Rouge: Louisiana State University, 1967), 121–22; Clement Eaton, *A History of the Southern Confederacy* (New York: Free Press, 1954), 158–59.

4. Numbers of Confederate captured are based on Mark M. Boatner III, *The Civil War Dictionary* (New York: Vintage Books, 1988), 397, and Ulysses S. Grant, *Memoirs* (New York: Literary Classics, 1990), 212.

5. Miers, *Lincoln Day by Day*, 3:68; J. Matthew Gallman, *The North Fights the Civil War: The Home Front* (Chicago: Ivan R. Dee, 1994), 47; James A. Rawley, *The Politics of Union* (Hinsdale, IL: Dryden Press, 1974), 49.

6. Gallman, *The North Fights the Civil War*, 98; Rawley, *The Politics of Union*, 50.

7. Gallman, *The North Fights the Civil War*, 96.

8. Henry S. Commager, ed., *Civil War Archive: The History of the Civil War in Documents* (New York: Black Dog & Leventhal Publishers, Inc., 2000), 813–16.

9. Roger L. Geiger and Nathan M. Sober, eds., *Land Grant Colleges and the Reshaping of American Higher Education* (New Brunswick, NJ: Transaction Publishers, 2013), 97–103.

10. Account of Lincoln hearing the news of Union victory at Vicksburg in Benjamin P. Thomas, *Abraham Lincoln: A Biography* (New York: Modern Library, 1968), 387.

11. Thomas, *Abraham Lincoln*, 387–88.

12. Robert E. May, ed., *The Union, the Confederacy, and the Atlantic Rim* (West Lafayette, IN: Purdue University Press, 1995), 10; Philip Van Doren Stern, *When the Guns Roared: World Aspects of the American Civil War* (Garden City, NY: Doubleday & Co., 1965), 208.

13. Brooks D. Simpson, "Great Expectations: Ulysses S. Grant, the Northern Press, and the Opening of the Wilderness Campaign," in *The Wilderness Campaign*, ed. Gary W. Gallagher (Chapel Hill: University of North Carolina Press, 1997), 15–19. *New York Tribune*, May 9, 1864, p. 1. *New York Times*, May 9, 1864, p. 1.

14. Lincoln quoted in John C. Waugh, *Reelecting Lincoln* (New York: Crown Publishers, 1997), 347.

15. Miers, *Lincoln Day by Day*, 3:294.

16. Miers, *Lincoln Day by Day*, 3:294.

17. Miers, *Lincoln Day by Day*, 3:295.

18. Thomas, *Abraham Lincoln*, 493–94.

19. For the evolution of Black Codes and Jim Crow laws, see Douglas A. Blackmon, *Slavery by Another Name: The Re-enslavement of Black Americans from the Civil War to World War II* (New York: Anchor Books, 2009); Eric Foner, *Reconstruction: America's Unfinished Revolution, 1863-1877* (New York: Harper and Row, 2001); and Daniel A. Novak, *The Wheel of Servitude: Black Forced Labor after Slavery* (Lexington: University Press of Kentucky, 1978).

20. Thomas, *Abraham Lincoln*, 513.

CHAPTER 16. LINCOLN'S LONG PATH TO FINAL REST

1. Gregory Coco, *A Vast Sea of Misery* (Gettysburg, PA: Thomas Publications, 1988), 51, 128–30; Gerard A. Patterson, *Debris of Battle: The Wounded of Gettysburg* (Mechanicsburg, PA: Stackpole Press, 1997), 122; William Frassanito, *Gettysburg: A Journey in Time* (New York: Charles Scribner's Sons, 1975), 24–29, 32–33, 190–91.

2. Philippe Ariès, *Western Attitudes towards Death* (Baltimore, MD: Johns Hopkins University Press, 1974), 87; *Illustrated Life, Services, Martyrdom, and Funeral of Abraham Lincoln* (Philadelphia: T.B. Peterson and Brothers, 1865), 203.

3. David Nasaw, *Going Out: The Rise and Fall of Public Amusements* (Cambridge, MA: Harvard University Press, 1999), 120. Christine Ammer, *American Heritage Dictionary of Idioms, 2nd Edition* (Boston: Houghton Mifflin, 2013), 113.

4. Edward Steers Jr., *Blood on the Moon: The Assassination of Abraham Lincoln* (Lexington: University Press of Kentucky, 2005), 120–22, 252. Timothy S. Good, ed., *We Saw*

Lincoln Shot: One Hundred Eyewitness Accounts (Jackson: University Press of Mississippi, 1995), 160–65.

5. Ariès, *Western Attitudes towards Death*, 12–14, 38.

6. Benjamin Thomas and Harold Hyman, *Stanton: The Life and Times of Lincoln's Secretary of War* (New York: Alfred A. Knopf, 1962), 399n.

7. *New York Times*, April 16, 1865, p. 1, *New York Times*, April 17, 1865, p. 1. Thomas J. Craughwell, *Stealing Lincoln's Body* (Cambridge, MA: Belknap Press, 2007), 5–9; *New York Times*, April 17, 1865, p. 1.

8. Coco, *A Vast Sea of Misery*, 128–30. Craughwell, *Stealing Lincoln's Body*, 9.

9. Drew Gilpin Faust, *This Republic of Suffering: Death and the American Civil War* (New York: Vintage Books, 2008), 156.

10. Faust, *This Republic of Suffering*, 156. Martha Hodes, *Mourning Lincoln* (New Haven, CT: Yale University Press, 2015), 143–44. Craughwell, *Stealing Lincoln's Body*, 13–15.

11. Hodes, *Mourning Lincoln*, 149–51.

12. Faust, *This Republic of Suffering*, 161.

13. Jeremy Prichard, "'Home Is the Martyr': The Burial of Abraham Lincoln and the Fate of Illinois' Capital," *Journal of the Abraham Lincoln Association* 38, no. 1 (Winter 2017).

14. "The Lincoln Monument," *Chicago Tribune*, June 4, 1865, p. 4; "The Lincoln National Monument," *National Republican* (Washington, DC), June 15, 1865, p. 2.

15. Craughwell, *Stealing Lincoln's Body*, 23.

16. Prichard, "'Home Is the Martyr,'" 28–35.

17. John C. Power, *Abraham Lincoln: His Life, Public Services, Death, and Great Funeral Service* (Chicago: H.W. Rokker, 1889), 302–3.

18. Power, *Abraham Lincoln*, 302–3. Merrill D. Peterson, *Lincoln in American Memory* (New York: Oxford University Press, 1994), 52–53.

19. Charles Lachman, *The Last Lincolns: The Rise and Fall of a Great American Family* (New York: Union Square Press, 2008), 162–64. "Lincoln," *Chicago Tribune*, September 22, 1871, p. 2.

20. Craughwell, *Stealing Lincoln's Body*, 104–10.

21. Craughwell, *Stealing Lincoln's Body*, 125–30.

22. Craughwell, *Stealing Lincoln's Body*, 178–79.

23. "Illinois' Hallowed Spot," *The Inter-Ocean* (Chicago, IL), April 15, 1887, p. 1; "Martyr Lincoln's Body," *Chicago Tribune*, April 15, 1887, p. 1; "The Lincoln Memorial," *Sterling Daily Gazette* (Sterling, IL), April 16, 1887, p. 1.

24. Craughwell, *Stealing Lincoln's Body*, 183.

25. Craughwell, *Stealing Lincoln's Body*, 195.

CHAPTER 17. ASSASSINATION CONSPIRACY THEORIES

1. *National Intelligencer*, April 15, 1865, p. 1. The article also initially reported that the two attacks might have been conducted by a single individual. Interestingly, the report identified the Lincolns' guests at the play as "Mrs. Harris" rather than her daughter, Miss Clara Harris, and her escort as "Major Rathburn" rather than Major

Henry Rathbone. *National Intelligencer*, April 15, 1865, p. 1; Chase quoted in Lately Thomas, *The First President Johnson* (New York: William Morrow, 1968), 313.

2. As late as April 16, the *New York Times* was reporting that John Surratt, not Lewis Payne, was Seward's attacker. *New York Times*, April 16, 1865, p. 1.

3. For further analyses of the Lincoln assassination conspiracy myths, see George S. Bryan, *The Great American Myth* (New York: Carrick and Evans, 1940); and William Hanchett, *The Lincoln Murder Conspiracies* (Urbana: University of Illinois Press, 1983).

4. *New York Times*, April 15, 1865, p. 1. Michael Kauffman, *American Brutus: John Wilkes Booth and the Lincoln Conspiracies* (New York: Random House, 2004), 280.

5. *New York Times*, April 16, 1865, p. 1; Peter Knight, ed., *Conspiracy Theories in American History* (Santa Barbara, CA: ABC-Clio, 2003), 1:435.

6. Steven Anzovin and Janet Podell, *Famous First Facts about American Politics* (New York: H.W. Wilson Co, 2001), 248.

7. Anzovin and Podell, *Famous First Facts*, 248; Benjamin Thomas and Harold Hyman, *Stanton: The Life and Times of Lincoln's Secretary of War* (New York: Alfred A. Knopf, 1962), 422–23. Sherman quoted in Kauffman, *American Brutus*, 281.

8. George Templeton Strong quoted in Jennifer L. Weber, *Copperheads: The Rise and Fall of Lincoln's Opponents in the North* (New York: Oxford University Press, 2006), 215. Soldier in the Ninth Ohio Battery quoted in "Camp Near Franklin, Tenn.," *Portage County Democrat* (Ravenna, OH), May 16, 1863, p. 3.

9. *Extra Star* quoted in *New York Times*, April 17, 1865, p. 1.

10. *New York Times*, April 26, 1865, p. 2; Estherville, Iowa, report from Kauffman, *American Brutus*, 236–38. *New York Times*, April 26, 1865, p. 2.

11. For details on Republican divisions that helped Democrats in the 1884, 1892, and 1912 presidential elections, see Mark Wahlgren Summers, *Rum, Romanism, and Rebellion: The Making of a President, 1884* (Chapel Hill: University of North Carolina Press, 2000); Arthur Schlesinger, ed., *History of American Presidential Elections, Vol. 2, 1844–1896* (New York: McGraw Hill, 1971); and James Chase, *1912: Wilson, Roosevelt, Taft, and Debs—The Election That Changed the Country* (New York: Simon and Schuster, 2004).

12. Franklin Pierce quoted in the *New York Times*, April 26, 1865, p. 2.

13. "Here is a very extraordinary communication," William C. Davis, *Jefferson Davis: The Man and His Hour* (New York: HarperCollins, 1991), 619. See also Kauffman, *American Brutus*, 281.

14. Davis quoted in Herman Hattaway and Richard E. Beringer, *Jefferson Davis, Confederate President* (Lawrence: University of Kansas Press, 2002), 413.

15. Thomas and Hyman, *Stanton*, 421–22.

16. Thomas and Hyman, *Stanton*, 462. Christopher Dell, *Lincoln and the War Democrats* (London: Associated University Press, 1975), 327; Andrew Johnson quoted in Dell, *Lincoln and the War Democrats*, 355n.

17. Booth note quoted in Kauffman, *American Brutus*, 222. Annette Gordon-Reed, *Andrew Johnson* (New York: Henry Holt, 2011), 90-93. Marli F. Weiner, ed., *Heritage of Woe: The Civil War Diary of Grace Brown Elmore, 1861-1868* (Athens, GA: University of Georgia Press, 1997), 117.

18. Thomas, *The First President Johnson*, 309. A 2006 publication alleged that both Johnson and Stanton conspired to kill Lincoln and take over the government, suggesting in addition that Andrew Johnson and John Wilkes Booth were "old friends," and the latter had been hired as a hitman: John C. Griffin, *Abraham Lincoln's Execution* (Gretna, LA: Pelican, 2006).

19. David O. Stewart, *Impeached: The Trial of President Andrew Johnson and the Fight for Lincoln's Legacy* (New York: Simon and Schuster, 2009), 14–17; Gordon-Reed, *Andrew Johnson*, 90–96.

20. Roy Basler, ed., *The Collected Works of Abraham Lincoln* (New Brunswick, NJ: Rutgers University Press, 1953), 2:323.

21. Floyd Risvold, ed., *Louis Weichmann: A True History of the Assassination of Abraham Lincoln and of the Conspiracy of 1865* (New York: A.A. Knopf, 1975), 9–10.

22. Father Chiniquy, *Fifty Years in the Church of Rome* (London: Robert Banks and Son, 1886). For other versions of the alleged Roman plot, see Justin D. Fulton, *Washington in the Lap of Rome* (1888), and Thomas M. Harris, *The Assassination of Lincoln* (1892). See also Risvold, *Louis Weichmann*, 417n; Knight, *Conspiracy Theories in American History*, 1:438; and Burke McCarty, *The Suppressed Truth about the Assassination of Abraham Lincoln* (Washington, DC: 1922), 51–53.

23. Thomas and Hyman, *Stanton*, 319, 393.

24. Otto Eisenschiml, *Why Was Lincoln Murdered?* (London: Faber and Faber, 1937). Theodore Roscoe, *The Web of Conspiracy: The Complete Story of the Men Who Murdered Abraham Lincoln* (Englewood Cliffs, NJ: Prentice-Hall, 1959).

25. W. Emerson Reck, *A. Lincoln: His Last 24 Hours* (Jefferson, NC: McFarland, 1987), 11–12; Matthew Pinsker, *Lincoln's Sanctuary: Abraham Lincoln and the Soldiers' Home* (New York: Oxford University Press, 2003), 153.

26. Thomas and Hyman, *Stanton*, 398.

27. David Balsiger and Charles Sellier, *The Lincoln Conspiracy* (Los Angeles, CA: Schick Sunn, 1977).

28. Knight, *Conspiracy Theories in American History*, 1:440; Hanchett, *The Lincoln Murder Conspiracies*, 228.

CHAPTER 18. LINCOLN TRIBUTES

1. "The Churches Memorialize the Lincolns," *Lincoln Lore* (July 29, 1940).

2. Emanuel Hertz, ed., *Lincoln Talks: An Oral Biography* (New York: Bramhall House, 1986), 3.

3. D. Mark Huddleston, "A Developing Frontier: Logan County, Illinois to 1876," MA thesis, Eastern Illinois University, 1976, pp. 17–19; Guy C. Fraker, *Lincoln's Ladder to the Presidency: The Eighth Judicial Circuit* (Carbondale: Southern Illinois University Press, 2012), 155–57.

4. James W. Savage and John T. Bell, *History of the City of Omaha, Nebraska* (Chicago: Munsell, 1894), 61.

5. Arthur B. Hayes and Samuel D. Cox, *History of the City of Lincoln, Nebraska* (Lincoln, NE: State Journal Co., 1889), 101–11; Ronald C. Naugle, John J. Montag, and

James C. Olson, *History of Nebraska*, fourth edition (Lincoln: University of Nebraska Press, 2014), 121–24.

6. Brian Matthew Jordan and Evan C. Rothera, eds., *The War Went On: Reconsidering the Lives of Civil War Veterans* (Baton Rouge, LA: Louisiana State University Press, 2020), 223–27.

7. *Lincoln's Birthday, Hearing before the Committee on the District of Columbia, House of Representatives, Sixty-Seventh Congress, First Session, H.R. 2310* (Washington, DC: Government Printing Office, 1921), 3.

8. *Whose Heritage? Public Symbols of the Confederacy* (Montgomery, AL: Southern Poverty Law Center, 2019), 12.

9. Christopher A. Thomas, *The Lincoln Memorial and American Life* (Princeton, NJ: Princeton University Press, 2002), 6–8; *Lincoln Memorial* (Washington, DC: US Department of Interior, 1986), 8, 36.

10. "Will Come Later," *Gettysburg Times*, January 25, 1913, p. 1. "The Lincoln Memorial," *New York Tribune*, January 22, 1913, p. 8. See also Elihu Root, *Latin America and the United States: Addresses by Elihu Root* (Good Press, 2019); Warren Zimmerman, *First Great Triumph: How Five Americans Made Their Country a World Power* (New York: Farrar, Straus, and Giroux, 2002).

11. "Lincoln Memorial to be Greek Temple," *The Sun* (New York), January 30, 1913, p. 4.

12. *Lincoln Memorial* (Washington, DC: US Department of Interior, 1986), 8, 36.

13. National Park Service, US Department of the Interior, *Lincoln Highway: Special Resource Study, Environmental Assessment* (Washington, DC: National Park Service, 2000), 3–5.

14. *Complete Official Road Guide of the Lincoln Highway* (Detroit: Lincoln Highway Association, 1916), 9.

15. *Complete Official Road Guide of the Lincoln Highway*, 13–17.

16. Drake Hokanson, *Lincoln Highway: Main Street across America* (Iowa City: University of Iowa Press, 1999), 84–86, 131.

17. "The Lincoln Penny," *Brooklyn Daily Herald* (Brooklyn, NY), April 18, 1909, p. 38.

18. Mary Ellen Snodgrass, *Coins and Currency: An Historical Encyclopedia*, second edition (Jefferson, NC: McFarland, 2019), 37–38.

19. "The Lincoln Penny," *Brooklyn Daily Herald* (Brooklyn, NY), April 18, 1909, p. 38.

20. "Newsboys Raid Wall Street by Cornering Coins," *St. Louis Post-Dispatch* (St. Louis, MO), August 5, 1909, p. 7.

21. *Daily Republican* (Burlington, KS), September 2, 1909, p. 8. *Fresno Morning Republican* (Fresno, CA), November 7, 1909.

CHAPTER 19. LINCOLN MYTHS AND MISCONCEPTIONS

1. Douglas L. Wilson, *Lincoln's Sword* (New York: Vintage Books, 2006), 79.

2. Lincoln quoted in Stephen B. Oates, *Abraham Lincoln: The Man behind the Myths* (New York: Signet, 1984), 106.

3. For the gradual transformation of the Proclamation from first draft to final signature, see Benjamin Thomas, *Abraham Lincoln: A Biography* (New York: Modern Library, 1968), 333–64.

4. As stated above, estimates of escapees to Union positions during the war range from Leslie Schwalm's conservative estimate of 320,000 to Ira Berlin et al.'s perhaps optimistic number of 474,000+. See Leslie A. Schwalm, "Between Slavery and Freedom: African American Women and Occupation in the Slave South," in *Occupied Women: Gender, Military Occupation, and the American Civil War*, ed. LeAnn Whites and Alecia P. Long (Baton Rouge: Louisiana State University Press, 2009), 138–39; Ira Berlin, Barbara J. Fields, Steven F. Miller, Joseph P. Reidy, and Leslie S. Rowland, *Slaves No More: Three Essays on Emancipation and the Civil War* (New York: Cambridge University Press, 1992), 178; John Hope Franklin, *From Slavery to Freedom* (New York: Vintage Books, 1967), 259–60; James M. McPherson, *Battle Cry of Freedom* (New York: Oxford University Press, 1988), 79–80; Eugene D. Genovese, *Roll, Jordan, Roll: The World the Slaves Made* (New York: Pantheon Books, 1974), 648–49.

5. Thomas, *Abraham Lincoln*, 49–51. Don E. Fehrenbacher, *Lincoln in Text and Context: Collected Essays* (Stanford: Stanford University Press, 1987), 246–69. Some authors present the Lincoln-Rutledge relationship as more fact than legend, though their positions stem more from the force of sentimentalism rather than from any significantly new evidence. Chief among the pro–love affair works is John Evangelist Walsh's *The Shadows Rise: Abraham Lincoln and the Ann Rutledge Legend* (Urbana: University of Illinois Press, 1993).

6. Philip Davis, *History Atlas of North America* (New York: Macmillan, 1998), 66; Lauren Schweninger, *Families in Crisis in the Old South: Divorce, Slavery, and the Law* (Chapel Hill: University of North Carolina Press, 2012), 163–64.

7. Gerald J. Prokopowicz, *Did Lincoln Own Slaves? And Other Frequently Asked Questions about Abraham Lincoln* (New York: Pantheon Books, 2008), 156. For the role of white death and property distribution in slave life, see Edward Ball, *Slaves in the Family* (New York: Farrar, Straus, and Giroux, 1998); Anne C. Bailey, *Weeping Time: Memory and the Largest Slave Auction in American History* (New York: Cambridge University Press, 2017).

8. For further analysis of Josiah Holland the biographer, see Merrill Peterson, *Lincoln in American Memory* (New York: Oxford University Press, 1994), 68–70.

9. Sarah Bush Johnston Lincoln quoted in Harold Holzer, ed., *Lincoln as I Knew Him* (Chapel Hill, NC: Algonquin Books, 2009), 14. Mary Todd Lincoln's observations from Prokopowicz, *Did Lincoln Own Slaves?*, 30–32. Herndon's views on Lincoln from Earl Schenk Miers, ed., *Lincoln Day By Day: A Chronology, 1809–1865* (Dayton, OH: Morningside, 1991), vii–viii.

10. *Lincoln Memorial* (Washington, DC: US Department of Interior, 1986), 22.

11. Prokopowicz, *Did Lincoln Own Slaves?*, 30–32.

12. Philip R. Reilly, *Abraham Lincoln's DNA and Other Adventures in Genetics* (Cold Spring Harbor, NY: Cold Spring Harbor Laboratory Press, 2002), 3–8.

13. Amy Stewart, *Wicked Plants: The Weed that Killed Lincoln's Mother and Other Botanical Atrocities* (Chapel Hill, NC: Algonquin Books, 2009), 14.

14. Reilly, *Abraham Lincoln's DNA*, 8–12. Peter N. Robinson and Maurice Godfrey, *Marfan Syndrome: A Primer for Clinicians and Scientists* (New York: Kluwer Academic/Plenum Publishers, 2004), 8–11.

15. Garry Wills, *Lincoln at Gettysburg: The Words that Remade America* (New York: Simon and Schuster, 1992), 31.

16. Louis A. Warren, *Lincoln's Gettysburg Declaration: "A New Birth of Freedom"* (Ft. Wayne, IN: Lincoln National Life Foundation, 1964), 61. Frank L. Klement, *The Gettysburg Soldiers' Cemetery and Lincoln's Address: Aspects and Angles* (Shippensburg, PA: White Mane Publishing, 1993), 86–89.

17. Warren, *Lincoln's Gettysburg Declaration*, 54.

18. James M. Cole and Roy E. Frampton, *Lincoln and the Human Interest Stories of the Gettysburg National Cemetery* (Hanover, PA: Sheridan Press, 1995), 11.

19. In the landmark volume on battlefield photography, *Gettysburg: A Journey in Time* (New York: Charles Scribner's Sons, 1975), author William Frassanito stated the memorial marked the spot. He changed his statement in later editions of his book.

20. Newspaper reporters at the cemetery commencement either failed to mention the rostrum's location or were vague. For a breakdown of theories old and new as to where Lincoln stood, see Wills, *Lincoln at Gettysburg*, 205–10. See also Martin P. Johnson, *Writing the Gettysburg Address* (Lawrence: University of Kansas Press, 2015).

21. Louis A. Warren, "The Sobriquet—'Honest Abe,'" *Lincoln Lore*, August 17, 1942. Robert Lincoln quoted in Mark Neely Jr. and Harold Holzer, *The Lincoln Family Album* (New York: Doubleday, 1990), 33.

22. "He was a good—obliging clerk" from Douglas L. Wilson, Terry Wilson, and Rodney O. Davis, eds., *Herndon's Informants: Letters, Interviews, and Statements about Abraham Lincoln* (Urbana: University of Illinois Press, 1998), 14. "You ask what gave him the title of honest Abe" from Wilson et al., *Herndon's Informants*, 76 (emphasis in original).

23. Warren, "The Sobriquet."

Chapter 20. Sites of Lincoln Historic Preservation

1. "Birthplace Farm Title," *Lincoln Lore* (July 10, 1939).

2. Robert W. Blythe, Maureen Carroll, and Stephen H. Moffson, revised by Brian C. Coffey, *Abraham Lincoln Birthplace National Historic Site: Historic Resource Study* (Atlanta, GA: US Department of the Interior, 2001), 2.

3. Blythe et al., *Abraham Lincoln Birthplace National Historic Site*, 30.

4. Lucy Lawliss and Susan Hitchcock, *Abraham Lincoln Birthplace National Historic Site: Cultural Landscape Report* (Atlanta, GA: US Department of Interior, 2004), 10.

5. Lawliss and Hitchcock, *Abraham Lincoln Birthplace National Historic Site*, 12.

6. Lawliss and Hitchcock, *Abraham Lincoln Birthplace National Historic Site*, 36; Blythe et al., *Abraham Lincoln Birthplace National Historic Site*, 33–36.

7. *Lincoln Boyhood National Memorial: General Management Plan/Environmental Impact Statement* (Washington, DC: US Department of Interior, 2005), 51.

8. *Lincoln Boyhood National Memorial*, 55.

9. *Lincoln Boyhood National Memorial*, 53.

10. Benjamin Thomas, *Lincoln's New Salem* (New York: Knopf, 1954), 103–10.

11. "New Salem Program Looks at Civilian Conservation Corps History," *The Courier* (Lincoln, IL), October 6, 2017.

12. Thomas, *Lincoln's New Salem*, 103–10.

13. "Occupants of the Springfield Lincoln Home," *Lincoln Lore* 1387 (November 7, 1855).

14. "Occupants of the Springfield Lincoln Home."

15. Lincoln Home National Historic Site, Hearings before the Subcommittee on National Parks and Recreation of the Committee on Interior and Insular Affairs, House of Representatives, 92-4, H.R. 3117 and Related Bills, 1971; *Vicinity, Lincoln Home National Historic Site: Abbreviated Final, General Management Plan/Environmental Impact Statement* (Washington, DC: US Department of the Interior, 2011), 6–22.

16. George J. Olszewski, *Restoration of Ford's Theatre* (Washington, DC: US Department of the Interior, 1963), 105.

17. John C. Waugh, *Reelecting Lincoln* (New York: Crown Publishers, 1997), 47.

18. Garry Wills, *Lincoln at Gettysburg* (New York: Simon and Schuster, 1992), 21. Waugh, *Reelecting Lincoln*, 47.

19. Kent Gramm, *November: Lincoln's Elegy at Gettysburg* (Bloomington: Indiana University Press, 2001), 132–33.

20. Louis A. Warren, *Lincoln's Gettysburg Declaration* (Fort Wayne, IN: Lincoln National Life Foundation, 1964), 81. Waugh, *Reelecting Lincoln*, 48.

21. Warren, *Lincoln's Gettysburg Declaration*, 137–38.

22. Matthew Pinsker, *Lincoln's Sanctuary: Abraham Lincoln and the Soldiers' Home* (New York: Oxford University Press, 2003), 189–91; "President Lincoln's Cottage Opens to Public, Brings Hidden Piece of History to Light in Washington," National Trust for Historic Preservation, Press Release, March 20, 2008.

23. Olszewski, *Restoration of Ford's Theatre*, xi.

24. Olszewski, *Restoration of Ford's Theatre*, 63.

25. Olszewski, *Restoration of Ford's Theatre*, xi; Brian Anderson, *Images of America: Ford's Theatre* (Charleston, SC: Arcadia, 2014), 95–125.

26. Benjamin Franklin Morris, *Memorial Record of the Nation's Tribute to Abraham Lincoln* (Washington, DC: Morrison, 1866), 40.

Bibliography

Newspapers
Brooklyn Daily Herald (Brooklyn, NY)
Chicago Tribune
The Courier (Lincoln, IL)
Daily Republican (Burlington, KS)
Fresno Morning Republican (Fresno, CA)
Gettysburg Times (Gettysburg, PA)
Illinois State Journal (Springfield, IL)
Illinois State Register (Springfield, IL)
The Inter-Ocean (Chicago, IL)
National Intelligencer
National Republican (Washington, DC)
New York Times
New York Tribune
Ottawa Free Trader (Ottawa, IL)
Portage County Democrat (Ravenna, OH)
Richmond Daily Whig (Richmond, VA)
Rock Island Argus (Rock Island, IL)
St. Louis Post-Dispatch (St. Louis, MO)
Sangamo Journal (Springfield, IL)
Sterling Daily Gazette (Sterling, IL)
The Sun (New York)
Washington Chronicle (Washington, DC)

Journals and Periodicals
Abraham Lincoln Quarterly
Civil War History
Documentary Editing
Early American Studies
Farm and Fireside
Harper's New Monthly Magazine
Journal of the Abraham Lincoln Association
Journal of the Illinois State Historical Society
Journal of the Senate of the Nineteenth General Assembly of the State of Illinois

Lincoln Legal Briefs
Lincoln Lore
Newsletter of the Abraham Lincoln Association

US CONGRESSIONAL MATERIAL AND
NATIONAL PARK SERVICE REPORTS

Blythe, Robert W., Maureen Carroll, and Stephen H. Moffson, revised by Brian C. Coffey. *Abraham Lincoln Birthplace National Historic Site: Historic Resource Study.* Atlanta, GA: US Department of the Interior, 2001.

Budget of the United States Government: Historical Tables, Fiscal Year 2007. Washington, DC: US Government Printing Office, 2006.

Lawliss, Lucy, and Susan Hitchcock. *Abraham Lincoln Birthplace National Historic Site: Cultural Landscape Report.* Atlanta, GA: US Department of Interior, 2004.

Lincoln's Birthday, Hearing before the Committee on the District of Columbia, House of Representatives, Sixty-Seventh Congress, First Session, H.R. 2310. Washington, DC: Government Printing Office, 1921.

Lincoln Boyhood National Memorial: General Management Plan/Environmental Impact Statement. Washington, DC: US Department of Interior, 2005.

Lincoln Memorial. Washington, DC: US Department of Interior, 1986.

Lincoln Home National Historic Site, Hearings before the Subcommittee on National Parks and Recreation of the Committee on Interior and Insular Affairs, House of Representatives, 92-4, H.R. 3117 and Related Bills, 1971.

Menz, Katherine B. *The Lincoln Home: Lincoln Home National Historic Site, Springfield, Illinois.* Harpers Ferry, WV: National Park Service, 1983.

National Park Service, US Department of the Interior. *Lincoln Highway: Special Resource Study, Environmental Assessment.* Washington, DC: National Park Service, 2000.

Olszewski, George J. *Restoration of Ford's Theatre.* Washington, DC: US Department of the Interior, 1963.

Vicinity, Lincoln Home National Historic Site: Abbreviated Final, General Management Plan/Environmental Impact Statement. Washington, DC: US Department of the Interior, 2011.

BOOKS

Abel, E. Lawrence. *A Finger in Lincoln's Brain: What Modern Science Reveals about Lincoln, His Assassination, and Its Aftermath.* Santa Barbara, CA: Praeger, 2015.

Algeo, Matthew. *Abe and Fido: Lincoln's Love of Animals and the Touching Story of His Favorite Canine Companion.* Chicago: Chicago Review Press, 2015.

Allen, Michael. *Western Rivermen, 1763-1861.* Baton Rouge: Louisiana State University Press, 1994.

Allen, R. L. *Domestic Animals: History and Description.* New York: C.M. Saxton, 1848.

Ammer, Christine. *American Heritage Dictionary of Idioms.* Second edition. Boston: Houghton Mifflin, 2013.

Anderson, Brian. *Images of America: Ford's Theatre.* Charleston, SC: Arcadia, 2014.

Angle, Paul. *"Here I Have Lived": A History of Lincoln's Springfield*. Springfield, IL: Abraham Lincoln Association, 1955.

——. *The Lincoln Reader*. New Brunswick, NJ: Rutgers University Press, 1947.

Anzovin, Steven, and Janet Podell. *Famous First Facts about American Politics*. New York: H.W. Wilson Co, 2001.

Ariès, Philippe. *Western Attitudes towards Death*. Baltimore, MD: Johns Hopkins University Press, 1974.

Armistead, Gene C. *Horses and Mules in the Civil War*. Jefferson, NC: McFarland, 2013.

Aubin, Jean-Pierre. *Time Is Money: How Long and How Much Money Is Needed to Regulate a Viable Economy*. New York: Springer, 2014.

Baber, Adin. *A. Lincoln with Compass and Chain*. Rochester, IL: Professional Land Surveyors Association, 2002.

Bailey, Anne C. *Weeping Time: Memory and the Largest Slave Auction in American History*. New York: Cambridge University Press, 2017.

Baker, Jean H. *Mary Todd Lincoln: A Biography*. New York: W.W. Norton, 1987.

Ball, Edward. *Slaves in the Family*. New York: Farrar, Straus, and Giroux, 1998.

Balsiger, David, and Charles Sellier. *The Lincoln Conspiracy*. Los Angeles, CA: Schick Sunn, 1977.

Baringer, William E. *Lincoln's Vandalia*. New Brunswick, NJ: Rutgers University Press, 1949.

Barondess, Benjamin. *Three Lincoln Masterpieces*. Charleston, WV: Education Foundation of West Virginia, 1954.

Barton, William. *The Women Lincoln Loved*. Indianapolis: Bobbs-Merrill, 1927.

Basler, Roy, ed. *The Collected Works of Abraham Lincoln*. New Brunswick, NJ: Rutgers University Press, 1953.

Bates, David H. *Lincoln in the Telegraph Office*. New York: Century Company, 1907.

Benner, Martha L., and Cullom Davis, eds. *The Law Practice of Abraham Lincoln: Complete Documentary Edition*. Second edition. Springfield: Illinois Historic Preservation Agency, 2009.

Berlin, Ira, Barbara J. Fields, Steven F. Miller, Joseph P. Reidy, and Leslie S. Rowland. *Slaves No More: Three Essays on Emancipation and the Civil War*. New York: Cambridge University Press, 1992.

Berry, Stephen. *House of Abraham: Lincoln and the Todds, a Family Divided by War*. New York: Houghton Mifflin, 2007.

Bestor, Arthur, David Mearns, and Jonathan Daniels. *Three Presidents and Their Books*. Urbana: University of Illinois Press, 1955.

Beveridge, Albert. *Abraham Lincoln, Vol. 1*. Boston: Houghton Mifflin, 1928.

Blackmon, Douglas A. *Slavery by Another Name: The Re-enslavement of Black Americans from the Civil War to World War II*. New York: Anchor Books, 2009.

Blair, Harry C., and Rebecca Tarshis. *The Life of Colonel Edward D. Baker: Lincoln's Constant Ally*. Portland: Oregon Historical Society, 1960.

Boatner, Mark M., III. *The Civil War Dictionary*. New York: Vintage Books, 1988.

Boggess, Arthur C. *The Settlement of Illinois, 1778–1830*. Chicago: Chicago Historical Society, 1908.

Boritt, Gabor S. ed. *Lincoln and His Generals.* New York: Oxford University Press, 1994.
———. *Lincoln and the Economics of the American Dream.* Memphis, TN: Memphis State University Press, 1978.
Branning, Rosalind L. *Pennsylvania Constitutional Development.* Pittsburgh, PA: University of Pittsburgh Press, 1960.
Briggs, Harold, and Ernestine Briggs. *Nancy Hanks Lincoln.* New York: Bookman Associates, 1952.
Brooks, Noah. *Abraham Lincoln: His Youth and Early Manhood, with a Brief Account of His Later Life.* New York: G.P. Putnam's Sons, 1901.
Bryan, George S. *The Great American Myth.* New York: Carrick and Evans, 1940.
Burlingame, Michael. *Abraham Lincoln: A Life.* Baltimore: Johns Hopkins University Press, 2008.
———, ed. *Lincoln Observed: Civil War Dispatches of Noah Brooks.* Baltimore: Johns Hopkins University Press, 1998.
Carpenter, Francis B. *Six Months at the White House with Abraham Lincoln.* New York: Herd and Houghton, 1866.
Catton, Bruce. *Terrible Swift Sword.* New York: Doubleday & Co., 1963.
Channing, Edward. *A History of the United States, Vol. 6.* New York: Macmillan, 1925.
Chase, James. *1912: Wilson, Roosevelt, Taft, and Debs—The Election That Changed the Country.* New York: Simon and Schuster, 2004.
Chiniquy, Father. *Fifty Years in the Church of Rome.* London: Robert Banks and Son, 1886.
Choron, Sandra, and Harry Choron. *Planet Dog: A Doglopedia.* Boston: Houghton Mifflin, 2005.
Clinton, Catherine. *Mrs. Lincoln: A Life.* New York: Harper, 2009.
Coco, Gregory A. *A Vast Sea of Misery.* Gettysburg, PA: Thomas Publications, 1988.
Cole, James M., and Roy E. Frampton. *Lincoln and the Human Interest Stories of the Gettysburg National Cemetery.* Hanover, PA: Sheridan Press, 1995.
Commager, Henry S., ed. *Civil War Archive: The History of the Civil War in Documents.* New York: Black Dog & Leventhal, 2000.
Complete Official Road Guide of the Lincoln Highway. Detroit: Lincoln Highway Association, 1916.
Connelly, Thomas L. *Army of the Heartland.* Baton Rouge: Louisiana State University, 1967.
Craughwell, Thomas J. *Stealing Lincoln's Body.* Cambridge, MA: Belknap Press, 2007.
Cronon, William. *Nature's Metropolis: Chicago and the Great West.* New York: W.W. Norton, 2009.
Davis, Philip. *History Atlas of North America.* New York: Macmillan, 1998.
Davis, William C. *Jefferson Davis: The Man and His Hour.* New York: HarperCollins, 1991.
Dell, Christopher. *Lincoln and the War Democrats.* London: Associated University Press, 1975.
Dennett, Tyler, ed. *Lincoln and the Civil War: In the Diaries and Letters of John Hay.* New York: Dodd and Mead, 1939.

DeRose, Chris. *Congressman Lincoln*. New York: Simon and Schuster, 2013.

Dirck, Brian. *Lincoln the Lawyer*. Urbana: University of Illinois Press, 2007.

Donald, David H. *Charles Sumner and the Coming of the Civil War*. Naperville, IL: Sourcebooks, 2009.

———. *Lincoln*. New York: Touchstone, 1995.

———. *Lincoln at Home: Two Glimpses of Abraham Lincoln's Family Life*. New York: Simon and Schuster, 2000.

———. *We Are Lincoln Men*. New York: Simon and Schuster, 2003.

Doyle, Don H., ed. *American Civil Wars: The United States, Latin America, Europe, and the Crisis of the 1860s*. Chapel Hill: University of North Carolina Press, 2017.

Dubin, Michael J. *United States Presidential Elections: The Official Results by County and State*. Jefferson, NC: McFarland, 2002.

Duff, John J. *A. Lincoln: Prairie Lawyer*. New York: Bramhall House, 1960.

Eaton, Clement. *A History of the Southern Confederacy*. New York: Free Press, 1954.

Eisenschiml, Otto. *Why Was Lincoln Murdered?* London: Faber and Faber, 1937.

Ellison, Betty Boles. *The True Mary Todd Lincoln: A Biography*. Jefferson, NC: McFarland, 2014.

Faust, Drew Gilpin. *This Republic of Suffering: Death and the American Civil War*. New York: Vintage Books, 2008.

Faust, Patricia. *Historical Times Illustrated Encyclopedia of the Civil War*. New York: HarperCollins, 1991.

Fehrenbacher, Don E. *Lincoln in Text and Context: Collected Essays*. Stanford, CA: Stanford University Press, 1987.

Finkelman, Paul, and Martin Hershock, eds. *The Political Lincoln: An Encyclopedia*. Washington, DC: CQ Press, 2009.

Foner, Eric. *Reconstruction: America's Unfinished Revolution, 1863–1877*. New York: Harper and Row, 2001.

Fraker, Guy C. *Lincoln's Ladder to the Presidency: The Eighth Judicial Circuit*. Carbondale: Southern Illinois University Press, 2012.

Franklin, John Hope. *From Slavery to Freedom*. New York: Vintage Books, 1967.

Frassanito, William. *Gettysburg: A Journey in Time*. New York: Charles Scribner's Sons, 1975.

Freemon, Frank R. *Gangrene and Glory*. Madison, NJ: Fairleigh Dickinson University Press, 1998.

Furgurson, Ernest B. *Freedom Rising: Washington in the Civil War*. New York: Vintage Books, 2005.

Gallagher, Gary W., ed. *The Wilderness Campaign*. Chapel Hill: University of North Carolina Press, 1997.

Gallman, J. Matthew. *The North Fights the Civil War: The Home Front*. Chicago: Ivan R. Dee, 1994.

Gary, Ralph. *Following in Lincoln's Footsteps*. New York: Carroll and Graf, 2001.

Geiger, Roger L., and Nathan M. Sober, eds. *Land Grant Colleges and the Reshaping of American Higher Education*. New Brunswick, NJ: Transaction, 2013.

Genovese, Eugene D. *Roll, Jordan, Roll: The World the Slaves Made*. New York: Pantheon Books, 1974.

Gienapp, William E. *Origins of the Republican Party, 1852–1856*. New York: Oxford University Press, 1987.

Good, Timothy S., ed. *We Saw Lincoln Shot: One Hundred Eyewitness Accounts*. Jackson: University Press of Mississippi, 1995.

Gordon-Reed, Annette. *Andrew Johnson*. New York: Henry Holt, 2011.

Gramm, Kent. *November: Lincoln's Elegy at Gettysburg*. Bloomington: Indiana University Press, 2001.

Grant, Ulysses S. *Memoirs*. New York: Literary Classics, 1990.

Gray, Ralph. *Following in Lincoln's Footsteps*. New York: Carroll and Graf, 2001.

Griffin, John C. *Abraham Lincoln's Execution*. Gretna, LA: Pelican, 2006.

Hall, Kermit L., ed. *The Oxford Companion to American Law*. New York: Oxford University Press, 2002.

Hanchett, William. *The Lincoln Murder Conspiracies*. Urbana: University of Illinois Press, 1983.

Hattaway, Herman, and Richard E. Beringer. *Jefferson Davis, Confederate President*. Lawrence: University of Kansas Press, 2002.

Hayes, Arthur B., and Samuel D. Cox. *History of the City of Lincoln, Nebraska*. Lincoln, NE: State Journal Co., 1889.

Henn, Robert L. *Lincoln and Darwin: Two Men Who Shaped the World*. Pittsburgh, PA: Dorrance Publishing, 2010.

Herndon, William. *The Hidden Lincoln*. New York: Viking, 1938.

Herndon, William, and Jesse Weik. *Herndon's Life of Lincoln*. New York: Da Capo Press, 1983.

———. *Herndon's Lincoln: A True Story of a Great Life*. Reprinted New York: Cosimo, 2009.

Hertz, Emanuel, ed. *The Hidden Lincoln: From the Letters and Papers of William H. Herndon*. New York: Blue Ribbon, 1940.

———. *Lincoln Talks: An Oral Biography*. New York: Bramhall House, 1986.

History of Sangamon County, Illinois. Chicago: Inter-State, 1881.

Hodes, Martha. *Mourning Lincoln*. New Haven, CT: Yale University Press, 2015.

Hokanson, Drake. *Lincoln Highway: Main Street across America*. Iowa City: University of Iowa Press, 1999.

Holland, Josiah. *The Life of Abraham Lincoln*. Springfield, MA: G. Bill, 1866.

Holzer, Harold, ed. *Lincoln as I Knew Him*. Chapel Hill, NC: Algonquin Books, 2009.

Honeck, Mischa. *We Are the Revolutionists: German-Speaking Immigrants and American Abolitionists after 1848*. Athens: University of Georgia Press, 2011.

Houser, M. L. *Lincoln's Education and Other Essays*. New York: Bookman Associates, 1958.

Huddleston, D. Mark. "A Developing Frontier: Logan County, Illinois to 1876." MA thesis, Eastern Illinois University, 1976.

Hunt, Robert E. *The Good Men Who Won the War: Army of the Cumberland Veterans and Emancipation Memory*. Tuscaloosa: University of Alabama Press, 2010.

Hunter, Alexander, and J. H. Polkinhorn. *History of the New National Theater*. Washington, DC: Polkinhorn, 1885.

Illustrated Life, Services, Martyrdom, and Funeral of Abraham Lincoln. Philadelphia: T.B. Peterson and Brothers, 1865.

John, Richard R. *Spreading the News: The American Postal System from Franklin to Morse*. Cambridge, MA: Harvard University Press, 1995.

Johnson, Martin P. *Writing the Gettysburg Address*. Lawrence: University of Kansas Press, 2015.

Jones, Edgar De Witt. *The Influence of Henry Clay on Abraham Lincoln*. Lexington, KY: Henry Clay Memorial Foundation, 1952.

Jordan, Brian Matthew, and Evan C. Rothera, eds. *The War Went On: Reconsidering the Lives of Civil War Veterans*. Baton Rouge: Louisiana State University Press, 2020.

Kauffman, Michael. *American Brutus: John Wilkes Booth and the Lincoln Conspiracies*. New York: Random House, 2004.

Keller, Ron J. *Lincoln in the Illinois Legislature*. Carbondale: Southern Illinois University Press, 2019.

Klement, Frank L. *The Gettysburg Soldiers' Cemetery and Lincoln's Address: Aspects and Angles*. Shippensburg, PA: White Mane Publishing, 1993.

Klooster, Wim. *Revolutions in the Atlantic World: A Comparative History*. New York: New York University Press, 2009.

Knight, Peter, ed. *Conspiracy Theories in American History*. 2 vols. Santa Barbara, CA: ABC-Clio, 2003.

Kunitz, Stanley, and Howard Haycraft, eds. *British Authors before 1800: A Biographical Dictionary*. New York: H.W. Wilson, 1952.

Lachman, Charles. *The Last Lincolns: The Rise and Fall of a Great American Family*. New York: Union Square Press, 2008.

Lamon, Ward Hill. *Recollections of Abraham Lincoln, 1847–1865*. Lincoln: University of Nebraska Press, 1994.

Leland, Charles G. *Abraham Lincoln and the Abolition of Slavery in the United States*. New York: G.P. Putnam, 1881.

Lepler, Jessica M. *The Many Panics of 1837: People, Politics, and the Creation of a Transatlantic Financial Crisis*. New York: Cambridge University Press, 2013.

Linklater, Andro. *Measuring America*. New York: Penguin Group, 2002.

Livermore, Thomas L. *Numbers and Losses in the Civil War in America: 1861–1865*. Bloomington: Indiana University Press, 1957.

Lodge, Henry Cabot. *George Washington, Vol. 2*. Berkeley: University of California Press, 1927.

May, Robert E., ed. *The Union, the Confederacy, and the Atlantic Rim*. West Lafayette, IN: Purdue University Press, 1995.

McCarty, Burke. *The Suppressed Truth about the Assassination of Abraham Lincoln*. Washington, DC: 1922.

McDermott, Stacey Pratt. *Mary Lincoln: Southern Girl, Northern Woman*. New York: Routledge, 2015.

McGuirk, Carol, ed., *Critical Essays on Robert Burns.* New York: Simon and Schuster, 1998.

McPherson, James M. *Battle Cry of Freedom.* New York: Oxford University Press, 1988.

———. *Tried by War: Abraham Lincoln as Commander in Chief.* New York: Penguin Press, 2008.

Meade, George Gordon, III, ed. *The Life and Letters of George Gordon Meade.* New York: Charles Scribner's Sons, 1913.

Miers, Earl Schenck, ed. *Lincoln Day by Day.* 3 vols. Dayton, OH: Morningside, 1991.

Miller, Richard Lawrence. *Lincoln and His World: The Early Years.* Mechanicsburg, PA: Stackpole Books, 2006.

———. *Lincoln and His World: Prairie Politician, 1834–1842.* Mechanicsburg, PA: Stackpole, 2008.

———. *Lincoln and His World: Vol. 3, The Rise to National Prominence, 1843–1853.* Jefferson, NC: McFarland, 2011.

Morris, Benjamin Franklin. *Memorial Record of the Nation's Tribute to Abraham Lincoln.* Washington, DC: Morrison, 1866.

Nagel, Paul C. *John Quincy Adams: A Public Life, a Private Life.* Cambridge, MA: Harvard University Press, 1999.

Nasaw, David. *Going Out: The Rise and Fall of Public Amusements.* Cambridge, MA: Harvard University Press, 1999.

National Portrait Gallery. *First Ladies of the United States.* Washington, DC: Smithsonian Institute, 2020.

Naugle, Ronald C., John J. Montag, and James C. Olson. *History of Nebraska.* Fourth edition. Lincoln: University of Nebraska Press, 2014.

Neely, Mark E., Jr. *The Abraham Lincoln Encyclopedia.* New York: McGraw-Hill, 1982.

Neely, Mark E., Jr., and Harold Holzer. *The Lincoln Family Album.* New York: Doubleday, 1990.

Nicolay, John. *A Short Life of Abraham Lincoln.* New York: Century, 1902.

Novak, Daniel A. *The Wheel of Servitude: Black Forced Labor after Slavery.* Lexington: University Press of Kentucky, 1978.

Nowlen, Robert A. *The American Presidents from Polk to Hayes.* Denver, CO: Outskirts Press, 2016.

Oakes, James. *The Radical and the Republican: Frederick Douglass, Abraham Lincoln, and the Triumph of Antislavery Politics.* New York: W.W. Norton, 2007.

Oates, Stephen B. *Abraham Lincoln: The Man behind the Myths.* New York: Signet, 1984.

Owens, Robert M. *Mr. Jefferson's Hammer: William Henry Harrison and the Origins of American Indian Policy.* Norman: University of Oklahoma Press, 2007.

Patterson, Gerard A. *Debris of Battle: The Wounded of Gettysburg.* Mechanicsburg, PA: Stackpole Press, 1997.

Paull, Bonnie E., and Richard E. Hart. *Lincoln's Springfield Neighborhood.* Charleston, SC: History Press, 2015.

Pease, Theodore C., ed. *Collections of the Illinois State Historical Library, Vol. 18, Statistical Series, Vol. I, Illinois Election Returns, 1818–1848.* Springfield: Illinois State Historical Library, 1923.

Peterson, Merrill D. *Lincoln in American Memory*. New York: Oxford University Press, 1994.

Phisterer, Frederick. *Statistical Record of the Armies of the United States*. New York: Charles Scribner and Sons, 1893.

Pinsker, Matthew. *Lincoln's Sanctuary: Abraham Lincoln and the Soldiers' Home*. New York: Oxford University Press, 2003.

Power, John C. *Abraham Lincoln: His Life, Public Services, Death, and Great Funeral Service*. Chicago: H.W. Rokker, 1889.

Pratt, Harry E. *The Personal Finances of Abraham Lincoln*. Springfield, IL: Abraham Lincoln Association, 1943.

Prokopowicz, Gerald J. *Did Lincoln Own Slaves? And Other Frequently Asked Questions about Abraham Lincoln*. New York: Pantheon Books, 2008.

Putnam, Elizabeth D. *The Life and Services of Joseph Duncan, Governor of Illinois, 1834–1838*. Springfield: Illinois State Historical Society, 1921.

Quaife, Milo M., ed. *Publications of the State Historical Society of Wisconsin, Vol. 1*. Madison, WI: State Historical Society of Wisconsin, 1916.

Randall, Ruth Painter. *Colonel Elmer Ellsworth*. Boston: Little, Brown and Co., 1960.

———. *Mary Lincoln: Biography of a Marriage*. Boston: Little, Brown and Co., 1953.

Rawley, James A. *The Politics of Union*. Hinsdale, IL: Dryden Press, 1974.

Rayback, Joseph G. *Free Soil: The Election of 1848*. Lexington: University Press of Kentucky, 1970.

Reck, W. Emerson. *A. Lincoln: His Last 24 Hours*. Jefferson, NC: McFarland, 1987.

Reep, Thomas. *Lincoln at New Salem*. Petersburg, IL: Old Salem Lincoln League, 1927.

Reilly, Philip R. *Abraham Lincoln's DNA and Other Adventures in Genetics*. Cold Spring Harbor, NY: Cold Spring Harbor Laboratory Press, 2002.

Remini, Robert V. *Henry Clay: Statesman for the Union*. New York: W.W. Norton, 1991.

Reynolds, David S. *Abe: Abraham Lincoln in His Times*. New York: Penguin Press, 2020.

Richardson, H. Edward. *Cassius Marcellus Clay: Firebrand of Freedom*. Lexington: University Press of Kentucky, 1976.

Risvold, Floyd, ed. *Louis Weichmann: A True History of the Assassination of Abraham Lincoln and of the Conspiracy of 1865*. New York: A.A. Knopf, 1975.

Roberts, Alasdair. *America's First Great Depression: Economic Crisis and Political Disorder after the Panic of 1837*. Ithaca, NY: Cornell University Press, 2012.

Roberts, Timothy Mason. *Distant Revolutions: 1848 and the Challenge to American Exceptionalism*. Charlottesville: University of Virginia Press, 2009.

Robinson, Peter N., and Maurice Godfrey. *Marfan Syndrome: A Primer for Clinicians and Scientists*. New York: Kluwer Academic/Plenum Publishers, 2004.

Roscoe, Theodore. *The Web of Conspiracy: The Complete Story of the Men Who Murdered Abraham Lincoln*. Englewood Cliffs, NJ: Prentice-Hall, 1959.

Rowan, Roy, and Brooke Janis. *First Dogs: American Presidents and Their Best Friends*. Chapel Hill, NC: Algonquin, 2009.

Salvatore, Susan Cianci, ed. *Civil Rights in America: Racial Voting Rights*. Washington, DC: US Department of the Interior, 2009.

Savage, James W., and John T. Bell. *History of the City of Omaha, Nebraska.* Chicago: Munsell, 1894.

Schaff, Jon D. *Abraham Lincoln's Statesmanship and the Limits of Liberal Democracy.* Carbondale: Southern Illinois University Press, 2019.

Scheele, Carl H. *A Short History of the Mail Service.* Washington, DC: Smithsonian Institute Press, 1970.

Schlesinger, Arthur, ed. *History of American Presidential Elections, Vol. 2, 1844–1896.* New York: McGraw Hill, 1971.

Schwalm, Leslie A. "Between Slavery and Freedom: African American Women and Occupation in the Slave South." In *Occupied Women: Gender, Military Occupation, and the American Civil War,* edited by LeAnn Whites and Alecia P. Long. Baton Rouge: Louisiana State University Press, 2009.

Schweninger, Lauren. *Families in Crisis in the Old South: Divorce, Slavery, and the Law.* Chapel Hill: University of North Carolina Press, 2012.

Sears, Stephen W. *Chancellorsville.* Boston: Houghton Mifflin, 1996.

———, ed. *The Civil War Papers of George B. McClellan.* New York: Ticknor and Fields, 1989.

Segal, Charles M. *Conversations with Lincoln.* New Brunswick, NJ: Transaction Publishers, 1961.

Selcer, Richard. *Civil War America: 1850–1875.* New York: Facts on File, 2006.

Shaw, Archer, ed. *The Lincoln Encyclopedia.* New York: Macmillan, 1950.

Simon, Paul. *Freedom's Champion: Elijah Lovejoy.* Carbondale: Southern Illinois University Press, 1994.

———. *Lincoln's Preparation for Greatness: The Illinois Legislative Years.* Urbana: University of Illinois Press, 1971.

Simpson, Brooks D. "Great Expectations: Ulysses S. Grant, the Northern Press, and the Opening of the Wilderness Campaign." In *The Wilderness Campaign,* ed. Gary W. Gallagher. Chapel Hill: University of North Carolina Press, 1997.

Snodgrass, Mary Ellen. *Coins and Currency: An Historical Encyclopedia.* Second edition. Jefferson, NC: McFarland, 2019.

Speed, Joshua F. *Reminiscences of Abraham Lincoln.* Louisville, KY: Bradley and Gilbert, 1896.

Steers, Edward Jr. *Blood on the Moon: The Assassination of Abraham Lincoln.* Lexington: University Press of Kentucky, 2005.

Stevenson, Louise L. *Lincoln in the Atlantic World.* New York: Cambridge University Press, 2015.

Stewart, Amy. *Wicked Plants: The Weed that Killed Lincoln's Mother and Other Botanical Atrocities.* Chapel Hill, NC: Algonquin Books, 2009.

Stewart, David O. *Impeached: The Trial of President Andrew Johnson and the Fight for Lincoln's Legacy.* New York: Simon and Schuster, 2009.

Stone, Geoffrey R. *Perilous Times: Free Speech in Wartime.* New York: W.W. Norton, 2004.

Stowell, Daniel W., ed. *The Papers of Abraham Lincoln: Legal Documents and Cases.* 4 vols. Charlottesville: University of Virginia Press, 2008.

Stringer, Lawrence B. *History of Logan County, Illinois*. Chicago: Pioneer Publishing, 1911.

Summers, Mark Wahlgren. *Rum, Romanism, and Rebellion: The Making of a President, 1884*. Chapel Hill: University of North Carolina Press, 2000.

Symonds, Craig L. *Lincoln and His Admirals*. New York: Oxford University Press, 2008.

Szasz, Ferenc Morton. *Abraham Lincoln and Robert Burns: Connected Lives and Legends*. Carbondale: Southern Illinois University Press, 2008.

Tarbell, Ida M. *Life of Abraham Lincoln, Vol. 1*. New York: Lincoln Memorial Association, 1900.

Thomas, Benjamin. *Abraham Lincoln: A Biography*. New York: Modern Library, 1968.

———. *Lincoln's Humor and Other Essays*. Urbana: University of Illinois Press, 2002.

———. *Lincoln's New Salem*. New York: Knopf, 1954.

Thomas, Benjamin, and Harold Hyman. *Stanton: The Life and Times of Lincoln's Secretary of War*. New York: Alfred A. Knopf, 1962.

Thomas, Christopher A. *The Lincoln Memorial and American Life*. Princeton, NJ: Princeton University Press, 2002.

Thomas, Lately. *The First President Johnson*. New York: William Morrow, 1968.

Transactions of the Illinois State Historical Society for the Year 1904. Springfield, IL: Phillips Brothers, 1904.

Trask, Kerry A. *Black Hawk*. New York: Henry Holt, 2006.

Traub, James. *John Quincy Adams: Militant Spirit*. New York: Basic Books, 2016.

Tucker, Spencer C., ed. *Encyclopedia of American Military History, Vol. 1*. New York: Facts on File, 2003.

Turner, Justin, and Linda Turner. *Mary Todd Lincoln: Her Life and Letters*. New York: A.A. Knopf, 1972.

Tweedy, John. *A History of the Republican National Conventions from 1856 to 1908*. Danbury, CT: J. Tweedy, 1910.

Unger, Harlow Giles. *John Quincy Adams*. Philadelphia, PA: Da Capo Press, 2012.

US Commerce Department. *Statistical Abstract of the United States*. Washington, DC: US Government Printing Office, 2005.

Van Doren Stern, Philip. *When the Guns Roared: World Aspects of the American Civil War*. Garden City, NY: Doubleday & Co., 1965.

Walsh, John Evangelist. *The Shadows Rise: Abraham Lincoln and the Ann Rutledge Legend*. Urbana: University of Illinois Press, 1993.

War of the Rebellion: A Compilation of the Official Records of the Union and Confederate Armies. Washington, DC: Government Printing Office, 1880–1901.

Ward, Geoffrey C. *The Civil War: An Illustrated History*. New York: Alfred A. Knopf, 1990.

Warren, Charles. *A History of the American Bar*. New York: Howard Fertig, 1966.

Warren, Louis A. *Lincoln's Gettysburg Declaration: "A New Birth of Freedom."* Ft. Wayne, IN: Lincoln National Life Foundation, 1964.

———. *Lincoln's Youth*. Indianapolis: Indiana Historical Society, 2002.

Waugh, John C. *Reelecting Lincoln*. New York: Crown Publishers, 1997.

Weber, Jennifer L. *Copperheads: The Rise and Fall of Lincoln's Opponents in the North*. New York: Oxford University Press, 2006.

Weems, Mason Locke. *The Life of George Washington*. Edited by Marcus Cunliffe. Cambridge, MA: Harvard University Press, 1962.

Weichmann, Louis. *A True History of the Assassination of Abraham Lincoln and the Conspiracy of 1865*. New York: A.A. Knopf, 1975.

Weiner, Marli F., ed. *Heritage of Woe: The Civil War Diary of Grace Brown Elmore, 1861–1868*. Athens: University of Georgia Press, 1997.

Welles, Gideon. *Diary of Gideon Welles*. Boston, MA: Houghton Mifflin, 1909.

Wheeler, Tom. *Mr. Lincoln's T-Mails*. New York: Collins, 2006.

White, Ronald C., Jr. *A. Lincoln: A Biography*. New York: Random House, 2009.

Whites, LeAnn, and Alecia P. Long, eds. *Occupied Women: Gender, Military Occupation, and the American Civil War*. Baton Rouge: Louisiana State University Press, 2009.

Whose Heritage? Public Symbols of the Confederacy. Montgomery, AL: Southern Poverty Law Center, 2019.

Widmer, Ted. *Lincoln on the Verge: Thirteen Days to Washington*. New York: Simon and Schuster, 2020.

Wiley, Bell I. *The Life of Johnny Reb: The Common Soldier of the Confederacy*. Baton Rouge: Louisiana State University Press, 1978.

Wills, Garry. *Lincoln at Gettysburg: The Words that Remade America*. New York: Simon and Schuster, 1992.

Wilson, Douglas L. *Honor's Voice: The Transformation of Abraham Lincoln*. New York: A.A. Knopf, 1998.

———. *Lincoln's Sword*. New York: Vintage Books, 2006.

Wilson, Douglas L., Terry Wilson, and Rodney O. Davis, eds. *Herndon's Informants: Letters, Interviews, and Statements about Abraham Lincoln*. Urbana: University of Illinois Press, 1998.

Wilson, Rufus R. *Lincoln among His Friends*. Caldwell, ID: Caxton Printers, 1942.

Winkle, Kenneth J. *Lincoln's Citadel: The Civil War in Washington, D.C.* New York: W.W. Norton, 2013.

———. *The Young Eagle: The Rise of Abraham Lincoln*. Dallas, TX: Taylor Trade, 2001.

Woldman, Albert A. *Lawyer Lincoln*. Boston: Houghton Mifflin, 1936.